apple

Start Your Own

e-BUSINESS

DISCARD

Additional titles in *Entrepreneur's* **Startup Series**

Start Your Own

Bar or Club

Bed & Breakfast

Business on eBay

Business Support Service

Car Wash

Child Care Service

Cleaning Service

Clothing Store

Coin-Operated Laundry

Consulting

Crafts Business

e-Learning Business

Event Planning Business

Executive Recruiting Service

Freight Brokerage Business

Gift Basket Service

Growing and Selling Herbs and Herbal
   Products

Home Inspection Service

Import/Export Business

Information Consultant Business

Law Practice

Lawn Care or Landscaping Business

Mail Order Business

Medical Claims Billing Service

Net Services

Personal Concierge Service

Personal Training Business

Pet-Sitting Business

Restaurant and Five Other Food Businesses

Self-Publishing Business

Seminar Production Business

Specialty Travel & Tour Business

Staffing Service

Successful Retail Business

Vending Business

Wedding Consultant

Wholesale Distribution Business

Entrepreneur
MAGAZINE'S

start up

2ND EDITION

Start Your Own

e-BUSINESS

*Your Step-by-Step
Guide to Success*

Entrepreneur Press and Lynie Arden

EP
Entrepreneur.
Press

Publisher: Jere L. Calmes
Cover Design: Beth Hansen-Winter
Production and Composition: CWL Publishing Enterprises, Inc., Madison, WI

This publication is designed to provide accurate and authoritative information in regard to the subject matter covered. It is sold with the understanding that the publisher is not engaged in rendering legal, accounting or other professional services. If legal advice or other expert assistance is required, the services of a competent professional person should be sought.

ISBN 13: 978-1-59918-192-9
      10: 1-59918-192-4

Library of Congress Cataloging-in-Publication available

Printed in Canada
13 12 11 10 09   10 9 8 7 6 5 4 3 2 1

Contents

▲

▲

▲

Preface

Like the mythical phoenix, the internet has risen from the ashes of the 2000 dotcom crash. This second surge, known as Web 2.0, continues to offer a virtual universe of opportunity. While venture capitalists and angels are more prudent about offering funding for dotcom startups, driven entrepreneurs with good ideas are still devising ways to build solid businesses that harness the power of the internet to reach millions of people worldwide.

Still, for every dotcom business that flourishes, hundreds—maybe thousands—go bust. What does it take to build a dotcom that will succeed? Read this book and you'll know,

▲

because in these pages you'll find recipes for success, road maps that pinpoint the hazards, and dozens of interviews with dotcom entrepreneurs who have proved they've got what it takes to survive in this sometimes fickle marketplace.

What separates the losers from the winners? Poor ideas, poor execution, poor marketing and poor funding.

Good ideas and smart business practices aren't always enough, though. The internet has become crowded with companies that were online innovators and with traditional companies that reconfigured their operations to include an internet component. In some cases, launching a national, full-scale consumer-oriented site today may require millions to cover marketing, hardware, software and staffing costs. Gulp! That's a big leap from the graduate school project days that gave rise to Yahoo.

Low-budget websites are still launching and making it to the big time—social media phenom Facebook was born in a college dorm room—but now more than ever, they require a unique combination of customer insight, business understanding, technical know-how, financial resources and entrepreneurial drive. The possibilities of success remain enticing, even when wallets are thin—if your ideas are smart and your execution persistent. The one inescapable fact is this: It's war on the monitors, and more websites will die than will survive. What will yours do?

The goal of this book is to give you the tools and knowledge you'll need to emerge among the victors. In these pages, you'll find the soup to nuts, the A to Z, of taking your idea through funding, building partnerships, launching, winning eyeballs and laughing all the way to the bank. This is not a technical book. It's a book about business and consumer psychology.

While the internet's roots are in technology, that technology has become much more accessible to a wider group of entrepreneurs through the efforts and investment of many companies and people. Today, there better software tools that make it easier than ever for anyone—technophobes included—to build and manage websites.

We'll tell you what you need and where to get it, and for hard-core do-it-yourselfers, there's even a chapter on building your own website. Either way, there's no longer a reason to say "I don't get this internet stuff." You've got to get it, or get out of business.

Some words about how this book is organized: Interspersed among the chapters are "Cheap Tricks," mini-interviews with low-budget website builders. The book also features interviews, called "e-Chats," with CEOs of big-budget name-brand sites—among them drugstore.com, Netflix.com, Proflowers.com, Autobytel.com, eBags.com and Zappos.com.

You'll also find three kinds of tip boxes designed to hammer home key points:

- **Smart Tip:** bright ideas you want to remember as well as online opportunities

- **Beware!:** pitfalls and potholes you want to avoid

- **Budget Watcher:** money-saving ideas and practices

Here's the promise of this book: If you need to know it to do business online, you'll find it between these covers. Read on to find out how to make your internet dreams a reality.

1

The Internet
Gold Rush

This is it—your second chance to strike it very rich because once again, the internet is changing all the rules. The first dotcom gold rush occurred roughly between 1995 and 2001. It began when a little startup named Netscape introduced a web browser—and the race for cash was on. Amazon, eBay, Yahoo, 1-800-Flowers.com, drugstore.com, Priceline.com, WebMD.com—they staked their claims to a piece of cyberspace and became billion-dollar businesses. Others, like Pets.com, WebVan and eToys, flamed out spectacularly when the bubble burst in 2001. Many wondered if the internet would ever amount to anything more than a few pie-in-the-sky ideas.

But today, e-commerce is back in a big way. Web 2.0 is here and many are referring to it as the second internet gold rush because so many new companies are once again making a big splash and changing the way people do business, spend time and purchase things online. Just as dotcom giants of the first wave did a decade ago, companies like Skype, YouTube, Facebook and Google are skyrocketing in value. And just as before, they've all been started by smart individuals who have faith in their ideas and the future of the internet. They are succeeding because the new rules favor companies that are innovative, smart and ultraquick to react to changing consumer interests. It also helps that Web 2.0 entrepreneurs have been able to learn from the mistakes and successes of the original dotcom pioneers.

Chew on these numbers: Online retail sales are projected to hit $204 billion in 2008, up from $175 billion in 2007, and should reach $300 billion by 2013, according to a study conducted by Forrester Research, an independent technology and market research company. During the 2007 holiday season alone, consumers spent more than $29 billion online, an increase of 19 percent over the same period in 2006. On 2007's "Green Monday"—the term eBay coined for the second Monday in December—online sales hit a record of $881 million, making it the heaviest online spending day in history.

The internet is for real, and in the 21st century, if you're not on it, you're not in business. That is today's reality byte.

A New Set of Rules

On the web, the advantage is yours—it belongs to the entrepreneur. Why? Consider Compaq, now a brand under the Hewlett Packard umbrella. It makes fine computers—maybe no better than its competitors, but certainly no worse. So why did Dell long ago surpass Compaq in market leadership? Dell leapt feet first into full-steam web retailing. It yanked its merchandise out of retail stores and threw the dice, betting the company's future on direct selling (via catalogs and the web) to corporations and individuals. Compaq, meanwhile, faltered at every step because it didn't want to alienate its established retail channels, convinced they would be irked if suddenly the same computers were available for less on the internet. So Compaq dithered during the infancy of the web, and that indecisiveness made it lose momentum and leadership while upstarts grabbed market share.

Compared with 20th-century business models, the web is both a new distribution channel and a new way of doing business. Don't miss either part of that statement. Think of the web only as a new channel—a different way of putting products and services in front of customers—and you miss the threat and the promise of the internet, which is that it has and will continue to utterly change the business world and how you do business.

For one thing, the web is ruthless in the squeeze it puts on pricing. Fat and waste have to go, and good riddance, because many large companies (and too many small companies) have grown comfortably wealthy by exacting indefensible margins out of the retail process. No more. The web stomps margins flat, and to make profits, companies have to rethink where their dollars will be earned. Big companies (most of them) have responded to these new rules by shutting their eyes and praying the moment will pass. (Think of the big banks that treat customers terribly, pay laughable interest rates and are forever hiking fees. Most are doomed to be dinosaurs.) All this is good news for you because it means you have a wide-open playing field before you.

> **! Beware!**
>
> Venture capital funding, billions of dollars' worth, is out there—but be prepared for a grilling like you've never had before any check is signed. Never forget that venture capitalists are in business to make money, lots of it, not to speculate on chancy business ideas.

Better still, the opportunities are unlimited. Would it be wise to go head to head against Google or Amazon? Not directly, because these companies are among the many internet businesses that can legitimately claim to have established major consumer brands. But at less than 20 years old, the web is still just a tot in the overall business world and, as so many of Dotcom 2.0's upstart entrepreneurs have shown, possibilities are still everywhere. Want proof? Read on for a few amazing stories of internet success popping up where most people would least expect it.

Getting Social

Consider Facebook. The ultra popular social networking site was started by a Harvard student in his dorm room. As a sophomore, Mark Zuckerberg had a hunch that his fellow university students would like to congregate, send messages, load photos and generally flirt with one another online. Within a year of launching Facebook, Zuckerberg took off for Silicon Valley and hasn't looked back since.

Facebook eventually opened its doors to all users, not just students, and it now has 66 million active users. In 2007, Microsoft purchased a 1.6 percent share in the social networking company. Do the math: That's a $15 billion valuation—and Zuckerman isn't even 25 years old yet.

News Corp. purchased social networking site MySpace for $580 million in 2005. Google paid $1.65 *billion* for video-sharing site YouTube in 2006. And AOL just recently picked up Bebo, a favorite social networking site in the United Kingdom, Ireland and New Zealand, for $850 million.

These are some big figures. While social networking can be a difficult game to enter, it does show the extreme possibilities are available in our new Web 2.0 world for innovative entrepreneurs with a good idea.

Claiming Success

Charles Brofman is an internet entrepreneur who has found success pairing fast-paced internet technology with the slow-paced process of settling insurance claims.

Brofman started Cybersettle Inc. (cybersettle.com), a White Plains, New York–based online dispute resolution company, in 1996. Its web-based system facilitates high-speed, confidential claim settlements by matching offers and demands. Parties can settle disputes instantly, 24/7, via the internet, or by calling its customer service center during normal business hours.

Why did he start the company? "The courts today literally cannot handle the onslaught of litigation they face," says Brofman, a seasoned trial attorney. "As a result, people who are entitled to get compensated for their injures have to wait long periods of time, and insurance companies that have an obligation to pay—and want to pay—have to wait a long period of time. Cybersettle really just came out of our frustration with this process."

> **Tip...**
>
> ## Smart Tip
> Just because your idea might seem a little out of the ordinary, don't quit if you're a believer. Charles Brofman didn't quit, and his Cybersettle is a big winner in reinventing the way insurance claims are settled.

Here's how Cybersettle works: An insurance company receives a statement of claim from a plaintiff's lawyer. When the insurance adjuster reviews the case and is ready to settle, he then enters three offers into the computer. The plaintiff's lawyer is informed that the insurer has made an offer, and the lawyer then enters three demands. The Cybersettle main server compares the lawyer's first offer with the insurer's, and when the demand falls below the offer, the software splits the difference and settles the claim. Brofman says the system mirrors the way the insurance industry does business.

To date, Cybersettle, which can be used in the United States and Canada, has handled more than 200,000 transactions and has facilitated over $1.5 billion in settlements, including bodily injury and other types of insurance claims.

In addition, Cybersettle has expanded beyond just insurance. One area is public entities. A pilot program with New York City started in 2004; by the end of the first year, the city estimated Cybersettle had saved the city about $11 million. By

2007, the City comptroller announced that the cost of claim handling for the city dropped $34 million in the prior fiscal year—and he attributed $27 million of that savings to Cybersettle.

Cybersettle is also launching a new consumer-to-consumer program in 2008 that will basically become an online small claims court for the world.

Brofman says there are several reasons why his internet venture is successful. One, his company has a "fabulous" investor, a strategic partner who understands his business. Another is that his business does what the internet was designed to do, and that is to conduct a transaction 24 hours per day, seven days per week. "If you are going to do something on the net," says Brofman, "you have to do something that the net was designed to do."

Reaching Their Peak

If you're willing to expand your horizons a little, as two entrepreneurs discovered, the sky's the limit. Consider Jim Holland and John Bresee, who founded Backcountry.com, a Herber City, Utah–based online retailer of outdoor gear for all things backcountry, in 1996.

Holland, a two-time Olympic ski jumper and six-time national champion Nordic ski jumper, and Bresee, a former editor of *Powder* magazine, founded the company with the purpose of providing outdoor adventure gear to the hard-core recreational athlete. Holland and Bresee's online store has seen triple-digit average annual growth for the past 10 years. Pretty amazing, considering the fact that they began the company without any outside investment.

"We developed the site ourselves and banked about $2,000 of our own money to get started, which we used for inventory," says Bresee. "We took a risk but knew there was an interest out there for what we were doing."

What's the company's secret to success? There's not one answer to that question, but a key reason is that the company decided to focus on a narrow niche—selling gear to hard-core sports enthusiasts—instead of competing with mass-market retailers like REI that might sell the same items, but without the same knowledge.

Backcountry.com, for example, populates its call-center staff with hard-core skiers and trekkers who are out there using the equipment the site sells. Therefore, when customers contact Backcountry.com with their questions, the customer solutions team, known as "Gearheads," can answer by drawing on their own unique personal experience.

Excellent customer service, in fact, is the company's mantra. "We make it very easy for our customers to communicate directly with real people at Backcountry.com, whether they have a question or want to make a purchase. Our phone number is on every page of our site, and people can just as easily opt to IM a Gearhead if they prefer," says Bresee.

Other reasons for its continued growth? The addition of other successful niche sports gear sites (Tramdock.com, Dogfunk.com, SteepandCheap.com, WhiskeyMilitia.com and BackcountryOutlet. com), cost-effective online and word-of-mouth advertising, and the company's philosophy that the risky way is the safe way.

"If it's safe, we're not interested in pursuing it," says Bresee. "To successfully grow a business, you have to take risks. In the case of Backcountry.com, we're lucky that the risks we've taken are working out pretty well."

Film Rentals for the 21st Century

Now, what about taking on an established business model and using the internet to completely turn it on its head? Travel back to 1997, a time when the dotcom era was in full bloom. It was also a time when the idea of renting movies via mail seemed ludicrous. In fact, many thought that Netflix founders Marc Randolph and Reed Hastings were nuts. DVD players had just started selling in the United States in March 1997, yet by October the guys were already executing their business plan. Despite the odds and the obstacles, they persevered to create Netflix, a pure-play dotcom that has revolutionized the movie rental industry.

At the start of this venture, there were plenty of naysayers asking why people would wait for movies to arrive in the mailbox when they could just go down the street to Blockbuster. But the founders stubbornly found a way around all objections and spent countless hours mapping out operational strategies.

Netflix launched in 1998, operating for the first five years with virtually no advertising money. Even they were surprised by the consumer response. The key was connecting with rabid early DVD adopters on Usenet discussion groups. Netflix made no public announcements about the site launch, hoping the soft launch might bring in volumes of more than 10 or so "friends and family" orders per day. But the first day, 500 orders arrived, almost exclusively from Usenet advocates who noticed the site was live and announced it to their networks. Within 30 days, the company was processing 1,000 orders per day; within three months, they were moving more than 2,000 orders per day, and their phenomenal growth continued from there.

Netflix has been one of the most successful dotcom ventures yet. Today, it's the world's largest online DVD movie rental service, serving 7.5 million members and offering 90,000 movie titles. Its appeal and success are built on providing an expansive selection of DVDs, an easy way to choose movies, and fast, free delivery.

Incredible stories? You bet, but the internet is filled with them because all the rules are new in the internet economy. Even the biggest players can be successfully challenged by the upstart who sees an opportunity, then seizes it.

Better yet, the odds are stacked in your favor because you are little. How? When a big company such as Toys "R" Us fumbles its e-commerce debut—which it did by disappointing many holiday season shoppers back in 1999—it makes headline news and even e-commerce history. That company has a well-established brand; consumers who shop there, offline or on, shop with expectations. When it made hash of its web storefront, it hurt.

What if you do likewise—drop a few balls at startup? Customers don't know you, don't have expectations, and odds are you'll be forgiven. A few years ago, business guru Tom Peters' mantra was that the moment had come for business to practice "Ready, Fire, Aim" because no longer was there latitude to spend months scoping the target. On the web, too, action counts. Take it—as Netflix did—and you just may come out way ahead.

Sweet Dreams

Sometimes even when your dreams aren't so lofty, the internet can still save the day, as Barbara McCann found out. She and her husband, Jim, owned The Chocolate Vault, a store in Tecumseh, Michigan, a village about 60 miles west of Detroit. They'd watched traffic—and customers—veer away from little towns, and they'd watched their cash flow dry to a trickle. Then they decided to give the internet a whirl.

On a skimpy budget—a few thousand dollars—Barbara McCann personally built her website, chocolatevault.com, and then she watched an amazing thing happen. "People from all over the country found us, and they started buying our chocolates!" she says.

McCann says the internet business has grown so much that she has decided to close the retail store. In 2005, she moved her internet business and home to another small town in southeastern Michigan and built a small factory-type facility that allows the company more space. McCann says the move was the best decision she could have made.

McCann doesn't have the money to buy major advertising space and instead puts all her energy into offering exceptional customer service. "We are trying to give our customers the kind of personal service online that they would receive if they walked into our store," she says. "We've also found ways to customize our products. For example, we make custom molds for our corporate clients."

McCann also says that most of her customers are return customers who keep coming back because the site is understandable and easy to maneuver.

▲

The E-Commerce Quiz

Think you're ready to become a "netpreneur"? Prove it. Before moving on to the next chapter, take this quiz. Answers are true or false.

1. I'm comfortable in a game in which tomorrow's rules are invented the day after tomorrow.
2. I see inefficiencies—waste and delay—in many current business practices.
3. I'm willing to delay this year's profits to potentially make more money next year.
4. I know how to size up customers I've never seen or talked with.
5. The net excites me—I honestly like surfing around and seeing what's new.
6. I can live with thin margins.
7. Customer satisfaction is the most important thing a business can deliver.
8. I'm not afraid of battling titans.
9. I see opportunity where others see risks.
10. I am willing to work harder and smarter than I ever could have imagined possible.

Scoring: Guess what—"true" is always the right answer for any netpreneur. But you knew that already because you're ready to compete on this merciless playing field.

Will The Chocolate Vault rise to the top and challenge the biggies in that space, such as Godiva and others? "Never," says McCann, who knows her budget and her ambition. But the big miracle is that "the internet has been a lifesaver for us," she says. "We would've closed our shop without it."

Set the scale of your internet ambitions—dream large in the way of Charles Brofman, or dream on a more diminutive scale like the McCanns—because there is no "right" approach to the internet. Good, steady money can be earned by strictly local players who open on the net and find a stream of global business pouring in. Or big bucks may be yours if you invent a new eBay or Monster.com.

10 Reasons You
Should Be Online

Need convincing that the web is the place for your business to be? It would be no sweat to list 25 reasons—even 50 to 100—but to get you started, here are 10 reasons you have to be online.

1. **It's cheap.** There is no less expensive way to open a business than to launch a website. While you can spend many millions of dollars getting started, low-budget

(opened with as little as $100) remains a viable way to launch an online business.

2. **You cut your order fulfillment costs.** Handling orders by phone is expensive. Ditto for mail orders. There's no more efficient—cheap, fast, accurate—way to process orders than via a website.

3. **Your catalog is always current.** A print catalog can cost big bucks, and nobody wants to order a reprint just to change one price or to correct a few typos. A website can be updated in minutes.

4. **High printing and mailing costs are history.** Your customers can

> ⚠ **Beware!**
> Not only can online catalogs be updated in seconds, they must be! A sure way to frustrate online shoppers is to take them through the buying process only to annoy them at the last moment with a "Sorry, out of stock" message. Never do that. If merchandise is out of stock, clearly note that early in the buying process. Customers can accept inventory problems, but they'll never accept you wasting their time.

download any product information you want them to have from your website. You can focus your marketing efforts on e-mail newsletters and online advertising rather than direct mail. Sure, you'll still want to print some materials, but lots can be distributed via the web.

5. **You cut staffing costs.** A website can be a low-manpower operation. With just a few free, easy-to-use tools, you can put your business on autopilot. If you do need help with web development, design, marketing or content, you can find other like-minded netpreneurs working from their home offices and hire them for one-off jobs as independent contractors—a much easier option than hiring a regular, full-time employee.

6. **You can stay open 24 hours a day.** And you'll still get your sleep because your site will be open even when your eyes are closed.

7. **You're in front of a global audience.** Ever think what you sell might be a big hit in Scotland or China, but feel clueless about how to penetrate foreign markets? The web is your answer because it's truly a borderless marketplace. Watch your site log, and you'll see visitors streaming in from Australia, Italy, Japan, Malaysia—wherever there's a way to access the internet.

8. **There are no city permits and minimal red-tape hassles.** This could change, but in most of the country, small web businesses can be run without permits and with little government involvement. As you expand and add employees, you'll start to bump into laws and regulations, but it certainly is nice to be able to kick off a business without first filling out reams of city, county and state forms.

9. **It's fast.** You can build a website on Saturday afternoon, open a Google AdWords account on Sunday, create a viral ad campaign to reach millions on

Monday, and have money from paid orders in your bank account by Tuesday. It's not always that simple, of course, but the potential for overnight results is always there. That doesn't mean you'll be rich on Tuesday, but your business could be well under way.

10. **It's easy to get your message out.** Between your website and smart use of e-mail and online advertising, you'll have complete control over when and

Budget Watcher

On a really tight budget? Hire local college students or interns and have them work part time. Many young people are willing to work for low or no pay in exchange for getting in on the ground floor of an e-business startup.

how your message goes out. You can even expand your reach—usually for just an investment of time—via social networking sites and through clever viral marketing techniques. You can't beat a website for its immediacy, and when a site is designed well and has a thorough marketing campaign, it's hard to top its ability to grab and hold the attention of potential customers.

You have other reasons for wanting a web business? Fair enough. The key is understanding your reasons, knowing the benefits of doing business online, and being persistent through the launch. This isn't always an easy road to take, but it's definitely a road that has transported many to riches, with much less upfront cash, hassle and time required than for similar, offline businesses. And that's a tough value proposition to top.

3

Dotcom Dreams vs. Dotcom Nightmares

Dotcom dreams are back. After the first bubble burst in 2000, many thought e-commerce really was nothing more than a dream—a bad dream at that. But since then, Facebook, MySpace, eBay, YouTube, Google and Wikipedia have become part of a daily information diet for millions. Dow Jones recently announced that venture capital for internet startups has reached almost $1 billion and global online advertising revenue is projected to rise to $55 billion by 2010. Google's shares topped $750 in late 2007, and younger Dotcom 2.0 companies are being snatched up by old-school giants like AOL and Yahoo!. Some call this the reincarnation of the internet. Even VC firms and angels are again envisioning an online future rich with possibility—and money.

It's taken seven years to rebound from the bust, but things are definitely on the upswing. After the dotcom crash of 2000, IPOs for internet-related companies languished for almost three years. Then, in 2003, several internet-related companies went public, including RedEnvelope (redenvelope.com), a gift e-tailer; Provide Commerce (providecommerce.com), which operates Proflowers.com; the popular travel company Orbitz (orbitz.com); and iPayment (ipaymentinc.com), which provides payment-processing services to small merchants for credit and debit card transactions. Even more promising, most of these IPOs exceeded investors' expectations.

In 2004, Salesforce.com went public, as did Google. In 2005, both Napster.com (napster.com) and Buy.com went public. Actually, this was the second time Buy.com had taken its shares public in less than five years. IPOs from the truly blockbuster Web 2.0 companies, such as Facebook (facebook.com) and LinkedIn (linkedin.com), may not happen until 2009. But 80 venture-backed companies went public in 2007, including standouts like web-based business applications company NetSuite (netsuite.com), which raised $161 million with its highly anticipated IPO.

Companies like these that find huge success with IPOs, big VC investments and pricey acquisitions are few and far between. You likely are not a richly funded dotcom and need not sit around worrying about the day the VCs show up at the door demanding some kind of return. So breathe normally—but don't rest on your laurels. Just because you're not a multimillion-dollar Web 2.0 wunderkind, it doesn't mean you're immune to big-time mistakes. Let's revisit the reasons so many dotcom 1.0 companies no longer exist—so you can avoid them:

- *Bad balance-sheet math:* At no point did the companies that crashed and burned generate financial statements that indicated any reasonable relationship between income and expenses. And yet they spent wildly, renting expensive offices in Silicon Valley and New York's Silicon Alley, hiring deep staffs (and often paying salaries upward of six figures for minor positions), and buying fantastic exposure in ads of every media. No genuinely small startup could long afford these lush business habits. Sure, every startup has a day or a week or a few months when income lags way behind outgo, but at least the math makes some kind of sense, and in the lean period, spending is lean, too. You don't need the ritzy office, the high-powered law firm or the Stanford MBA employees, so you should be able to keep your expenses in some kind of rational alignment with income.

- *No revenue model:* The core question for dotcom startups is "What is your revenue model?" This is shorthand for "How do you envision bringing in income?

> ## ! Beware!
>
> Of course you'll start off in the red—that's the norm. But when can you honestly project seeing black ink? You need to know that answer and work hard to make it a realistic forecast. So many dotcoms have been shut down because they never had honest forecasts of when investors could expect to see black ink. Don't let that happen to you.

What will be your revenue streams? How do you expect to make a profit?" Potential investors will ask this, as will would-be employees, partners and anybody considering a financial future with your dotcom. Strangely, however, when the question has been asked, the questioners have typically accepted formulaic answers. In the past, dotcoms have vaguely explained that their revenue model involved a mix of ad dollars and e-commerce, and in most cases, the answer was accepted. It was a mistake because, as the failed dotcoms proved, nobody had ever really put flesh on the revenue models.

Never open a business without understanding your revenue source. This seems so elemental, but in the heady days when vaporous businesses such as Pets.com, Kozmo and Boo.com quickly snagged multibillion-dollar market caps, many people abandoned this axiom.

Will your predictions be on target? Probably not. They may even be wildly wrong, but that doesn't mean they didn't serve a good purpose. Simply articulating realistic, workable revenue models is good discipline. In practice, businesses usually evolve in ways the founders did not anticipate—a fact that is all the more true in the wild and wooly net—so early drafts of revenue models likely will get discarded, fast. But always know where, approximately, money will originate.

Incidentally, the unspoken revenue model of many dotcoms apparently had been additional rounds of funding—either from VCs or public markets—but, at the end of the day, those spigots will get turned off. Why? Read on.

- *No clearly defined exit strategy:* Every well-conceived startup comes equipped with an exit strategy for investors. An exit strategy is how investors will get their money out of the business and when. Founders with hands-on roles in the business probably don't need to know their exit strategy, but angels, VCs and such want to know how and when they'll see a return on their investment. What are possible exit strategies?
  1. Going public: a prime choice for many dotcoms
  2. Getting bought by a bigger fish: not as popular as going public, but attractive when public markets turn turbulent
  3. Bringing in new investors to buy out others: another option, but rarely used in the years of net mania, probably because later-round investors were unwilling to pay the inflated prices sought by early investors

  There is no saying which exit strategy is best, but what can be said is that no

CEO needs anxious investors calling every few minutes to ask when they might cash out. And that happens all too often when there's been a lack of clarity—even realism—about the investment. This means that in early talks with investors (even if it's your folks who put up the money), you need to be honest about how you see them getting their money out and when. Be as pessimistic as possible. Sure, you might spook investors, but better to do it now than have them hassling you as you're trying to build the business.

- *Building market share to the detriment of the business:* Market share is not God, although CEOs of the many

Budget Watcher

When you start with little funding, do as small businesses have always done: Operate on a shoestring. Dell Computers, for instance, got its start in a dorm room. Apple started in a garage. Your quarters needn't be that humble, but never, ever spend money you don't have to for the sake of "making an impression." If anything, it's the wrong impression you'll make because investors aren't looking to put money in the hands of CEOs who spend like drunken sailors. Frugality is always a good thing for a startup.

failed dotcoms who pursued a strategy of building market share at any cost wanted you to believe otherwise. Look through the financial filings of many of the best-known dotcoms, and what's stunning is that a common practice is selling merchandise for less than they paid for it. Pay $300 to a wholesaler for handheld computers, and no matter how many you sell for $250, you won't do anything but go broke.

Yet, the wacky mantra-infected Silicon Valley of the late 90s held that somehow, market share was the end-all. Sure, you will get market share when you sell items below cost because nobody can compete. But when pressures build and you have to tweak prices up to survive, how much of that precious market share will you lose? Lots, you can bet, which is why the only method for long-term survival is to price rationally to begin with. It makes sense to use loss-leader pricing on an item or two if that strategy generates orders that, in a short-term horizon, will produce profits.

Smart Tip

Tip...

You probably don't need to hire an expensive consultant to write a fancy business plan; it's a waste of time and money. But you do need to write down the basics of your business, no matter what. And you do need a formal business plan if you're seeking venture capital or angel funding. As the business evolves, and as fundamental assumptions change, take out the business plan and update it. Are you still on track to hit your targets?

But it makes no sense whatsoever to consistently sell goods at below-cost prices. How can anybody wonder why so many dotcoms have nearly slid into extinction with such practices?

- *Ignoring stakeholders:* Who has a stake in your business? Investors, your community, your employees, management, your vendors and your customers. Long debates can explode around attempts to prioritize these stake-holders—whose stake is meatiest or weakest?—but probably the best strategy for most dotcoms is to assume that all stakeholders carry about equal weight (except for your community, which, in the case of an internet startup, likely carries no weight at all).

  To succeed, businesses want to satisfy all stakeholders. That doesn't mean all will get what they want (stakeholders quite commonly are in conflict with each other, and a management task is seeing that everybody gets enough to feel happy), but it does mean you need to stay aware of your stakeholders, their wants and what you're delivering. You won't last long if investors, employees, management, vendors or customers get and stay cranky. Failed dotcoms often had little or no awareness that any stakeholders existed (at least any who were not on Wall Street), but stakeholders always exist and will always demand their due.

- *Forgetting what industry you're in:* Guess what? Your online store is still a store, meaning you're competing in a retail universe. Yet CEOs of stumbling dotcoms talk as though they're in any industry but retail, throwing around terms like "new media," "content" and "consulting." Never fool yourself about your industry.

- *Having more ego than profits:* Not only did many CEOs of defunct dotcoms forget what industry they were in, some actually seemed to forget that they were in business at all and that the essence of a business is to make money from revenue—not from bedazzled stock market speculators and frenzied angel investors pouring cash into the till. The sad fact about many failed dotcoms is that they could have been successful—maybe not on the lavish scale hoped for by the founders, but profitable nonetheless. And they blew it by forgetting that in the end, business is business. While it might be fun to appear on the cover of a magazine, it's ultimately more fun to be on top of a steady stream of black ink—and it's no fun at all to manage a business that's dripping red ink.

The message for you: Don't be discouraged by the stumblings of the name-brand dotcoms. They had it coming. That sounds cruel, but really, they did. You can avoid their mistakes and thereby create a very different outcome for your business.

Should You Shut Down Your Brick-and-Mortar Store?

s it time to lock the door of your brick-and-mortar store forever to focus exclusively on online retailing? That's a question many small-business owners have asked when adding online locations. The web and its many opportunities are certainly exciting—often more exciting than Main Street. E-commerce and offline retailing can coexist and, in many cases, the result is greater than the sum of the parts. Sometimes online retailing turns out to be the far better way to go, but not always. Every business is different and you'll have to decide for yourself if it's a good idea to shut down your storefront.

E-tailer Sherry Rand has a definite opinion on the subject. "The smartest thing I've done in business is shutting down my store and going exclusively as an online retailer," she says. "Now I have a really neat business. I love it." Rand has an online store that focuses on a very specific niche—gear for cheerleaders. You want pompoms in various styles and colors? You want megaphones for leading cheers? Then you should know about Pom Express (pomexpress.com), where Rand has conducted e-business for nearly 10 years since she shut the doors of her brick-and-mortar store.

"Online, I don't have to carry the great overhead of a store, and from a quaint town, North Hampton, New Hampshire, I'm selling globally," says Rand. "We get lots of orders from Europe, where cheerleading is really picking up." Rand, herself a cheerleader from fourth grade until she graduated from college, sold cheerleading supplies as a manufacturer's representative until she opened her own store. Now that she's operating solely on the web, she says, "This is a great niche. And on the internet, I can conduct business wherever I want to be."

Moving Out

Sounds good—but good enough to persuade you to dotcom? The temptations are potent. Close a brick-and-mortar operation, go strictly cyber and whoosh—you've distanced yourself from monthly rent payments and dealing face to face with grumpy customers, not to mention that you've positioned your business to sell globally. At least that's what it seems like in theory. But can you count on it happening for you?

Probably not, says Jackie Goforth, a partner for PricewaterhouseCoopers who focuses on retail and e-commerce companies. While she says a great example of an industry that has shifted to online is antique and collectible retailing, "I would say for the average retailer, this is not the time to shut down your shop. I think we will find that retailers will use their online presence as a great complement to their stores. It may actually drive in traffic by allowing the customer to do some online browsing."

Additionally, she says the appeal of being able to return merchandise pur-

Tip...

Smart Tip

What about returns? They're proving to be a real hassle in online retailing—both to e-tailers and to consumers—and that's where e-tailers with brick-and-mortar storefronts have a big advantage because consumers who want to return products can simply take them to the storefront. Smart e-tailers stress this perk, so if it's true for you, flaunt it!

chased online at the local brick-and-mortar store gives shoppers confidence in their online purchases. "There still appears to be some fear that online purchases are difficult to return," she says. "The retailer who carries unique and exclusive merchandise could potentially tap into a much larger market by utilizing the web to reach a broad customer group."

You have to keep in mind, though, that for every dotcom that thrives, there are more that flop, says Mark Layton, president and CEO of Profits in e-Business, a think tank for internet commerce-related business activities and research. "Many dotcoms will become dot bombs—they'll fail," says Layton. "Online or offline, you need a sustainable business model. If you don't have that, you don't have a business."

Having It Both Ways

Experiencing second thoughts about burning the lease on your storefront and going strictly virtual? Consider Vino! (vino2u.com), the online complement to a Winter Park, Florida, wine store, both owned by Rhonda Gore-Scott. Built around the tasty proposition that all the wines it sells are rated 85 or higher by a prestigious publication (such as *Wine Spectator*), both the storefront (opened in 1998) and the online store (launched a month later) are profitable, according to Gore-Scott. "Once you do a little foundation work," she says, "the website offers a very convenient and efficient way to manage another arm of our business."

But she has no intention of shutting down the brick-and-mortar store, for a flock of reasons. For starters, an online operation still needs some real-world warehousing for merchandise such as hers, and the brick-and-mortar store provides that. But it's the second reason that's the clincher: The site sells to many customers outside the area, but there are also many locals coming into the store with shopping lists they've printed out on the web. For those customers, the combination of the website and the store offers a great convenience—they hunt for wines they want online, at midnight or 6 a.m., and then they can get in and out of the brick-and-mortar store in a matter of minutes. "I enjoy the brick-and-mortar portion very much because of the face time with our customers. The two parts are very complimentary," says Gore-Scott. "They combine the human element with the efficient, quick 24/7 element."

Double Vision

Still, isn't this dual-channel strategy an unnecessary complication that forces an entrepreneur to focus on two distinctly different venues? The experts don't think so, and in fact, it has worked exceptionally well for many business owners. "There are tremendous advantages to be had by leveraging net sales with a brick-and-mortar store," says Bart Weitz, a marketing professor at the University of Florida, Gainesville. Case in point: "You can use the store to promote the website," and that means printing your URL on bags, sales slips and advertising fliers. That can be a big step in overcoming the obstacle facing every dotcom today. "It's gotten very expensive to attract people to a site," says Weitz. "Stand-alone sites incur very high marketing expenses because they have to spend the money to get eyeballs."

"A [brick-and-mortar store] can be a billboard for your website," says Bentley College e-commerce professor Bruce Weinberg, who points to clothier Gap as an example. It already has massive brand awareness, and whenever a customer walks in—even walks by—a storefront, there's a reinforcement of the URL,

gap.com. Your business might not be a Gap, but even so, says Weinberg, the fact that you are in a physical location with signage and various advertising campaigns to promote the store will mean that you are also building awareness for your website.

Another argument in favor of a dual-channel strategy: "Different consumers want different things," says William Gartner, the Spiro professor of entrepreneurial leadership at Clemson University in Clemson, South Carolina. "Some customers want the kind of personal interaction that can only happen in a traditional retail setting. For others, it's simpler to log on to the net. The smart, consumer-oriented business makes it easy to buy, no matter the customer's preferences."

Who's Minding the Store?

But the big, worrisome question is "Isn't all retailing heading to the web anyway?" Not necessarily. Explains PricewaterhouseCoopers' Goforth, "There are certain merchandise categories that'll be slow to succeed online—but I would anticipate it will follow the trends seen with the catalog industry. Unique product that is hard to find in stores and expensive for the brick-and-mortar retailer to stock will be the logical players online."

Other types of businesses are going to have a tough time prospering if they're not online as well. Cases in point: bookstores, consumer electronics sellers and travel agen-

Fortunetelling

Want an easy rule of thumb for assessing how your business might fare online? College of William & Mary business professor Jonathan Palmer shares the three factors that shed a green light on this decision:

1. You sell a product line that can be delivered economically and conveniently.

2. You have a desire to market to customers outside your own geographic location and a product with broad appeal.

3. There are significant economic advantages involved in going online.

Chew especially hard on points one and two because if they are on your side, the profits implied in the third point likely will follow.

A fourth decision factor just might be "Can you economically draw customers to your site?" Chasing a mass market—and going belly to belly against Amazon, Drugstore.com, Travelocity and the like—means you had better bring a seven- or eight-figure advertising/marketing budget to the table to keep up with your competitors. But the good news is that there is still plenty of room for thinly funded players who have targeted shrewd niches and have a solid business plan. The experts agree: Those are tomorrow's dotcom success stories.

cies, to name a few. Margins are getting squeezed ever lower as multiple internet vendors and internet-savvy consumers create a situation with increasingly competitive pricing, and that means it will only get tougher to succeed in a brick-and-mortar context. But other types of businesses—from furniture sellers to clothiers—just may find the going stays smooth in brick-and-mortar stores.

"Some products are ideal for online; others just work better in a brick-and-mortar store, where customers want to test the look, feel and fit," says Jonathan Palmer, a business professor at the College of William & Mary in Williamsburg, Virginia.

Worried about being a merchandiser in an endangered category? Don't

Tip...

Smart Tip

With smaller, nonbrand-name sites, a big consumer worry is that your e-commerce site is a fly-by-night scam. When you have a brick-and-mortar storefront, you also have solidity in the minds of consumers. Don't hide it. Put up a photo of it on your website, and definitely show the street address. Bingo—you're an established retailer. Consumer worries will vanish.

panic, says Goforth. "We heard that catalogs would put traditional retailers out of business, and it didn't happen. In fact, some catalog retailers eventually backed into opening brick-and-mortar stores. Now we hear that the web will put B&Ms out of business, and that certainly has not happened. We may see e-tailers going for brick-and-mortar stores."

Website
Building 101

What's stopping you from putting up a website for your business? A big and persistent hurdle is the belief that doing it is hard, technically demanding work. While that might have been true when the World Wide Web first took flight, web page authoring is no longer solely the province of propeller heads. Plenty of easy-to-use software is on the market, and a web newcomer can usually get an initial

▲

page up within a few hours. Better still, all this can be accomplished at a very low cost. "Even the smallest businesses can afford to be on the web," says Mary Cronin, a business professor at Boston College and editor of *The Internet Strategy Handbook* (Harvard Business School Press).

Believe it or not, this is probably the least important chapter in this book. Why? Because putting up a website has become so simple, it's scarcely worth mentioning. And if you don't have time to spare, a small outlay of cash will buy you the services of a local college student or even an outsourced programmer from another country fluent in HTML. Web page creation may be fun for purists, but it is no litmus test of your "right" to be on the web.

But for those of you who want to do it yourself, this chapter provides step-by-step tips for producing your website—from picking the right tools and putting them into use to testing your creation. Set aside a few hours, follow the steps and you, too, will be in business on the web.

Know Your Purpose

The starting point for putting up a website is to determine what you want it to do—and know what it likely won't do. The bad news is that you won't get rich quick with a website. Very few startups have achieved overnight success on the web—the most notable being Amazon. The web just isn't the fast track to Easy Street that too many commentators have depicted it to be.

Then why do it? Of course, persistence and ingenuity may eventually be rewarded with profits. But there are other sound reasons for putting up a website. Even if your home page is little more than an electronic billboard for your company, it's still a powerful tool for building a business. On the web, for instance, "distance means nothing," says Jerry White, director of the Caruth Institute of Owner-Managed Business at Southern Methodist University in Dallas. A small business in the United States can use the web as a low-cost tool for reaching customers in other states, even other countries.

The clock, too, no longer matters. "On the web, your business can be open 24 hours a day, seven days a week," says Gail Houck, a consultant and web strategist. Another reason for building a web presence: The web lets you serve customers in ways that would be unimaginable in a traditional retail environment. On the web, it's easy to offer far deeper product selection, for instance, and—with clear thinking on your side—prices, too, typically can be driven down.

All good reasons? You bet, and you may have many more. Whatever your motivations, the single most important step you can take is this one: Define your goals and expectations. Do that, and the rest—including the mechanics of site design—will fall into place.

Where so many small businesses (and a few very large ones, too) go wrong is that they haven't taken this clarifying step. The resulting sites are fundamentally confusing because nobody ever took the time to specify their purpose. It's perfectly fine to erect a site that amounts to a company information brochure, but that site cannot be expected to function as a retail platform.

Getting Started

In the not-too-distant past, building a website meant hours of writing HTML code, line by line. Today's leading web-authoring tools are solidly WYSIWYG, which is computer-speak for "what you see is what you get." Building a page now involves little more than clicking a mouse.

Which tool to use? The top choice—both for usability and affordability—is WebExpress from MicroVision Development (about $70), available for download and purchase at mvd.com/WebExpress. It is super easy to use and you don't have to know a thing about HTML code; WebExpress will walk you through the process. You'll be able to create a professional-looking website that will have you up on the web in no time.

Another option is Visual Site Designer from CoffeeCup Software (coffeecup.com). For only $49, you can get a super simple-to-use website builder that allows you to build a customized site from scratch or from one of 60 templates. Newbies should probably choose a template, and then tweak it to get it just the way you want it. One of the advantages of CoffeeCup is you don't have to buy an expensive bundled package. There are dozens of special applications you can buy ($39 to $49) separately to build forms, add killer Flash effects, provide live chat and so on. It doesn't include a shopping cart program, but it will support any outside shopping cart program you designate.

Budget Watcher

Try WebExpress for free by downloading the software from vd.com/WebExpress/download.htm. This is full-featured trialware, about 4.5MB. And even if you decide not to buy the software, any pages you have created are yours to use on the web.

If you want the best web-authoring tool out there, check out Adobe's Dreamweaver (adobe.com/products/dreamweaver). It's the top choice for most professional web developers. You can build a sophisticated website from scratch either in text (code) or visually (WYSIWYG). It doesn't come with its own templates, but it will support any template you want to use. There are hundreds of free templates available on the net. Pick one you like, and Dreamweaver will automatically use the template design throughout your website. Dreamweaver lists for $399, but you can find it for a lot less if you shop around, and you can try it out for free.

▲

On File

You've created umpteen wonderful web pages, so now how do you get them onto your website? You need another piece of software, a program that handles FTP (file transfer protocol). An FTP program lets you shift files from your computer to another via an internet connection, and that makes it an essential piece of any net toolkit.

FTP is built into CoffeeCup's Visual Site Designer and many other web page editors, but personally, I have long found it faster and easier to use a specialty FTP program. For years I've relied on WS_FTP. Its newest version is WS_FTP Home 2007 ($39.95 from Ipswitch Inc., ipswitch.com). A free trial version is available for download.

An alternative is Cute FTP ($39.99 for the Home version, $59.99 for the Professional version), available from GlobalSCAPE at cuteftp.com. Hunt for still others at CNET's downloads site—download.com. Type in FTP, and you'll be presented with dozens of apps that do this work.

Check out several apps and pick the one that works best for you—and know that, even if you've never FTP'd, once you get into website construction and maintenance, your FTP application will become one that's put to daily use.

A word of caution: FTP software generally seems tricky to use. That's because you need to precisely specify your user name, password, etc., and you must also correctly type everything in the right case (upper or lower). It can be a bit maddening to get an FTP program working right, but once you do, settings will be saved and future transfers will be no harder than a few mouse clicks. For more tips, head to "FTP 101—A Beginner's Guide" at ftpplanet.com/ftpresources/basics.htm. It's a helpful, free guide that should get you up and running in a matter of minutes.

Oh, a vocabulary point: When you transfer a file to your website, that's uploading. When you transfer a file from a website to your computer, that's downloading. Keep those words straight, and all you read about FTP will suddenly make more sense.

On a Shoestring

Do you need new software to create a website? Not necessarily. Most web hosting services offer site-building tools as part of their package. But these are web-based, not software you have on your own computer. This is where most new e-tailers start because it's free, easy, convenient, and you get free 24/7 handholding if you get stuck. Most offer templates only, but templates limit what you're able to do. Look for a host

Image Boosters

When you use images on the web, you need specialty software that will let you change the image's size, resolution and more. Good image-editing software will even let you touch up photographs. There's a stain on your white shirt in that photo? Whoosh! An image editor will wipe away all such problems.

Such software used to be tricky to use and expensive and was mainly aimed at professionals working in graphics and photography. Nowadays, there's a boatload of good, cheap, easy-to-use programs. A top choice is Adobe Photoshop Elements (adobe.com/products/photoshop/family/), which costs $99.

More good choices come from Ulead (ulead.com), a Taiwan-based software developer that excels at creating wonderful and very cheap graphics-editing tools. For instance, SmartSaver Pro ($59.95) allows nearly instant changes in an image's format and size. Why is that important? On a web page, you generally want small images that display fast, and with SmartSaver Pro, it's simple to save many versions until you get the right balance of size and graphical quality for your site.

Another must-have Ulead program is PhotoImpact ($89.99). The poor man's Photoshop, PhotoImpact is the solution when you cannot lay hands on Photoshop Elements. It's easy to use, versatile and powerful, and it will allow for creative reshaping of images to suit your website.

You can't create quality web pages without owning image-editing software—but you don't need to spend big bucks or enroll in college courses to master sophisticated software. For most of us, less than $200 will buy all we need. A big plus with Ulead is that most of its programs are available for free trial downloads. Next time you wish you could tweak an image, visit Ulead, download the tool you need—and just do it!

that will provide both templates and tools to create your own design. Best option: GoDaddy.com will also build your site for you. So if you run out of time or just don't have the patience to figure it out, $49 is all it takes to get you up and running fast.

Puttin' on the Glitz

The web is a graphical medium—words matter, but images are just as important in attracting and holding viewers. That's why both WebExpress and Visual Site

Designer come bundled with collections of free art—textured page backgrounds, buttons, arrows and other visual elements for helping readers navigate a site.

Want to go a visual step beyond? Check out these options:

- *Get flashy:* Add some Flash to your site with CoffeeCup Firestarter (free to try, $49 to buy). You can quickly create complex image and sound effects with just a few clicks of the mouse—Flash Intro pages, graphic logos, MP3 sounds, special effects or whatever you want.

- *Another artistic option:* Forget trying to make your own images and just roam the web in a hunt for free art that has been uploaded by graphic artists who are happy just to get their work in the public view and gladly let others download their images. Start enhancing a web page's graphics with a visit to FreeGraphics (freegraphics.com), where you'll find hundreds of buttons, bars, photos, clipart and things that spin, wiggle, crawl and fly (animated graphics). There is even free graphic viewing and editing software and a list of websites where you can create your own buttons, logos and 3D art—all without downloading or purchasing software. Most—but not all—of the graphics can be used free for commercial as well as personal websites. However, there are a number of different sources, so you'll want to be sure and check the guidelines for each.

- *How about this great source?* You can get very high-quality imagery at iStockPhoto (istockphoto.com). You'll find royalty-free stock photography, vector illustrations, Flash files and videos for as little as $1 and no higher than $20—a small price to pay for enhancements that will make your site much more polished.

Many days can be spent downloading images—the web is swamped with terrific free art. But the chief beef of surfers is long waits for pages to load, invariably caused by creating a page with too many graphics. You want a clean, uncluttered site that not only loads easily but looks professional. So use images sparingly. A few brighten a page; too many drown it. Follow these rules for a light, clean site:

- *Keep it small:* Another reason graphics take so long to load is that they may be too big. Graphics are measured in pixels, and web page display sizes can differ. In an old-school small monitor, a 640-by-480 pixel web page rendered nicely. However, most people are now using monitors that can render 800-by-600 pixel or 1024-by-768 pixel sites.

Tip...

Smart Tip

Don't go crazy with colors—this is one of the biggest goofs of new web page designers. Stick with maybe two colors for fonts (words) and use a simple, basic color for the page background (white, off-white and pale yellow are good choices). Always test your page on a laptop with a very cheap screen—don't assume surfers have high-end monitors. If it doesn't look good on a small, cheap screen, it's bad page design.

Most images shouldn't be any wider than 500 pixels and no higher than about 300 pixels. To avoid bringing a surfer to a screeching halt on your website, make sure your images are no bigger than 20K. For maximum downloading speed, each web page—including images and text—should be under 45K.

- *Another caveat:* Before uploading any images you didn't create yourself to your website, carefully read the fine print on the artist's page. Some prohibit use on commercial sites. If in doubt, ask for permission. That is a sure cure against future complications. Always assume an image is copyrighted, unless there is an explicit statement that says it can be used for free.

- *Something to keep in mind:* Simple is best with a web page. Better an unglamorous page that loads rapidly than a state-of-the-art page that causes the browsers of half your visitors to crash. When a mania seizes you and you want to design pages with fancy looks and the newest bells and whistles, put that stuff on a personal page, not your business site. All those toys are fun to play with—but web visitors hate them.

- *A reliable rule of thumb:* The more times you say "wow" as you design your web page, the worse it is. You want to create a page where the wow factor is minimal in terms of design but high in terms of functionality.

Testing, Testing

Gremlins often play tricks with web pages, and that's why no professional webmaster announces a new page to the public before testing it. Surf the web enough, and sooner or later you'll stumble into a test site mounted by a brand-name business that has put it online in a "beta" version so that insiders can find the bugs before the public does. Do the same thorough testing before publicizing your page.

A crucial test: Make sure pages work equally well in Microsoft Internet Explorer and Mozilla's Firefox, which is quickly gaining on Internet Explorer in the browser race. Ignore this advice at your own peril. It's also easy to forget all the Mac users out there. Test on a Windows machine and a Mac, using Apple's Safari and Firefox browsers. (Microsoft no longer supports an Internet Explorer browser for Mac users.) If you're a Windows user and you don't have access to a Mac, find a friend who has one to test for you.

If, in testing your own site, you find bugs, don't fret. Few pages get put up

Smart Tip
When updating pages, always go through your testing procedure as soon as you put up the changes. It's tempting to neglect this, but don't. Too often I've put up updated pages that, somehow, turned out to be bug-ridden. And never do page changes during your peak traffic periods! That's inviting calamity.

without at least some kinks, and a good place to start is to pinpoint things that show up on your screen offline but don't work online. One standard problem is that an image (or two or three) isn't displaying, caused by a botched hyperlink. Strip down any web page to its essentials, and you'll find a little text interspersed with many hyperlinks, which are web directions to images and other files stored elsewhere. Put in the wrong hyperlink—and sometimes even web-authoring programs do it—and the online page will show up as a jumble.

This is when it's time to do a spot of dirty work with HTML code. In your web-authoring program, find the button that says something like "View HTML" or "View code" and click on it. A screen filled with gibberish will open. Hunt for the code pointing to the image or text that is not displaying. A good bet is that the link reads <img src="C:\Windows\temp\bluediamond.gif"> or something like that. No link that includes directions to local drives will work online ("C:\" is your local drive). The cure? Erase everything that comes before the image's name—the result will read <img src="bluediamond.gif">—and it should work exactly right online, but only if the image is saved in your main folder. If you've saved it to an images folder or in another subfolder, you will need to include the entire file path. For example, if you have your "bluediamond.gif" image in a file called "products/womens/images" then your code needs to read "img src= products/womens/images/bluediamond.gif."

Another common mistake: getting either the name of the image or the extension wrong. If you downloaded a photo with the name "bluediamonds" (plural), but wrote "bluediamond" (singular), it won't work. Likewise, if your photo is in a JPEG format, it should read "bluediamond.jpg," not "bluediamnond.gif."

Follow the same drill with anything that's not displaying properly. HTML is intimidating at first glance—and at second glance, too. But tinker with it, and soon enough, all images and links will display the way you intended.

Keep It Fresh

A sure way to go wrong with a website is to put it up and leave it there. To keep viewers coming back, a page needs regular updating. "If your page is aging, static, it says, 'I don't get it,' " says Boston College's Cronin.

How often does a site need updating? Probably once a month at a minimum for a brochure-type site, weekly for an e-commerce site, and daily for a content-driven site. Updating takes time, but the investment is warranted, says White at Southern Methodist. "The internet is a new frontier with limitless possibilities," he says. "Now is the time to experiment...before lack of competency puts you out of business."

Hosted e-Commerce Solutions

Pssst. Want to know a shortcut that eliminates much of your need to know how to build a website and still puts you in an e-commerce business? Then you want to know about Yahoo! Merchant Solutions, a service that allows you to easily create an online store (smallbusiness.yahoo.com/ecommerce).

As opposed to doing it yourself, Yahoo! Merchant Solutions allows small businesses to get major league e-commerce capabilities in an easy-to-use and affordable solution.

Here's the promise of the service: You don't need to know a speck of HTML code, but within a short period of time, you will have an online store that looks good—and all you have to do is follow a form-driven set of instructions. Think of it as akin to cooking with a recipe. If you follow the instructions that Yahoo! provides, the result will be a credible, attractive site. A plus is that Yahoo! helps customers obtain a merchant account so they can accept credit card payments online.

Keep in mind that while Yahoo! does everything it can to make it easy to create an online store, it still takes a few hours, or if a customer needs to set up a merchant account for online credit card payments, several days.

Basically, when you purchase a Yahoo! Merchant Solutions package, you get web hosting and a full suite of e-commerce software to build a product catalog, create a custom checkout process, manage orders and track your performance. Yahoo! also helps merchants succeed online by providing 30 days of free consulting, easy-to-use tools, extensive online help and 24-hour toll-free support. Another important plus—you get featured on Yahoo! Shopping at a 20 percent discount, a fantastic source of traffic.

Are we recommending Yahoo! Merchant Solutions over stand-alone, do-it-yourself storefronts? It depends on what you want and how much time you are willing to invest.

As any surfer knows, the web is cluttered with millions of poorly constructed, nonfunctional storefronts that get little or no traffic. It is easy to construct a viable store with, say, Visual Site Designer—but "easy" does not mean effortless. Many, many hours go into the job, and your time investment can be slashed dramatically by turning to the templates offered by Yahoo! Merchant Solutions or a similar provider. Unfortunately, many

Budget Watcher

A Yahoo! location in particular may be real gold because of how it promotes its stores. Search for "Turkish coffee" on Yahoo!, for instance, and it's a fast hop into a couple of small e-tailers selling that brew as well as pots, cups and so forth. Just as a suburban mall brings its merchants traffic, Yahoo! attracts shoppers to its stores.

aspiring e-tailers end up with a poorly-designed website when they go the do-it-yourself route. So think hard about the Yahoo! Merchant Solutions option. This could be the solution you need.

How much does it cost to have a Yahoo! Merchant Solutions online store? After the initial $50 setup fee, you pay $39.95 per month for hosting, and a 1.5 percent fee on all transactions. Here's a tip: Yahoo! routinely offers deals like 25 percent off and no setup fee. The sale announcement goes up and down frequently on the site, so ask for it if you don't see it. If you decide to participate in Yahoo! Shopping, there is a 20 percent savings on the cost of per-click fees for all traffic that is sent to your storefront.

Other e-tailers turn to eBay (ebay.com) for their online storefront services—especially those e-tailers who are already experimenting with eBay. eBay Stores allow you to sell your fixed-price and auction items from a unique destination on eBay. You can build your own eBay Store through an easy series of steps: Create customized categories, include your own logo or choose one of eBay's online images, and list item descriptions and policies.

Your eBay Store is promoted to more than 204 million eBay users in several ways: All your listings will contain an eBay Store "red door" icon inviting buyers to visit your eBay Store; the eBay Store icon is attached to your user ID for extra visibility; buyers will be driven to your store through the eBay Store Directory, which is designed to promote all stores; and you will receive your own personalized eBay Store website address to distribute and promote.

The price is right, too. eBay offers three subscription fees: $15.95 per month for a Basic Store, $49.95 per month for a Premium Store, and $299.95 per month for an Anchor Store. In addition to the insertion and final value fees for regular online auction and fixed-price formats, eBay Store owners can use the longer duration store inventory format for a lower insertion fee (3, 5, or 10 cents for insertions depending on the price of the listed item, and 1 cent for gallery images) for up to 30 days. The insertion fee increases after that based on the duration of your listing, and your final-value fees are based on the final sale price of your item. You'll also need to be registered as an eBay seller by putting your credit card on file, and have a minimum feedback rating of 20, pay $5 to become ID-verified or have a PayPal account in good standing. For more information on eBay Stores, visit pages.ebay.com/storefronts/start.html and check out Entrepreneur's Startup Guide *eBay Business*.

Another storefront option is Amazon. For only $59.99 (plus 7 percent commission), Amazon's WebStore (amazonservices.com/webstore) will give you your own branded web business backed by the support, selection and expertise of Amazon. It's so easy to set up, you can start selling online in minutes. WebStore comes with a number of great marketing features like product recommendations, customer reviews, and recently viewed items for your own store.

Because your WebStore is associated with Amazon, existing Amazon customers can use their Amazon customer account to buy products from your WebStore. If customers don't have Amazon accounts, they can simply create one as they place an order on your site. Your customers get the safety and protection of the Amazon shopping cart and you get the fraud protection of Amazon's checkout system.

Seller Central is the online interface used to manage all aspects of WebStore. Through Seller Central, you can add product information, make inventory updates, retrieve orders and design your WebStore through a suite of web-based and downloadable tours. And you can take advantage of Amazon's fulfillment service—a great idea if you don't have much space. Just send your inventory to Amazon's fulfillment center, and when orders are placed through your store, Amazon will pick, pack and ship the products to your customers.

There are other options as well: Small merchants can use hosted e-commerce solutions from companies such as Volusion (volusion.com), Affinity Internet (affinity.com) and 1 and 1 Internet Inc. (1and1.com). In general, like the Yahoo! and eBay solutions, these sites provide everything you need to do business online, but without taking a bite out of your profits. They offer a combination of shopping cart technology, merchandising, payment, shipping, marketing smarts and, of course, hosting. For most people, these solutions are a lot better than doing it yourself.

Free Online Store

Another option for e-tailers is osCommerce (oscommerce.com), an open-source online e-commerce solution that is available for free. It allows store owners to set up, run and maintain their online stores with minimum effort and with no costs, license fees or limitations involved.

The services provided on the network of osCommerce support sites are continually improved to match the growing community the project has attracted in its seven years of operation. Today, this community consists of more than 12,800 registered online stores around the world, and more than 1,100 community members and project enthusiasts who help make the project succeed.

For more on web hosting, see Chapter 10, and for more on payment options, see Chapter 27.

Advanced Tools
and Tricks

Now that your site is up, how do you make it special and filled with content that attracts visitors and keeps them coming back? That mission consumes site-builders, both full-time professionals and part-timers, but if there is one fact we now know to be absolutely true, it is this: Simplicity is best.

Case in point: The website for a luxury hotel chain based

▲

in India features a huge soundtrack of classical music, which is just annoying. Maybe some sitar tracks—authentic Indian music—might make sense, but classical? It's bandwidth-hogging craziness. Resist the temptation to put something on your site just because you can. Never put up content that slows access to a page, especially if it doesn't demonstrably improve your users' experience on your site.

What works? Content that gives users reasons to linger, to absorb more of what you're offering. You'll find there are many, many ways to introduce this content, and you are going to have to exercise real discretion here. Pick a few tools, try them out, monitor user responses, and then delete the ones that don't prove their value. Be ruthless here, and never forget that simple is better.

That understood, here are many tasty tools for you to consider using to beef up your site. Just remember, this may be an all-you-can-eat buffet, but the more you put on your plate, the more discomfort your website visitors will feel.

- *Polls:* Polls, where surfers register their opinion on an issue, are at the heart of the net because this is interactivity in its most basic form. You can use surveys to improve any aspect of your business—and everything and anything can be surveyed. Thinking about launching a new product? Conduct a survey to find out if anyone is interested, what benefits they'd like to see, and how it could beat the competition. For existing products, survey your customers to learn how your products rank with similar ones and what they think could be improved. A particularly effective (and popular) survey uncovers interesting new ways to use products—you can't ask for a better marketing tool than that!

Writing a survey from scratch is a tricky bit of coding, but free polling templates are readily available for insertion into your site. All you have to do is fill in the blanks in a template and copy and paste a bit of code into your site, and you're in business. Sources of such templates are plentiful, but good ones are available from surveymonkey.com or freepolls.com.

- *Blogs:* At its most basic, a blog is a frequently updated, timed and dated online journal with a good dose of links involved. That may not sound like much to get excited about, but it has gone beyond fad to become a full-fledged internet phenomenon. The elements of interactivity, community and collaboration are key as growing businesses adopt blogs for customer relations, advertising, promotion and even internal communications.

There has been an explosion of blog marketing since 2006. Companies ranging from IBM to Stonyfield Yogurt are using blogs as effective marketing tools. They've realized this simple method of getting their message out can increase exposure, generate buzz, and even elevate their website's position on search engines. Most web hosts today provide blogging tools, but you can also pick one up for free from WordPress (wordpress.org).

- *RSS feeds:* Originally built to distribute syndicated news, RSS instant notification promises a host of other uses—including innovative marketing for your business.

The fast-spreading internet standard lets you instantly publish or receive bits of text and graphics. While it's currently used to show the latest news and blog updates, there's no limit to what it could be used for. RSS, originally created by Netscape as a simple way to swap news headlines between consenting languages but later picked up and improved on by UserLand, stands for Really Simple

Smart Tip

Use web tools sparingly. Best advice: Introduce one, and only one. If it proves popular, leave it up and add a second. If users ignore it, put up another but take down the unloved tool. Always keep it simple, and you'll invariably do better.

Syndication. (RSS, in earlier versions, also stood for Rich Site Summary or RDF Site Summary.) RSS is based on XML, which XML.com defines as "a markup language for documents containing structured information," which really just means a language that allows you to easily markup, sort and display data.

To see RSS in action, either download and install an RSS reader (also known as an RSS aggregator) from the web or use a web-based service. Open the reader, and you'll see a few sample RSS "feeds" with the latest headlines for each. Depending on the reader, the headlines may appear in your browser, in a separate application that looks much like an e-mail application, or within another application such as Microsoft Outlook. Simply click on a headline to bring up its associated web page.

Budget Watcher

Most RSS readers are free. NewsGator (newsgator.com/ Individuals/Default.aspx) offers several free, downloadable readers, including FeedDemon for PCs, NewNewsWire for Macs, NewsGator Go! for mobile devices, and NewsGator Inbox for Outlook Express. You can also easily read RSS feeds in a browser by signing up for free on sites like Bloglines (bloglines.com), Google Reader (google.com/reader) or My Yahoo! (my.yahoo.com).

While this will appeal to the news junkie in you, RSS' marketing skill may prove more powerful for your firm. In the simplest example, you could spiff up your website by adding RSS feeds from news services or blogs that will intrigue site visitors. More strikingly, in the future, RSS may handle marketing tasks where e-mail now falls flat. For example, as with e-mail, visitors can sign up for marketing alerts (for instance, useful product news plus discount coupons). Unlike e-mail, visitors can rest assured that they can't be spammed. If you don't like what you're getting via RSS, just pull the plug.

Where do you get RSS feeds for your website? There are several good sources of free RSS feeds, but be aware that most of them are ad-supported. At Moreover.com (moreover.com/site/products/ind/rss_feeds.html), a premier provider of real-time news and information, you can search for the perfect RSS feed from dozens of categories. You can even create your own customized feed. One caveat is that when you feature RSS feeds from other sites and they don't include the full text of the news or blog item, readers may click out to that site to view the full item. If you worry about people leaving your site and not returning, outside RSS feeds may not be for you.

An RSS feed can be especially effective as a marketing tool if you create your own messages rather than republish someone else's content. Creating RSS feeds from scratch is not really that difficult and you don't need a degree in XML programming. There are many tools available for do-it-yourselfers, including free Internet tools and low-cost software with wizards that walk you through the process. Most blog programs also have RSS feed creation functions.

RSS Feed Creator from Webvigour Software (free to try, $23.95 to buy, webvigour.com) is a good desktop RSS editor that allows you to create and maintain your own RSS newsfeeds with easy-to-use WYSIWYG editing. All you have to do is give your feed a title, write a short summary, enter the link to the web page URL that contains the full text, and hit "finish."

- *Podcasting:* A podcast is an effective method of publishing recorded audio and video presentations through the internet, in a way that will automatically tell your listeners when your new material is available. With a podcast, you can have your own radio show heard round the globe. Your listeners can tune in at their convenience on their own iPods or mp3 players.

You don't have to know anything about RSS or learn any programming code to create your own podcast. There are many free and low-cost websites and software that will help you easily create your podcast, host your files and help you distribute them. If you can click a mouse, you can create a podcast.

Want to know how easy it is to start podcasting? Check out ClickCaster (clickcaster.com), a business podcasting service that ranges from free to $29.95, depending on how fancy you want to get. ClickCaster's demo will walk you through the process so you'll have a good idea of what's involved—which isn't much. ClickCaster offers several enhancements such as embedding video into a blog or social networking profile, plus a worldwide distribution system designed with businesses in mind.

- *CGI scripts:* These are easy-to-use scripts (prewritten code) that you simply pop into your page to create a guest book, display images in different ways, add tests and quizzes, or gain the ability to track visitors. CGI (or Common Gateway Interface, a programming tool that lets many small applications run within a web environment) is one of the web's oldest resources. Newer, slicker ways to do much of what can be accomplished via CGI are plentiful, but the real plus is their price tag and simplicity: Scripts put together by enthusiasts are free and available for anyone to use. Always test any CGI script thoroughly before going public with a page, however. Because they're free and created by hobbyists, they may contain errors or not be up to snuff for the latest browsers.

Thousands of free CGI scripts exist, and one of the best resources for finding the scripts you need is The CGI Resource Index (cgi.resourceindex.com). If you can't find the script you want here, it probably doesn't exist.

- *JavaScripts:* Feeling patriotic? Add a flag waving in the breeze. Want your customers to know what time it is? Add a clock that ticks away in real time. You can add just about anything—calculators, interactive games, security passwords, e-mail forms, ticker tapes and special effects (like those fireworks)—with a JavaScript. It's an easy-to-use programming language that can be embedded in your web page's code. You don't have to be a programmer to come up with one. There are thousands of free JavaScripts on the net. Just browse through the categories on JavaFile.com (javafile.com) to find what you want. Adding the code to your page is very simple; unless you want to change any background colors, text colors or images, it's a basic cut-and-paste job. Visit JavaFile.com's "Help" section (javafile.com/help.php) for basic instructions.

- *Chat rooms and instant messengers:* It's easy to put up a private, real-time chat room on your site, and free from FreeJavaChat (freejavachat.com). Just click on the chat code generator to build a customized chat room for your website. Before you do, however, mull this over: Empty chat rooms look very, very dumb. Will you have enough traffic to put people into a chat room on a regular basis? Do you want to monitor it? How frequently? Know that you won't be on call 24 hours a day, seven days a week—but the chat room will, theoretically, be available that often. My advice: For most small sites, this is a tool to avoid.

Better by far is to set yourself up with a free instant messenger account from companies such as AOL (aim.com), Yahoo! (messenger.yahoo.com), MSN (webmessenger.msn.com) or Google (google.com/talk), where visitors can fire off questions to you if you're online. This gives surfers instant gratification and an alternative to e-mail for finding information, but doesn't expose you to the ridicule that comes with offering an unpopulated chat room. Do this in combination with providing a message board, and surfer needs ought to be very adequately handled.

- *Forums/message boards:* Message boards or forums are a great way to get feedback and encourage interactivity with your visitors. Createmybb

> **Tip...**
>
> **Smart Tip**
> If you decide to offer original content in your site's e-mail newsletter, be sure to archive that content on your website—otherwise, you're just letting that information go to waste. Giving visitors a taste of what your newsletter offers may also entice newcomers to sign up as well. For more information on e-mail newsletters, turn to Chapter 22.

(createmybb.com) is a free forum hosting service that's easy to set up and administer—simply fill out a short series of forms. You can even customize the appearance and features of your message board to match the style of your website.

At least in the beginning—and possibly long after that—you'll have to nurture discussions on your forums. After all, someone has to post first, and someone has to police the joint in case any conflicts and heated arguments break out. If your forums get really popular, you may be able to hire a local college student to manage them or give your most trusted users administrative status so they can do the policing for you.

- *News feeds, content and more:* A secret traffic-builder of the big websites is regularly updating content. Usually, that means paying writers and other content creators big bucks to produce copy, but you don't need to spend that kind of money.

There are plenty of legitimate ways to get new content without having to write it all yourself. If you see an article you like somewhere on the net, you may be able to get permission to reprint it. Or if you have a special-interest site, many of your readers may enjoy contributing occasional stories just for the thrill of seeing their names in virtual print.

This type of user-generated content (UGC) has been a huge trend on many sites for the past few years. Consider how much Amazon uses content created by its users, from product reviews to its Listmania section, where customers create lists of products on their favorite topics, like science fiction or knitting. Other examples of UGC are user-generated video site YouTube (youtube.com), reviews site Yelp (yelp.com) and the social bookmarking site Digg (digg.com), where users bookmark an interesting site, video or news story, and other users comment on that link.

Of course, the best part of UGC is that it's created for free by users. The difficulty is sifting through piles of nonsense to find the gems and managing your community to weed out offensive or inappropriate material. If you don't want to open the floodgate, ask a select few of your site's most ardent fans to contribute testimonials, expert reviews of products, or a guest entry on your company blog.

Another common content-gathering technique is to incorporate a newsfeed onto your site. This can be done a lot cheaper than you would imagine, and it automatically keeps your site updated with a fresh news section. The process is simple: The newsfeed provider simply gives you a piece of code, which you paste directly onto your web page. They take it from there. The news window that this code makes appears on your site links back directly to its own news server, constantly updating the content in the background. One place to look for newsfeeds is Moreover (w.moreover.com/site/products/ind/rss_feeds.html). If you're on a tighter budget, there are free or very low-cost models that often supplement their content with advertising. You can find a list of free sources at FreeSticky (freesticky.com). But examine the content carefully before incorporating it—some of the free content may be nothing more than a thinly disguised advertisement for something unrelated to your website's mission.

- *Daily content:* Many website visitors appreciate sites that offer a "tip of the day" and visit them on a daily basis, often in the morning, to glean the day's tip. Or they subscribe to a daily newsletter full of tips—and advertising. Some companies—like Daily Candy (dailycandy.com)—have even been founded just on the premise of providing free daily tips via an e-mail newsletter. Types of daily content include philosophical tips, household hints, jokes, obscure word definitions, hip events, poignant quotes or puzzles. To start, you don't have to come up with 365 of them; instead, work on a few months' worth of tips. Just be sure you're committed to your project—you don't want to get customers addicted to your daily dose of wisdom or fun, only to leave them high and dry when you run out of ideas. (For more on ways to make your site sticky, see Chapter 22.)

> **Tip...**
>
> ## Smart Tip
>
> Have you ever visited a website, intending to grab a quick bit of information only to look up and realize two hours have passed? You've landed on a "sticky" website. A sticky website is one that has somehow managed to grab and hold your attention so you "stick around" a while. Top websites invest a lot of money and effort to get sticky. Why? Because the longer surfers stick around, the more likely they'll become a paying customer.

- *Video:* Companies of all sizes are taking advantage of the YouTube phenomenon and so should you. Although there are other video-sharing sites where you can upload and share videos (like Vimeo, Google Video and Flickr), YouTube is the place to be if you want a potential audience of millions.

You could put your videos on your own website, but this giant video-hosting site can save you valuable storage space on your own web server while delivering all those viewers. Plus, you don't have to worry about all the bandwidth that's being used when visitors watch your videos. If you're lucky enough to have a video go viral, you don't risk having your servers overload and shut down—YouTube's servers will handle the load. If you want, you can still display the video on your own site by embedding a short snippet of code provided by YouTube. This is also free of charge. YouTube then serves the video from its site to appear on your web page. It's a good compromise.

If you already have a business-related video, you're about five minutes away from sharing it with the world. Uploading is free and easy—just follow the simple YouTube instructions. If your video runs longer than 10 minutes or is bigger than 100MB, use a free program like Microsoft Movie Maker to split the video up and compress the file size. Add transitions and splice together the clips with YouTube Remixer. You can find the Remixer from your account page by going to "My Videos" and clicking the "Remix Video" button next to any video that you'd like to remix.

▲

If you don't have a video yet, think carefully about the type of video you'd like to create. It might be a commercial, a message from your company president, or a "how-to" that educates your potential customers. Remember, the idea is to expand your audience and your customer base—not entertain random viewers with clever razzle-dazzle.

- *Bookmarking/sharing:* Social bookmarking, a trend that started in 2004, is a quick and effective way of getting targeted traffic to your website. It's a method for internet users to store, organize, search and manage bookmarks of web pages with the help of metadata (data about data). There are now tons of social bookmarking sites where users can save links to web pages that they want to remember and/or share. Users can categorize their links, personalize the links by adding comments, and allow other people to see the bookmarks and add their own comments.

Social bookmarking is a form of viral marketing. It works like this: Bookmarks are categorized according to the tags placed on them by users. Users can add ratings and comments, e-mail the bookmarks, and share them with other social networks. The people who are searching for similar tags or keywords will click on the bookmarks and visit the websites for more information. Targeted traffic is generated organically, boosting your search engine rankings at the same time. A great deal, especially considering it's absolutely free.

One of the oldest and most popular social bookmarking sites is Digg (digg.com). A prime example of social networking, traffic spikes from Digg have been known to crash websites—it's that good at driving traffic. Everything on Digg is submitted by users: news, videos, blogs, podcasts and more. When a bookmark is submitted, Digg users vote to "Digg it" if they like it or to "bury it" if they don't. If your submission rocks and receives enough "Diggs," its promoted to the front page for the millions of Digg visitors to see. If that happens, you'd better be prepared with some major bandwidth to handle the traffic.

Want to make sure visitors create a buzz for your site? Check out AddThis (addthis.com), a free bookmarking and sharing button. The button is very easy to install and it can be customized to match the look and feel of your website. Once installed, users can just click the button to bookmark your site on dozens of social bookmarking and networking sites (Facebook, Digg, Reddit.com, StumbleUpon.com, etc.). It even provides valuable statistics about your users' bookmarking and sharing activities.

The 10 Most
Deadly Mistakes in Web Design

This chapter could probably be called the 100 most deadly mistakes in site design—there are so many goofs site builders make—but let's narrow the focus down to the most disastrous 10. Avoid these gaffes, and your site will be far better than much of the competition.

1. **Disabling the back button:** Evil site authors long ago figured out how to break a browser's back button so that when a user pushes it, one of several undesired things happen: There's an immediate redirect to an unwanted location, the browser stays put because the "back" button has been deactivated, or a new window pops up and overtakes the screen. Pornography site authors are masters of this—their code is often so malicious that frequently the only way to break the cycle is to restart the computer. This trick has gained currency with other kinds of site builders. Our advice: Never do it. All that's accomplished is that viewers get annoyed.

2. **Opening new windows:** Once upon a time, using multiple new frames to display content as a user clicked through a site was cool—a new thing in web design. Now it only annoys viewers because it ties up system resources, slows computer response and generally complicates a surfer's experience. Sure, it's easy to use this tool. But don't. With tabbed browsing common in browsers like Firefox, users who wish to open links in new tabs can do so easily—and you can trust that other users know how to open entirely new pages or how to use the back button.

3. **Failing to put a phone number and address in a plainly seen location:** If you're selling, you need to offer viewers multiple ways to contact you. The smartest route is to put up a "Contact Us" link that leads to complete info—mailing address, phone, fax number and e-mail address. That link should be on each and every page of the website. Even if nobody ever calls, the very presence of this information adds real-world legitimacy to your site and comforts some viewers.

4. **Broken links:** Bad links—hyperlinks that do nothing when clicked or lead to "404" error pages—are the bane of any surfer. Test your site—and do it weekly—to ensure that all links work as promised. Include a "Contact the webmaster" link in your site's footer (the area at the bottom of each page of your site) so users can quickly let you know if they find a broken link or other mistake on your site—and fix those errors immediately.

5. **Slow server times:** Slow times are inexcusable with professional sites. It's an invitation to the visitor to click away. What's slow? A recent study by Akamai Technologies, commissioned through Jupiter Research, showed that online shoppers, on average, will wait only four seconds for a site to load before clicking away. If your site is loading significantly slower than this,

Budget Watcher

Check your site for broken links, automatically and free, with a stop at Keynote NetMechanic (netmechanic.com). Type in your URL, and—whoosh!—you will get a report on broken links and page load time, and even a freebie spell check. It can also give a free report on browser compatibility on the spot.

put it on a diet—images may be too large or special add-ons, like a Flash intro-duction, may be slowing things down.

6. **Outdated information:** Again, there's no excuse, but it's stunning how many site builders lazily leave up pages that long ago ceased to be accurate. When informa-tion changes, update the appropriate pages immediately—and this means every bit of information, every fact, even tiny ones. As a small business, you cannot afford the loss of credibility that can come from having even a single factual goof.

7. **Poor navigation:** The internet promises speed. If surfers can't figure out where to go next quickly and get there easily, they'll simply surf on to the next web-site—your competitor's! It's very frustrating to be forced to go back two or three pages to get to other areas of a site. It's also a waste of time. There should be a naviga-tion bar on every page that guides visitors to other areas of the site. Position the bar along the top of the page or along the left side so that it will always be visible regardless of screen resolution. Add an easy-to-find site map in your main naviga-tion bar and/or footer to provide visitors with an at-a-glance view of every page on your site.

> **Tip...**
>
> ## Smart Tip
>
> OK, there are exceptions to the "no orphans" rule. If you want a special page set aside only for invited viewers, send out the URL, but offer no links to the page from any of your other pages. When might you use it? For instance, if you're offering big discounts to a special group of customers, that price list might be put on an orphan page.

8. **Too many font styles and colors:** Pages ought to present a unified, consistent look, but novice site builders—entranced by having hundreds of fonts at their fingertips, plus dozens of colors—frequently turn their pages into a garish mishmash. Use two or three fonts and colors per page, maximum. The idea is to reassure viewers of your solidity and stability, not to convince them you are wildly artistic.

And be wary of font size for older viewers and those with weak eyesight. A 12-point font is good if you're targeting that audience; a 10-point font is good for a general audience. If you code your own site or hire someone to do it, make sure to code all font sizes in relative terms, meaning use percentages in your code—120 percent for big text, 100 percent for normal, 80 percent for tiny—which makes your site's font easily adjustable via a user's browser. Try it yourself using the "View" menu in either Microsoft's Internet Explorer or Mozilla's Firefox, and then selecting "Text size."

9. **Orphan pages:** Memorize this: Every page in your site needs a readily seen link back to the home page. Why? Sometimes users will forward a URL to friends,

▲

who may visit and may want more information. But if the page they get is a dead end, forget it. Always put a link to "Home" on every page and make your site logo (usually found near the top left side of the screen) link back to your home page—that will quickly solve this problem.

10. **Using leading-edge technology:** Isn't that what the web is all about, especially since a study by ThirdAge and JWT Boom found last year that more than 63 percent of online households are connecting to the internet via broadband? Nope, not when you're guaranteed to lose most of your viewers whenever your site requires a download of new software to be properly viewed. 3-D VRML pages are way cool—no question

Smart Tip

How do you know which browsers your customers are using or how big their screens are? You can usually check your website's log report (see Chapter 33) for this information, but for a broader view, go to W3Schools.com, an all-around excellent site full of free web development and design tutorials. Their "Browsers" section (w3schools.com/browsers) offers current browser statistics collected from W3Schools' own log files. W3Schools' users are a bit more tech savvy than the average Joe, but it's a good way to gauge general browser and display size usage.

about it—but if nobody actually looks at them, they're a waste. Never use bells and whistles that force viewers to go to a third-party site to download a viewing program. Your pages need to be readable with a standard, plain-Jane browser, preferably last year's or earlier. State-of-the-art is cool for techno wizards but death for entrepreneurs.

e-Chat With
Headsets.com's Mike Faith

Time out. So far, you've absorbed the theory of building a website, but to really understand what is going on, you need to hear from the experts—the entrepreneurs who are really doing it. Throughout this book, you will find two types of interviews—some with top executives

Headsets.com • Mike Faith, CEO and President
Location: San Francisco • Year Started: 1998

at the internet's most distinguished sites and others who may not be heading up sites that are as well-known as the major sites, and certainly smaller, but still successful in their own right. Why both types? The top execs offer their perspective on how successful online businesses are run, but it's the lesser-known yet still successful execs who give us insight into the nitty-gritty of the process. Mix them together, and what you have is the reality of success.

You want to stick with learning how to build a site into a monster business success? Skip over the next two chapters and carry on. But we strongly recommend you read the words from the real builders because they truly know where you are and how you can get to the next level. Even if you jump over this material now, come back to it later—because what you learn will pay big dividends.

Meet Mike Faith of Headsets.com, a leading provider of headsets that has been consistently successful online.

Entrepreneur: Tell me about your background. Why did you start Headsets.com? When was it founded?

Mike Faith: I emigrated to the United States from England, where the business climate is so stifling that it felt like "entrepreneur" was a dirty word. I wanted the freedom to do business in a way that supported my creativity, and the United States seemed like the perfect place. So in 1990, I jumped on a plane and never looked back. I started a few ventures that were moderately successful. They taught me some of the fundamentals of running a business and generated enough capital for me to start Headsets.com in 1998. Those early companies were call-center based, so we used a lot of telephone headsets. Finding good quality units at a reasonable cost and with decent supplier support turned out to be harder than it should have been—impossible, in fact—and that tripped my opportunity radar.

Entrepreneur: With how much money did you start Headsets.com? Did you get venture capital money? Was it self-funded?

Faith: Six weeks after realizing the opportunity, and with $40,000 of my own money, we were in business selling headsets. It was 1998, and we had a single product. The simplicity and cost of our offering was an instant hit, and we quickly grew revenues to the point that I was comfortable putting up the shutters on my other businesses to concentrate on the opportunity. Two years later, in 2000, our competitors were slashing prices and their margins. We were losing our differentiator. We looked at our business and the original opportunity and realized we had only served two of the three needs of the market. [We offered] a good product at a low cost, [but] we were missing that vital third part—service. So in 2000, as we incorporated from an LLC, we accepted a small round of funding, and that allowed us to fund a cultural shift in the organization to deliver what we think is world-class customer service.

Entrepreneur: Where did you open up shop? Why?

Faith: My wife and I were living in San Francisco when I started the business, so naturally that's where we opened shop. The Bay Area is a wonderful region with a near endless pool of world-class talent and an attitude [about] business innovation that, for me at least, captures all the reasons I moved to the United States. Many times over the years people have questioned the premiums we pay running a call center in the middle of one of the most expensive cities in the country, but every time it comes up, we can't help but see it as a strength. If you want the best, you have to pay for it. We want the very best!

Entrepreneur: What's been the biggest challenge you've had in building your company?

Faith: The biggest challenge we've faced, I'm proud to admit, has been my own growth. I'm an entrepreneur—I make decisions like you'd expect me to—and I've had to learn to involve others, think longer term and more strategically, and deal with a lot more formality and "corporate stuff" than I'm used to. It took a while before I built a team that I could trust to share the load, to execute my vision and my passion. Now we are just crossing that 50-employee threshold, and our challenges are to continue to build a strong, robust organization that is growing at 50 percent annually, without losing the things that made us successful—our adaptability, agility and efficiency. It's a challenge I relish.

Entrepreneur: How have you broadened your offerings or diversified your company since starting out? Why is this important for e-tailers to do?

Faith: I'm going to give you an answer that perhaps will go against conventional wisdom. The world's greatest marketer, Al Ries, taught me about ruthless focus years ago—and it's been an invaluable lesson. We sell headsets, and we sell only headsets. Because of this, we know more about selling headsets than anybody else, and we sell more headsets than anybody else. The more headsets we sell, the better we get at it. It's a wonderful virtuous cycle. I believe that other e-tailers would do well to stay focused, do less, do it better and reach deeper into a narrower

Secrets to Success

What is Headsets.com's secret weapon against some of the bigger companies that sell headsets? For one, they're experts—headsets are all they sell. In addition, they offer great prices, unbeatable guarantees, a solid reputation, free product trial, and it's all backed up by knowledgeable, smart, professional reps offering what Faith calls the "world's best customer service." These are all weapons any small e-tailer or online business owner can use to compete against the big guys—and win.

market. Of course, we've been tempted to diversify—we have this fantastically efficient, high-service model for selling business-to-business productivity tools. Why shouldn't we apply that to as many products that fit the mold as possible? Well, we dabbled in a few areas but found that even trying to pick up incremental sales in similar categories like audio headphones and telephone conferencers complicated our business to the point that the whole became less than the sum of the parts—not more.

Many people warn us of disruptive technologies and saturated markets, and we aren't cavalier or arrogant enough to believe that these risks aren't real—they are, but for us to tackle these risks through diversification means abandoning our core strengths, and that's just not an acceptable trade.

Entrepreneur: Who is your competition? Are they big guys? If so, how do you find your niche against them?

Faith: You can get headsets from lots of places, but it's almost always part of a diverse offering of products. A headset is still for the most part a consultative sale, despite their widespread adoption and the simplicity of the product relative to other things on the corporate desktop. So we make sure we remain true to our company tagline "America's Headset Specialists" and we serve the market's needs better than generic telecom suppliers, or office equipment suppliers who try to bolster volume by slashing margins and the all-important expert knowledge and service. For the longest time, we were the little guys, carving out a niche with the small companies and new headset users, while our big rivals squabbled over the large call-center market. But now we look around the competitive landscape and find the call-center market dwindling as it moves increasingly offshore and new headset adoption in the small-office sector driving all the growth in the industry, with us leading the charge and the historic big guns standing eerily silent. It's exhilarating.

Entrepreneur: Have you thought about going public? Why or why not?

Faith: I've often thought of taking Headsets.com public, but I usually talk myself out of it the same day. Then a month later, I'll think of it again. The shift to a public company would change our business and our ability to compete on the terms that I know will win. Public companies maintain their stock price by focusing on growth. But like success and happiness, growth is a byproduct of doing something to the best of your ability. The pursuit of growth for growth itself will always come up short. As a private company, we are free to focus on delivering what the customer wants—the best product at the best price, and with the best service. The irony is, of course, that by not focusing on growth, we are enjoying it in abundance, around 50 percent annually.

Entrepreneur: How do you market your site? What works? What doesn't?

Faith: We don't market our site specifically. Our website, as proud of it as we are, is nothing more than a way for our customers to place an order as quickly and efficiently as possible. We do market our products, of course (which ultimately drives traffic to our web servers and our call center), and we do that through a pretty significant business-to-business direct-mail program using a catalog and solo product offerings. We also use pay-per-click online advertising and do phenomenally well in natural search rankings and have a lively affiliate program. Of course, it helps that our company name (Headsets.com) and 800 number (800-HEADSETS) say pretty much everything you need to know to find us and what we sell. But above all of our marketing efforts, we've found that we've reached a critical mass, with repeat and referral business now becoming our largest source.

> ## Smart Tip
>
> You don't have to spend a lot of money on a big, traditional mass media advertising campaign to be successful. Look at Headsets.com: It sends out targeted, business-to-business direct-mail catalogs and uses search engine marketing. It helps that the company also has a memorable name (Headsets.com) and 800 number (800-HEADSETS) that say pretty much everything you need to know about them.

Entrepreneur: How do you up your look-to-buy ratio?

Faith: We simply remove all the barriers to buying our products. I know that sounds trite, but it's true. We offer great prices, unbeatable guarantees, a solid reputation, free trial of our products, all backed by knowledgeable, smart, professional reps offering the world's best customer service. I challenge anyone who needs a headset to not buy from us—why would you go anywhere else? Hey—even I want to buy a headset from us, and I'm a skeptic!

Cheap Tricks With
BlueSuitMom.com's Maria Bailey

T he ability to carve out niches on the web is amazing. Just ask Maria Bailey. A onetime marketing executive with AutoNation, she launched BlueSuitMom.com on Mother's Day 2000 with the aim of meeting the needs of

BlueSuitMom.com • Maria Bailey, President and Founder
Location: Pompano Beach, Florida • Year Started: 2000

Smart Tip

Tip...

Building a web business is a road filled with ups and downs for any entrepreneur, but a wonderful thing about it is that it provides a space of genuinely equal opportunity. Color, race, gender, creed—none of it matters because all cybercitizens are created equal. Better still, whatever you are, if there are others like you, that's the basis for creating an internet community that just may become a profitable business.

executive working moms. Her take on the net was that there were sites geared for working moms in general—but none aimed specifically at executives who also happen to be moms. So she decided to build one to offer networking opportunities, news geared for executive moms, and tips (how to manage time, for instance).

What started as a single website and a big dream has now grown into BSM Media (bsmmedia.com), a full-service marketing firm specializing in marketing to moms. Bailey has launched several other media properties as well since she began BlueSuitMom.com, including Newbaby.com, a video sharing and storing site for new and expectant moms, and Mom Talk Radio, which can be heard online and on traditional radio stations such as WLVJ 1040 in South Florida. Bailey also hosts a TV show on Lifetime TV called The Balancing Act and is the author of *Marketing to Moms: Getting Your Share of the Trillion-Dollar Market* (Prima Lifestyle) and *Trillion Dollar Moms: Marketing to a New Generation of Mothers* (Dearborn).

Today, BSM Media and its media properties connect some of America's most well-known brands such as Disney, HP and Precious Moments with the mom market and enjoy sales of more than $2 million.

Brilliant as the idea for BlueSuitMom was, the ramp-up of Bailey's site wasn't smooth. Read on for her candid—and helpful—comments on building a site.

Entrepreneur: How much funding did you start with? Where was it raised?

Maria Bailey: We started with a commitment for $1 million from a former boss—but, unfortunately, the money did not become a reality. So we truly began with $100,000 raised from personal savings and a few friends.

Entrepreneur: What were the first big obstacles you encountered in building a web business?

Bailey: Our biggest obstacle has been getting interested investors to actually write the check. That stems from a historical obstacle: Career women have done such a good job at proving to the wealthy/powerful men they work with that they have obtained work and family balance that it is difficult to help my potential investors understand the needs of our market. And on top of it, these men are most likely not married to a woman who is a vice president or CEO. So you say "mother," and they envision their spouse, who is [usually] a stay-at-home mom.

There has been a bit of challenge in learning to manage the young technology pros you need to grow your site. There is little loyalty, and they convey an attitude that they have you by a leash and without them you wouldn't be able to execute your business plan. They realize that their talents are in demand and are used to changing jobs often. Also, their confidence in technology has led many of them to believe that they also know how to run a business based on that technology. There is a short learning curve to adapt your management style to the new breed of employee you find in the web world.

Entrepreneur: How do you promote the business?

Bailey: We promote our business mainly by creating very strategic partnerships. For instance, we have a partnership with Stork Avenue, the largest retailer of birth announcements. They were willing to put our logo on 5 million catalogs in exchange for driving traffic to their site. We are relying too on the strong word-of-mouth network moms and businesswomen create and networking within women's professional organizations, HR departments and parenting organizations. We have also been featured in the media, including *The Wall Street Journal* and *USA Today*. Also, we are sponsoring events such as parenting conferences and distributing our content to other websites to build brand recognition, and we have been very lucky in creating great press.

Entrepreneur: What's the business's goal? What's the end game?

Bailey: Our exit strategy is not to go public. Our goal is to create a prequalified niche market that may be attractive to content aggregators, such as iVillage or a search engine. Because there is no one out there exclusively targeting our market, we feel we have a good shot at it. We monitor the women's market regularly and watch the internet strategies of others so that we can identify possible acquirers.

Entrepreneur: What unique advantages do you have vs. other websites?

Bailey: We felt the best advantage we could have was to be the first to market—and we were. We have used this as our strategy for every one of our media properties. With Newbaby.com, we are the first site offering video storage and sharing for new moms, and with Mom Talk Radio, we were the first radio show for moms. Because BlueSuitMom.com was the first site aimed at executive working mothers, it has allowed us to create all the great press we've received. The other advantage we have is that anytime we are working with a woman to make deals or create partnerships, we almost always get what we need because the woman on the other side of the phone relates immediately to the elements of our site.

Smart Tip

Tip...

eMarketer, a market research firm that specializes in e-business and online marketing, has found that more than 40 percent of all women who go online in the United States—approximately 35 million of them—are mothers of children under age 18.

▲

Entrepreneur: What's been your biggest surprise in building this business and your biggest disappointment?

Bailey: The biggest surprise has been how quickly the company has grown and morphed into other businesses with even greater opportunities. The response we have gotten from other internet companies and offline retailers, marketers and associations has been overwhelming. We can't keep up with the people who want to do business with us. Also, the international response we have received has been incredible. In addition to the growth of our marketing business, it's always rewarding to receive e-mails from women all over thanking us for our vision to create something that is valuable to them. It is personally fulfilling to know that your business is touching so many lives.

The biggest challenge is managing our growth. We have so much growth opportunity now. One of the biggest challenges is not going after every single opportunity, but selecting the smart opportunities.

The Nuts and Bolts of Web Hosts and Domains

With your website designed, you need a place to stow it so that visitors can access it, and the best way to do this is to hook up with a web hosting company.

Where to find one? Where else? The internet. After a small amount of research, you'll learn that some of the leading web hosting companies for small businesses today are Hostway, Blue Genesis, 1&1 Internet, IPOWER, DreamHost,

Web.com and Go Daddy. There are also many small local hosting companies, and many small e-tailers swear by them. Why? Because they are usually available any time of the day if there is a snag and offer excellent customer serivce.

When picking a host, you first and foremost want to know if a host can handle e-commerce activities. Some of the most bare-bones companies simply are not equipped. Other criteria that are important to most users: setup and monthly fees (a typical range for basic web hosting is $3.99 to $29.95 monthly, but the price usually goes up when adding e-commerce functionality, with a setup fee equal to one month's fee); amount of available storage space (you want at least 5 to 25 GB to start, as well as the option to add more space as your needs expand); and connection speed (some very low-budget hosts rely on T1 or T3 connections, but the rest use high-perform-ance T3 lines and above).

Comparing hosts is difficult, so a good policy is to quietly set up an account and test the host—kick the tires, so to speak—for several weeks before announcing your presence to the world. Isn't that expensive? You bet, when setup fees are factored in. But more expensive—and embarrassing—is to make a big push for traffic, only to have your host drop the ball and leave you with cranky visitors who cannot quite make it in. Better to know your host is operating smoothly before inviting guests to the party.

Master of Your Domain

Before setting up your site, you also need to stake out your domain name, which is the word between "www." and ".com" or ".net" in web addresses. So what name suits you? Come up with some possibilities, then head over to any number of web hosting companies—many offer CCTLD (country code top-level domain) registration.

A leading hosting provider in space-name registration is Go Daddy (godaddy.com). The price is right, too: $9.99 per year per domain name. Keep in mind, however, that if you are working with an e-commerce hosting provider to set up your online business, it will most likely be able to offer you domain registration as well. The drill is simple: You type in a name, and Go Daddy tells you if it's available. When you strike out—that is, the name you want is taken—the company offers similar pos-sibilities available for registration. Go Daddy traffics in the main U.S. top-level domains—".com," ".net" and ".org"—as well as newer domains like ".info," ".biz," ".us," ".cc," ".biz" and ".tv."

What's in a Name?

There's wide agreement that nothing matters as much as a good name. Yet who would have thought Amazon was one? What most matters in a name is that it's easy to spell and easy to remember. For my money, that's an argument against using a catchy name with an unorthodox country code suffix. Most U.S.-based computer users just automatically type ".com," ".net," ".edu," or ".gov." Throw a weird ending at them, and you may lose them. So I would recommend a clunky name with a ".com" or ".net" ending over a catchy name with an unorthodox ending.

Another argument against really off-beat endings: How stable are some of these countries? In revolutions, it's common to nationalize—that is, grab—holdings of foreign companies. What's to stop a new government from nationalizing its web and taking back all the names sold by

Tip...

Smart Tip
Want a fast take on comparative features of web hosts? Log onto Compare Web Hosts (comparewebhosts.com), where a few mouse clicks let you specify what's important to you and check out which hosts likely will serve your needs best. For a second opinion, head to TopHosts (tophosts.com), a site with a bit less functionality but more layers of detail—meaning it's not the easiest resource to use, but it has lots of information.

a prior government? Here we're venturing into speculation. It has not happened, but it could. Don't forget that when picking your domain. You want something that will last, that's worth investing time and money into building its traffic. And ".com" and ".net" names just may be the best bang for those dollars.

One reason you may want to consider picking up a CCTLD from a country that's not your own is if you plan on expanding to that country. Europeans, for example, prefer to interact with local businesses and will often search for companies with a CCTLD extension rather than a company with a .com extension. The appropriate CCTLD can make a difference for your business. Many companies offer these CCTLDs right now, but besides Go Daddy, a leading one is AllDomains.com (alldomains.com), an accredited registrar of the .com, .net, .org, .biz, .info and .us top-level domains. Keep in mind that CCTLDs are generally more expensive.. A recent look at Go Daddy shows that a .at domain costs $59.95 for a one-year registration of a website with an Austrian address. A Belgian CCTLD was much less, at $17.49 per year.

What is a good domain name worth? Stories abound of names selling for seven figures or more, but such transactions are rare. Zetetic, a domain name value research firm, says only 36 domain names have ever been known to fetch more than $1 million—including Chinese.com, vodka.com and business.com. Nonetheless, if you think you have a zingy, sellable name that you want to market, try Sedo.com (sedo.com), the leading marketplace for buying and selling domain names and websites. The site claims to have more than 1 million domains for sale.

How do you buy a domain name? Sedo's model is an offer-counteroffer model. This means that you negotiate directly with the domain's owner until you both agree on a price. This system takes away the uncertainty of an auction model, reduces the potential for fraud, and gives you control over how much you pay. Also, try Go Daddy, which offers auction sales of domain names in addition to its domain registration and web hosting services. The Domain Name Aftermarket (tdnam.com) is another domain marketplace that offers customers four different ways to buy and sell domains. "Buy Now" enables customers to purchase domains at a single, set price. "Expired Domain Auctions" enables customers to bid on an expired domain, with the winning bidder receiving full ownership of the domain name after a two-week (post-auction) waiting period. "Offer/Counteroffer" allows users to extend an offer on any domain, with The Domain Name Aftermarket staff acting as an intermediary. And "7-Day Public Auction" permits sellers to set a minimum starting bid, with potential buyers placing bids.

Beware!

Can you "park" a domain name for free? When you park a domain, you reserve it but haven't yet mounted a site. Many outfits tout that they offer free parking, but that's not exactly true: You still have to pay the registration fee. Free parking only means they'll put up an "under construction" sign that anyone who hunts for your domain will find. Be aware that some companies will also place copious amounts of advertising on your parked site. Google specifically targets owners of parked pages for revenue possibilities using its AdSense program (google.com/domainpark).

11

The Scoop on
Business-to-Business
e-Commerce

U sed to be, the dream was starting the next McDonald's, or maybe inventing a new widget everybody would need, putting you on the fast track to wealth so immense it could scarcely be counted. Today, of course, the dream is to come up with the new Amazon or Yahoo!—but that might be the wrong dream.

Isn't this book all about launching the Next Big Thing? Nope. It's about building viable businesses on the internet. Nowadays, a very good argument can be made that there's a smarter way to go than scouting around for the idea that will spawn a new Amazon.

Taking Care of Business

Consider Walt Geer. It was in late '98 that Geer, a partner in an Atlanta promotional products company, faced up to reality. His little business—which sold logo merchandise such as pens and coffee mugs to companies to distribute to employees and customers—was chugging along OK, but it was just one of 19,000 promotional products companies in the country. Plainly put, Geer's company was lost in the mob. So he decided to take the plunge. He cut the cord on his traditional company, dumping his existing customers and putting his business online as eCompanyStore (ecompanystore.com).

How is he doing now? Well, Geer has since left the company, although he is still a shareholder, and formed his newest company, Phenix Direct (phenixdirect.com), an overseas importer that serves larger promotional product distributors like eCompanyStore.

However, Geer says that in Phenix's early days, there were a couple months of hard swallowing: "We had no revenue coming in," recalls Geer, "but we had to focus our energy on the internet. We didn't have the resources to do it and run our traditional business." But, he says, "in just a few months, the internet let us move from being a small company to a national player. Before, we serviced lots of little accounts. Now we have Microsoft, for example. The internet lets us go after big accounts." In addition, Phenix grew at an average annual rate of 55 percent in 2006 and 2007.

eCompanystore and Phenix Direct are just two of hundreds of business-to-business (B2B) enterprises, where companies sell not to consumers but to other businesses. These internet companies may not be winning wide press attention, but they are creating a real buzz in big-money circles. According to a Forrester Research February 2007 report, The ePurchasing Software Market, e-procurement and e-sourcing are the norm today for the vast majority of firms, including 75 percent of the Global 2000.

Why the rush by businesses to purchase on the internet? Simply put, businesses are realizing that using the internet allows them to drive down costs. How much? One statistic says that when shifting purchasing to the web, a business can eliminate about 90 percent of the cost of a transaction. But more than just cost savings are propelling this mushrooming of business trade on the net, says Geer. "The real drivers are speed and efficiency," he says. "And besides, our web store is always open. These advantages are as attractive to our customers as the savings. The internet is a better and faster way for businesses to shop."

The Many Faces of B2B

Just who is making it in B2B e-commerce? Beyond big-name B2B players like Staples.com, OfficeDepot.com and ThomasNet.com, the web is filled with enticing companies that illustrate the breadth of this marketplace. That's because B2B e-commerce offers diverse opportunities, with some players seeking to establish themselves as marketplaces where buyers and sellers meet to do deals, while others are positioning themselves to provide services and products to business customers in a wholly new, web-based way. The bottom line: B2B e-commerce entrepreneurs are limited only by their own imaginations. There are plenty of possibilities in this still expanding space.

Want concrete examples of how businesses on the web are serving other businesses? Read on for a sampling of the strategies B2B websites are pursuing.

In the Know

What industry do you know, and know well? Substantial expertise is needed to create a viable B2B. What industries have you worked in? Which ones interest you enough that you'll enjoy the long hours of research you'll need to put in? Which industries are currently underserved—or not served at all—on the internet?

Marketing glitz doesn't go as far in a B2B context as getting down to the nuts and bolts of what you have to offer businesses that will positively affect their bottom line. Business executives tend to be more cold-blooded about these things, so show them where they will save time and money, and they will follow you.

Liquidity Services Inc.

The success of eBay, online discount retailers such as Overstock.com and Amazon.com, and click-and-mortar discount shops have proven that consumers and businesses want high-end products but want to pay less-than-high-end prices. As the market for less-than-new items grows for both consumers and business purchasers, those with an entrepreneurial heart are eager to capitalize on selling to these markets. The challenge, though, is where to find this type of inventory for prices low enough to make a profit on the resale.

Washington, DC–based Liquidity Services Inc. (LSI) is a business that helps organizations shed unwanted inventory through online auction marketplaces and has

▲

amassed more than 700,000 registered buyers of wholesale and surplus goods. LSI provides a consistent flow of new and used assets, including overstock, returned, refurbished and seasonal items on its online auction marketplaces Liquidation.com, govliquidation.com and liquibiz.com. The merchandise comes from LSI's contracts with Fortune 500 companies, public sector agencies, top retailers, manufacturers, wholesalers and distributors.

Buyers often resell the merchandise as individual units or in multiple quantities to small retail chains, through eBay, to small businesses, and even in export markets. "Our business model is very simple and transparent for both sellers and buyers," says Bill Angrick, chairman and CEO of LSI. "Not only do we convert surplus assets to cash for large and medium-sized organizations, but we enable buyers to find and purchase this inventory through secure online marketplaces."

The LSI marketplaces offer buyers a total solution to source inventory in bulk through an online auction process. The sites have thousands of auctions to bid on at any given time in more than 500 categories, including consumer electronics, computers and networking equipment, clothing and accessories, general merchandise, building and do-it-yourself hardware tools, vehicles, and many others.

LSI has contracts with major domestic and international shippers that enable significantly reduced shipping costs. This means buyers are able to resell the merchandise at more competitive prices while still maintaining a profit margin. Liquidation.com also allows buyers the opportunity to arrange their own shipping for inventory that is stored in LSI's six warehouse facilities located throughout the United States.

Dedicated to providing excellent customer service, LSI also offers a Buyer Relations team that is available to assist buyers throughout the buying process. On the seller side, LSI offers a full range of value-added services, including reconciliation of surplus, de-labeling, auction creation, marketing to current and potential buyers, buyer assistance, payment arrangements, and complete and transparent tracking.

"The overall goal of our asset remarketing activities is to provide a solution that maximizes the recovery value of surplus property," says Angrick. "We have more than 724,000 registered buyers that consistently use our marketplaces to source bulk and wholesale inventory, which ensures a competitive market price on the surplus inventory we handle for our sellers. Our buyers have confidence bidding on these items and

know that they will receive winning purchases in an easy and trusted manner."

According to Angrick, sellers can obtain 20 to 200 percent higher recovery using LSI's marketplaces, as well as save a significant amount of time, resources and money associated with traditional liquidation options.

In 2004, LSI launched its Advertising Solutions Division, which includes its GoWholesale search portal for small businesses and the wholesale industry. The site, GoWholesale.com, enables middle-market wholesale buyers and sellers in the United States to find, buy and sell everything wholesale. The site gen-erates more than 2 million business searches per month for wholesale goods and business services.

The key elements of GoWholesale's offering are pay-per-click (PPC) keyword search advertising and banner advertising that generate relevant search results for wholesale buyers. GoWholesale also provides business users with industry-related content such as articles, blogs, trade show information and community forums.

With more than $100 billion of surplus assets in the United States per year, LSI has focused on bringing the right services and expertise together in a single offering. "We provide the technology, buyers, product sales knowledge, compliance expertise and value-added services to maximize revenues and reduce overall costs," says Angrick. In the past eight years, LSI has stayed true to this focus and has grown from a raw startup to a global market leader within the surplus asset disposition industry, increasing its 2007 revenue to $198 million with $234 million in gross merchandise volume, or total sales across its marketplaces.

Elance

Elance (elance.com), based in Mountain View, California, is a highly successful online marketplace used by small and midsize businesses to outsource projects across 50 service categories—from website development and graphic design to bookkeeping and administrative support—through a large, global pool of service providers that bid for business.

Using the marketplace, buyers post projects and qualified service providers with the relevant skills bid on them. Buyers then determine the service provider that's best for their projects by reviewing proposals, experience and project portfolios, as well as feedback on each supplier aggregated by Elance from previous buyers. Buyers can

Smart Tip

The best news about B2B e-commerce? Launching a B2B site is significantly less expensive than trying to create a winning consumer site. Usually it's cheaper to target an audience and pursue it in B2B. If you have narrowed down a business niche and know how to cost-effectively target it, a B2B site can gain traction fast and on a minimal budget.

also browse service provider descriptions, and, if they find service providers they would like to work with, simply invite them to bid on their particular project.

Typically, buyers create a short list of service providers, and begin a dialogue with them through the marketplace. Once a buyer selects a provider and the project is accepted, buyers and service providers use the marketplace's online work space and message boards to manage their projects, and, upon completion, use the system to securely pay their providers online.

While buyers post projects for free, service providers pay a subscription fee to Elance to gain access to the buyer network. Additionally, Elance collects a small fee from the service providers once projects have been completed and they have been paid. Prices are extremely competitive due to the strength of the supplier network and nature of the bidding process.

The Elance Marketplace continues to grow, particularly as small and midsize businesses are seeing the benefits of outsourcing their projects and service providers look for additional channels to market their services.

"The Elance Marketplace is the top spot for accessing high-quality, affordable service providers across the broadest number of service categories," according to Elance president and CEO Fabio Rosati. "We enable small and midsize businesses to source their projects at a fraction of the cost of what they would pay at 'retail' rates. Now, in 2008, we have several service providers who have each derived more than $1 million in revenues from projects arranged through Elance."

Elance experienced significant growth in 2007 as more small and medium businesses (SMBs) signed on to work with Elance service providers. As of April 2008, more than 40,000 small and midsized buyers were active on Elance, up 60 percent from April 2007. More than 4,000 new projects are posted every week, worth more than $2 million.

Bulbs.com

Steve Rothschild is passionate about bulbs—lightbulbs, that is. He sometimes even closes his e-mail messages with "Have a Bright Day!" Perhaps that's why his privately held company bulbs.com is thriving. "Bulbs.com simplifies the purchase of lighting for business and consumers across the U.S.," says Rothschild, founder and CEO of bulbs.com. "Bulbs.com clients love the fact we are fast, easy and complete. Clients are

able to procure consistent lighting products for all their facilities, including the latest energy-saving lighting, and to save money, too. Many of the energy-saving products are simple retrofits that fit into existing sockets."

The company has a straightforward business model in which customers—85 percent of which are businesses—order lightbulbs directly from the company's website or via phone from their staff of lighting specialists. Bulbs.com has distribution agreements with Philips Lighting and a host of other manufacturers.

Budget Watcher

Do you buy anything for your business that could be more efficiently purchased on the internet? That thought alone can be the trigger to launch a B2B website. Get thinking about what you buy and here— and whether the net would make the process cheaper and faster.

Since its launch in 1999, Bulbs.com has received orders from more than 75,000 companies, and 65 percent of its business clients reorder on a regular basis. Major customers include Central Parking Systems, Samsonite Stores, Perfumania and Verizon Wireless, as well as the U.S. military and the National Park Service.

Why did Rothschild decide to set up a website that sold lightbulbs? "I was searching for my next opportunity, which I knew was going to be e-commerce related, and I knew that for it be successful, I had to find a product that would be identifiable via the web, had to be replaced on a regular basis, and its cost-to-freight ratio had to be viable," says Rothschild. "Lightbulbs were the obvious choice for me." Rothschild also says there was a need for this business in the marketplace.

Adding "C" to B2B

As these examples show, there are many small B2B web companies thriving despite the current economy. Some traditional B2C (business-to-consumer) companies are also entering the B2B e-commerce fray. Consider eBay. At any given time, there are approximately 102 million items available on eBay worldwide, and approximately 6 million new items are added each day. To make business buying easier for SMBs, eBay provides a section on its site called eBay Business (pages.ebay.com/businessmarketplace), which includes a business-oriented search engine bringing together all of eBay's business and industry listings under one easy-to-browse destination, focusing heavily on office technology products, such as computers and networking devices, as well as lots of consumer goods and services (think insurance and shipping) at wholesale prices. EBay reported that in the third quarter of 2007, businesses bought more than $2.1 billion worth of merchandise on the site worldwide—approximately 14.5 percent of all items purchased.

A Slam Dunk?

Hold on, however, because the sailing for new B2B entrants won't be entirely smooth. In key respects, the bar may be higher in B2B e-commerce than it is in B2C, and the requirements for succeeding will likely be stiffer. "B2B is different from B2C," says John J. Sviokla, vice chairman of Diamond Consultants, a global management firm that helps companies develop and implement growth strategies. "To succeed in this space, you will need deep domain knowledge." You don't need to know much about farming to successfully peddle peaches to consumers, but to build an exchange for farmers, you have to grasp the fundamental issues in that industry. Lack that, and there will be no trust on the part of your target audience."

Another hitch: B2B involves long selling cycles, and, likely as not, before big deals are nailed down, you'll need to do face-to-face selling. It is one thing to buy a $10 book with a mouse click. It's an entirely different matter to buy $100,000 worth of coffee mugs. "A website won't close deals for you," stresses Geer. "To make B2B deals, often you've still got to put feet on the street."

And there are times when a B2B model doesn't work. Consider Winery Exchange (wineryexchange.com), which was founded by Peter Byck in 1999 in Novato, California. The company now offers private-label wine brands for large, global wine retailers and creates and delivers strategic information to assist wineries and spirits companies in building, growing and managing their brands.

But when it started, its website allowed suppliers of wine, grapes, equipment and services to sell their wares in bulk to wine growers, wineries and retailers in a secure, user-friendly environment. "We are not trading online anymore," says Byck. "That didn't really work because there are a lot of relationships in the business, and people want to deal with people when they are buying these products. Also, some exchange models may work, but if you are trading bulk wine and grapes, it's just not a big enough industry with enough buyers and sellers to make a big business."

The company switched its focus to the private-label wine brand and strategic information sides of the business "because at the end of the day, you have to go where the growth and opportunities are," says Byck. "There were demands for those products, so we followed those paths."

Some analysts are somewhat suspicious of pure-play B2B e-commerce companies in general (these "pure plays" are purely online—they don't sell out of storefronts). But not everyone agrees. Many experts believe that it is indeed a great time to be in B2B e-commerce if you are a small company because with the technology and services available, you can appear to have the resources of a bigger company. Plus, you can reach buyers all over the world.

e-Chat
With Autobytel's Jim Riesenbach

Do you wish you could get a glimpse into the mind of a CEO at the helm of a dotcom that has evolved into a diversified and successful automotive marketing services company? Read on. Below, Jim Riesenbach, president

Autobytel Inc. • Jim Riesenbach, CEO and President
Location: Irvine, California • Year Started: 1995

▲

and CEO of Autobytel Inc., offers an in-depth look at the world of internet car buying and selling.

When Autobytel was founded in 1995, the internet and e-commerce were still relatively new, unproven concepts, and the word "tel" in Autobytel's name stood for telecommunications, which included fax and internet communications. Within the first year of business, the internet became the dominant means of communication. Consumers all over America began logging on to Autobytel and asking, electronically, for the vehicles they wanted to buy—say, a dark green four-door sedan with a six-cylinder engine and ABS. This electronic "Purchase Request" was routed to a local dealer based in the car buyer's ZIP code. The dealer was trained to get back to the consumer with a firm competitive price usually aimed below the sticker price.

A major goal of the company is to enable the dealer to make a better profit on online sales because its advertising/marketing costs—a big spend for dealerships—are often much lower for Autobytel-generated customers. In addition, a steady stream of incremental business can be generated through Autobytel—i.e., customers whom dealers likely wouldn't have seen otherwise. So it's "win-win-win" for Autobytel, the dealer and the consumer.

A veteran of online and digital media, Jim Riesenbach was named president and CEO of Autobytel in 2006. When he first joined Autobytel, Riesenbach was struck by how similar and limited the consumer experience was at the leading third-party automotive sites—all of which were built around new and used "buying funnels" that effectively push consumers to the transaction moment while walling out relevant information. Having witnessed the shortcomings of this "walled garden" approach during his tenure at AOL, he recognized that Autobytel's future should be guided by its pro-consumer past—and set out to create a more convenient, open, flexible and comprehensive consumer resource.

As a result, the company launched its flagship site, MyRide.com, under Riesenbach's leadership. Riesenbach says, "Myride.com combines original content with the first fully integrated vertical search experience for the automotive marketplace." MyRide.com is designed to enable consumers to quickly access relevant, organized information on everything automotive from across the web, without having to jump from site to site or sift through overwhelming, disorganized general search engine results.

To put Autobytel's impact on the automotive industry in perspective, since 1995, millions of car shoppers have visited Autobytel, generating billions of dollars in vehicle sales for Autobytel member dealers.

Entrepreneur: As the CEO of Autobytel, what is your goal for the company?

Jim Riesenbach: My goal is to continue what has been our mission since 1995—empowering consumers with the information they need to make smart, well-informed vehicle ownership and buying decisions while also offering automotive dealers and manufacturers marketing services that help them sell more cars efficiently.

Key to fulfilling our mission is our new flagship consumer site, MyRide.com, which we launched in fall 2007. From a consumer's perspective, MyRide.com is a true departure from anything else on the web. It's the first automotive site to incorporate search and community in a meaningful way—in fact, MyRide launched as the first automotive vertical search experience on the internet. It also has a much broader focus than the typical third-party buying site, serving not only the needs of car buyers, but also parts and accessories shoppers and vehicle owners looking for service and community.

In the long term, the goal is to continue to evolve MyRide.com and really establish it as the de facto place where people go to begin to look for information relating to "all things automotive." By doing that, we'll obviously have a great opportunity to grow our lead generation and advertising business—it's all predicated on providing a great consumer experience.

Entrepreneur: What's been the biggest surprise you've experienced since coming on board as CEO?

Riesenbach: I think that the stall in innovation in the online automotive space was the biggest surprise, especially in the face of the dramatic migration of automotive marketing dollars from traditional media to the internet in what is arguably the largest industry in the world.

Before I came on board, it was clear to me that the market opportunity was huge. With 90 percent of all car buyers using the internet to shop for a vehicle, it was profoundly obvious to me that the internet was the place for automotive marketers to find their customers. This was borne out by the hunger among automotive marketers for more and more online inventory and leads. To enter a space as a marketer where there is such a high demand for exposure is very exciting. However, I found

> **Beware!**
> Success breeds nearly instant imitation on the net. That's the irony: The more you prosper, the tougher you have to fight. How will you stay a step— better still, two steps—ahead of those who will follow?

> **Smart Tip**
> One reason Autobytel is a market leader is that the company hasn't fallen in love with how it does things. As market conditions change, Autobytel quickly adapts. That way of thinking and acting is essential for any dotcom. So once you've launched a site, prepare to continually retool your site and, perhaps, even your business model. Adaptation is the only way to survive on the web.

that there was a huge gap between the percentages of dollars the industry was spending on digital media and the percentage of consumers who were actually using and/or most influenced by that medium.

For example, although the vast majority of car buyers use the internet, the internet accounts for only a fraction—about 7.6 percent—of the overall $31 billion automotive advertising pie. The good news is that in an industry this large, even a small slice coupled with an increasing growth rate—online ad spending is projected to grow to $4 billion in 2010—has massive dollar implications. And experts agree that this growth continues to accelerate. In fact, Borrell Associates estimates that by 2010 online auto advertising will become the second-largest medium for automotive advertisers, surpassing newspapers, cable, radio, direct mail—everything but broadcast TV.

So, with perhaps the most compelling market opportunity in any industry, it was very surprising to me that online automotive sites had barely innovated since the auto dotcom glory days of 2000. In fact, if you stacked the leading automotive sites next to each other, autobytel.com included, and removed the branding, you would not be able to tell them apart. It appeared to me that, generally speaking, the third-party sites were taking their online visitors for granted. Essentially, they operated as "walled gardens" focused on driving consumers into the buying funnel. Our challenge was to change all that and, at the same time, create new media opportunities for the automotive industry by providing an entirely new experience that fit today's online automotive consumer.

We knew that 90 percent of all internet new vehicle shoppers used a search engine to search for car-related information, so we set out to create a site that would meet the behavior of online automotive consumers head on and allow them to experience automotive information from around the web in an organized and engaging fashion.

Here was another surprise: While the buying funnel is a critically important component of automotive marketing, only 6 percent of the population is actually in the market to purchase a new vehicle each year. And with 45 percent of internet users visiting automotive sites, we knew that there was a large underserved community of automotive consumers out there. The third-party sites were essentially ignoring these consumers and that surprise turned into another opportunity for MyRide. We designed the MyRide site to provide a wide variety of content that addressed consumers before, during and after the buying process, incorporating research, service, parts, accessories, social media and user groups with the goal of providing numerous new marketing touch-points for this industry.

Entrepreneur: What's your biggest challenge?

Riesenbach: I think it is—and will always be—to keep ahead of the rapidly evolving online automotive consumer. This is why it is so important to me to have people on our team who are both veterans of online automotive media as well as marketing innovators who know that looking one step ahead of not only our industry but the digital industry as a whole, is what's going to keep us on top of today's consumer. And the consumer comes first at Autobytel. While it can be challenging to balance the many different needs of all our constituents—automakers, auto dealers and auto consumers—by providing a superior consumer experience, we firmly believe that the results will be more site traffic, better lead volume and quality, and more valuable and diverse ad opportunities.

Entrepreneur: What's your strategy for coming out ahead of competitors?

Riesenbach: The strategy is to focus on providing the best consumer site and the best dealer programs in the industry. We launched MyRide.com to address what I think are some glaring automotive consumer needs—namely the ability to quickly find information beyond the confines of a single site, via search and user-generated information, and to provide an experience that, while incorporating the buying funnel, is also about every automotive need and experience.

At the same time, we've been busy innovating new services for our member dealers. For example, we recently rolled out our Autobytel LocalConnect program, which enables dealers to present inventory-specific ads to local

> **! Beware!**
> Autobytel's diversified company certainly gives its users and customers a unique experience. Can you offer your customers a similarly unique experience? Consumers today—more than ever—are looking for special experiences on the web. If you can't offer them something they can't get elsewhere on the web, they probably won't bother coming to your site.

shoppers on our sites who are actively searching for that inventory. We've also had a lot of success with the Rapid Response program we created to connect dealers via phone with customers immediately following purchase request submissions. Our revamped used vehicle program is another big advantage for dealers, providing premium placement and enhanced listings atop the web's largest used inventory (approximately 3.5 to 4 million vehicles) along with a pure pay-per-lead/pay-per-call pricing model.

Entrepreneur: What advantage do you, as a dotcom, have over the big automakers?

Riesenbach: Since Autobytel helped pioneer the online automotive marketing landscape back in 1995, we've always had a complementary relationship with the manufacturers. We've had great success in helping both automakers and dealers sell more while spending less.

We think our value in the industry will only grow with MyRide.com because it offers so many things that automaker sites don't—like a nationwide directory of local service providers, social networking content that covers a vast range of automotive subjects, and a search tool that scours the web for relevant used car listings, reviews and accessories. By serving multiple automotive information needs, we're in turn creating multiple marketing touch points for automakers and, for that matter, dealers.

e-Chat
With Zappos'
Tony Hsieh

I t's surprising what you can sell on the web.
Ask Tony Hsieh. When Zappos founder Nick Swinmurn
approached him with the idea of selling shoes online, Hsieh was
ready to hang up the phone. Then Swinmurn mentioned the

Zappos.com • Tony Hsieh, CEO
Location: Las Vegas • Year Started: 1999

size of the shoe market—$40 billion in the United States. What's more, $2 billion of that was sold by mail-order catalogs. If shoes—a highly personal and tactile item—could be sold through mail order, why not over the internet?

It was 1999, the heady days of dotcom dreams. Anything seemed possible, even an online shoe store. Convinced that the nonexistent e-commerce market for shoes would someday be even bigger than the $2 billion mail-order market, the pair started Zappos.com.

Today, online footwear is a $3 billion business, and Zappos is the undisputed leader in footwear retailing on the web. With 4 million customers, the Las Vegas company has doubled its sales every year since 1999 and is on track to hit an astounding milestone: $1 billion in revenue in 2008.

How did they do it? It's all about service. In fact, according to the company's philosophy, Zappos is a service business that sells shoes, not a shoe retailer that provides service. The company's service policies would make most e-tailers cringe. The call center, with its staff of more than 1,300 people is open 24/7. So is the warehouse. But the clincher that turns browsers into customers for life is the 365-day return policy with free shipping—both ways! That's right, you can shop till you drop and send back anything that doesn't fit or doesn't look just right with that new outfit. No harm, no foul. No wonder Zappos.com is on Time's most recent list of "25 sites we can't live without." For eight years, Tony Hsieh has presided over this internet phenomenon, carefully cultivating a corporate culture based on stellar service.

Entrepreneur: You've built Zappos on great customer service, but how?

Tony Hsieh: Part of it is the very fast shipping. We run our warehouse 24/7. It's not the most efficient way to run a warehouse, but it gets the shoes out to our customers as quickly as possible. We also run our call center 24/7. We're unlike most websites where it's hard to find a phone number to contact the company. Our 800 number is on the left corner of every single page of the website. And when you call a member of our customer loyalty team, they really strive to go above and beyond, making the experience very different from calling most other call centers. Our call center isn't outsourced either. It's right here at our headquarters in Las Vegas. As an example of what we believe is service, imagine a customer is looking

> **Tip...**
>
> **Smart Tip**
> Today, many CEOs keep in touch with customers through corporate blogs. Want to start your own blog? Go for it. But first do your research and understand what you're getting yourself into. Blogs can be fun, but they can also be demanding. A great resource is *The Rough Guide to Blogging* (Rough Guides). The book is the ultimate reference for anyone who wants to know more about blogging, whether you're a casual reader or an experienced professional blogger.

for a specific pair of shoes. Now let's say we're out of stock in their size or that particular style. We will actually search other online retailing websites and if we find them there, we'll direct the customer to that competitor.

Entrepreneur: Zappos started out as the first online shoe retailer. Who are your competitors now?

Hsieh: We don't think of our main competitors as anyone online. It's really more about getting customers used to the idea of buying shoes online. When most people hear that, it's a scary concept because of fit issues. So our biggest challenge is educating customers on how easy and quick it is to get the shoes. Some people order 10 pairs of shoes, try them on with 10 different outfits and then ship back the five that don't fit or don't look good. They've got 365 days to return them and we pay the shipping back to us. A lot of people don't know or realize that when they first hear about Zappos. We try to do everything we can to minimize the perceived risk for the customer.

Entrepreneur: How do you attract new customers to your site?

Hsieh: In terms of paid advertising, we do buy key words on search engines and we also have an affiliate program. But really, we started out in 1999 with pretty much zero dollars in sales and this year we are expected to break $1 billion in gross merchandise sales. It's been fast growth and the vast majority of that growth has been from repeat customers and word-of-mouth. So our philosophy is that all the money we might have otherwise spent on marketing, let's instead put it back into the customer experience. Things like offering free shipping both ways is very expensive. Things like running the call center and warehouse 24/7 is very expensive. But we really view those as our marketing expenses, and let our customers tell each other about our service.

> **Tip...**
>
> **Smart Tip**
>
> If you offer extraordinary service—like 24/7 customer service via a toll-free number or free shipping and returns—announce it prominently on your site. Let customers know how great your service is! On Zappos.com, you can find their 800 number and free shipping and returns declaration right below their logo and navigation on every page of their site.

Entrepreneur: You received several rounds of venture capital along the way. How important was venture capital to your success?

Hsieh: It allowed us to accelerate our growth because as our sales grew, our inventory requirements needed to grow as well. Funding that inventory growth was the reason we needed to raise the money. If we hadn't done that then we would have continued to grow, but just at a slower rate because we wouldn't have been able to warehouse as much inventory.

Entrepreneur: Do you have any advice for entrepreneurs wanting to attract venture capital?

Hsieh: Generally, VCs are looking for a business that is growing at a rapid rate and is in a large market. Plus, they want to see that the people in the company are passionate about whatever the company is about, that they're not in there just to try to make a quick buck.

Entrepreneur: Why did you expand into other merchandise besides shoes?

Hsieh: We got into handbags several years ago and then started selling apparel maybe a year or so ago. Then, over the past few months, we've added electronics and other accessories. We even have some cosmetics on our site now. Our plan was always for the Zappos brand to be known for great service, and not necessarily for shoes. In fact, hopefully 10 years from now people won't even realize we started out selling shoes online.

Entrepreneur: If you had to pinpoint one thing, what would be the secret to your success?

Hsieh: The company culture. Our number one priority as a company is to make sure that, as we grow, we continue to maintain a really service-focused culture. When we hire people, for example, we do two sets of interviews. One set is a standard set that the hiring manager's team does. Then, our HR department does another set of interviews to assess culture fit. And they have to pass both in order to be hired.

Then after they are hired, everyone in our Vegas office—it doesn't matter what position, accountant, lawyer or whatever—you go through the same four-week training program. We go over our customer service philosophy, company history, the importance of company culture, and then they get on the phone and talk to customers for a couple of weeks. After that, we send them to our warehouse in Kentucky to spend a week picking, packing, sending and receiving. So it's a total of five weeks of training, being immersed in company culture, before starting the as an accountant or lawyer or whatever you're hired for. It's pretty hard to go through that five weeks without understanding our focus on customer service and company culture. It gets everyone on the same page. I think when everyone's moving in the same direction, it moves the company forward that much faster.

Entrepreneur: What's next on the horizon for Zappos.com?

Hsieh: We're just going to continue what we've been doing for the past eight years. On an ongoing basis, we look for ways to improve service and slowly experiment with adding other product categories based on what customers tell us they'd like us to sell.

Secrets of

Venture Capital
Funding

Venture capital may have slowed down after the dotcom crash, but it's been slowly building up ever since. How much venture capital is there? We're seeing the most investment activity since the days of the dotcom boom. And the statistics are pretty impressive: VCs put some $30 billion into 2,648 deals in 2007. While that's still far from the more than $49 billion invested in 4,591 deals by venture capital firms in 1999, today's companies are pulling down large deal sizes from their investors. The overall median size of a venture round is $7.6 million, a new high-water mark for the industry, according to industry data provider Dow Jones VentureSource.

Yes, there are fewer deals, but more capital is often invested in individual deals today, according to Adam Wade of VentureSource. "This is partly because in 1999 about 54 percent of the deals were seed and first-round deals, which are often smaller in terms of dollars invested," says Wade. "However, today, these smaller early-stage deals make up only 38 percent of deal flow. Venture capitalists are holding on to companies longer and longer, and are focusing more resources on navigating older companies to liquidity."

Wade also points out that it's still tough going—for every young startup that wins venture funding, about 100 go away empty-handed, and probably another 100 or more didn't even get their foot in the door. But the news is getting better for web-related startups, according to Wade. "At the peak of the bubble in 2000, the 'information services' sector that includes most of today's Web 2.0 companies attracted an incredible $11.9 billion in investment," he says. "In 2007, the sector attracted $3.7 billion, which is quite a bit lower. Yet, it's still 43 percent more than in 2006. It's a sign that the industry is seeing a lot of investor interest but isn't overheating, or at least not just yet."

The primary driver of the current rise in venture capital activity is a big upswing in the number of venture-backed companies completing mergers and acquisitions (M&As) or initial public offerings (IPOs). In 2007, VentureSource found that 398 U.S. companies were acquired for approximately $46 billion. Another 74 companies completed IPOs, raising $6.7 billion.

Wade says that 65 information services companies raised $6.3 billion in M&As in 2007, while six others raised $587 million via IPOs. The largest M&A was for Oxygen Media, an internet and cable content provider that was acquired by NBC for $875 million. The largest IPO for the sector belonged to Switch and Data, an internet networking company that raised $198 million in its February debut on the NASDAQ exchange.

Funding in Hard Times

There's no doubt about it: Left behind in the rubble caused by the dotcom bust in 2000, venture capitalists are taking a more critical look at dotcom startups.

But, as we just noted, dotcom companies are still managing to get venture funding. Which ones are winning? The ones that can demonstrate they have a winning idea and a solid business model that is focused on the bottom line.

Consider Brickfish, a social media site that was founded by internet veterans in 2005. In 2007, the company secured first-round funding of $11.2 million from

Money Hunt

Want a source to tap for timely, practical information on how to start, manage and expand your business? Try Kauffman eVenturing (eventuring.kauffman.org), a website from the Ewing Marion Kauffman Foundation, a Kansas City, Missouri–based private, nonpartisan foundation that works with partners to advance entrepreneurship in America.

Kauffman eVenturing offers a guide to entrepreneurs on the fast-paced journey toward high growth. The site offers rich content, including new articles created by entrepreneurs exclusively for the site, and an in-depth aggregation of existing information on the web on a wide array of subjects—from accessing capital to implementing successful recruiting strategies and competing in global markets.

The Kauffman eVenturing site is organized around six subject areas—finance, human resources, sales and marketing, products/services, operations and the entrepreneur. New collections of articles are featured once a month, rotating among those subjects. The site is very easy to search and navigate, so entrepreneurs can find the information they need quickly. Keywords in every article are "tagged" so that information about a specific query is assembled immediately.

DCM, a Silicon Valley VC firm. President and CEO Shahi Ghanem, who was originally an angel investor in the company, has a unique dual perspective—he is also a limited partner in several different venture funds and has raised over $100 million in VC during his career.

Ghanem was able to secure VC funding for Brickfish because he had a good track record and he targeted VCs he thought would be a good fit for the investment. Ghanem says, "VCs are always looking for four things: A big market, a great team, a strong business strategy and the ability to build a profitable business. We made sure we had all four of those things lined up, then I brought them forward very clearly to the investors when I met with them."

Brickfish also had definite plans for the money. "We intended to use the new capital to accelerate our sales efforts and to build new viral propagation and reporting systems." That's exactly what it was used for, and quite successfully, too. "We launched our sales efforts and started to move forward. Since receiving the VC funds, we've worked with about 45 different customers, including a lot of well-known brands like Samsung and Kodak. Our team has grown over threefold and our revenues have grown 70 percent quarter-to-quarter. The use of our funds is exactly as anticipated."

Investors today are obviously concerned about reality vs. fantasy. If you have good business fundamentals and a track record you can prove, there's plenty of money out there. But if you're highly speculative and haven't proved yourself yet, VC backers aren't going to give you the time of day—let alone millions of dollars. Ghanem says investors are always looking for an extraordinarily compelling proposition with the market, the team, the strategy and potential profit, but it's important for you to vet the investor as well. "You also have to make sure the investor fits the investment.

⚠ Beware!

Bring in VC money, and you could lose control of your business. That's just a reality. For every Jeff Bezos who stays on top, there are several entrepreneurs with ideas that are good enough to get funded who don't personally inspire confidence—and they get pushed aside.

Look for guys that bring you more than money. They should bring you relationships, the culture, the board presence, and the knowledge and experience of people you really want to work with. Remember, these people are going to be tied to your hip for three to six years."

Brickfish is not the only company that received venture funding recently. Internet-specific companies received $4.6 billion in 748 deals in 2007, an increase of 12 percent and 8 percent, respectively, over 2006. Social networking giant FaceBook received a cash infusion totaling $240 million from various VC firms in 2007. And Reunion.com, the people search-and-find site, attracted $25 million from Oak Investment Partners in April 2007. Reunion's success in securing such a whopping amount for first-round funding is due, in part, to a revenue model that places paid-for services on par with advertising.

Big Winners

On paper, scoring VC funding looks simple. You write a business plan wherein you pay very close attention to the possible payday ahead (typically this is made vivid with charts that forecast revenue and profits). VCs do not want to hit singles. They swing for the bleachers, and to win funding, an idea has to have the clear potential to be a major winner.

Why do VCs want big winners? Simple. They're realists who know that out of every 10 ventures they fund, maybe eight will vanish without a trace, one will be a modest success and one will be a home run. But that one home run will generate so much cash, it will make all the losses forgettable as it propels the firm deep into black ink. So don't be conservative. Think big.

Also think of the exit strategy. That's key. VCs don't invest to hold; they want a way to translate a business success into an economic success. Usually, that means the company gets bought by a big fish—like Bebo.com, the third most popular social networking website in the United States, which was purchased by AOL for around $850 million. Bebo co-founders Michael and Xochi Birch used the opportunity to cash out of the company. Either way, early investors want to know how they will get out of this deal before they go into it.

Smart Tip

Tip...

Where to find venture capital firms? Check out the VC links on vFinance (vfinance.com) for leads to many VC firms.

Once you have your plan in hand—with an exit strategy and a payday spelled out—you look for every way possible to get it (and yourself) in front of VCs. It isn't easy. So often internet entrepreneurs complain, "I have a great business plan, and nobody will fund it." Maybe the plan is great, maybe it isn't, but step one in proving you've got what it takes to prosper in the rugged internet economy is finding a way to get in front of VCs.

You've tried and can't seem to land VC money? Take what cash you can from the legitimate investors you can get, of course, whether that's your parents or your neighbor's uncle's ex-wife. Get the business afloat and then maybe VCs will come calling with cash in their hands. Even better, once a business is prospering, you can usually get much more favorable terms from VCs. The earlier they come in, the bigger piece of the company they want, which means second-stage VC financing may actually be more desirable.

The moral: When the idea is good, the money will follow.

A Friend of a Friend

Who do you know? If you want a hearing at a VC firm, find a way in via friends and friends of friends. The "six degrees of separation" theory claims we all know everybody else—or at least we know somebody who knows somebody who knows somebody. Check it out: When a friend told me about this idea, I scoffed and said, "No way I'm within six degrees of the Pope." She told me: "You know me, and the father of a good friend of mine has met the Pope many times." The lesson: If you really want VC money, find out whom you know who knows somebody. That's the way in the door.

One way to find out who your friends know is to join business network LinkedIn (linkedin.com)—if you haven't already. There, you'll be able to browse the networks of your friends, colleagues, customers and acquaintances, and request introductions to their connections.

Inside Information

Don't get discouraged about finding VC money. Garage Technology Ventures, a venture capital investment bank for emerging technology companies, encourages submissions of business plans at its website (garage.com). Here, Guy Kawasaki, a managing director at the firm, and the author of *The Art of the Start* (Portfolio), eagerly tells how to win funding from Garage Technology Ventures. Kawasaki's trademark is irreverence—his wit is quick and pointed—but read between the lines in this Q&A, and you'll discover he's telling you what your chances are and how to make them better.

Entrepreneur: What does an entrepreneur need to get venture funding?

Guy Kawasaki: Circa 2005, the single most important factor was to show traction—that is, that someone is already paying you for your product. If not traction, then at least you need to show that someone is testing your product and will/might pay for the product soon.

Entrepreneur: What's your ballpark estimate of the percentage of business plans that get funded?

Kawasaki: We get about 2,000 to 2,500 plans per year and fund 10 of them. We used to receive many more plans during the 1997 to 1999 time frame, but the quality is now much higher.

Entrepreneur: A typical complaint is "I know nobody—where do I start looking?" What's your answer?

Kawasaki: Raising capital today is very challenging. You can't leave any stone unturned. This means friends, fools, family and potential customers … not to mention your own pocket. The days of raising a few million with a sketch on a napkin are gone—maybe not forever, but for a few years.

Entrepreneur: What's the minimum (realistic) funding for launching a B2B site? A B2C site?

Kawasaki: This is tough to answer because you can't glom all B2B- or B2C-type businesses together. You could start a company with $250,000 or $250 million. It all depends. Having said this, too much

Tip...

Smart Tip
Don't assume that you'll need to have all your ducks in a neat row to win venture funding. Quite the contrary. In many cases, VCs like helping to shape a business idea, to put their marks on a plan. And as they get more involved, their willingness to fund increases. You still need to be savvy—and to have good answers for questions—but keep your ears open to VC suggestions, and be ready to incorporate the good ones.

money is worse than too little [because people are usually less disciplined about the way they spend when funds are plentiful].

Entrepreneur: What's the one thing an entrepreneur can do that's sure to turn you off?

Kawasaki: Ask me to sign an NDA [nondisclosure agreement]. Actually, there's one more thing: Show up with a PowerPoint presentation containing 50 or so slides.

Entrepreneur: What's the one thing an entrepreneur can do that's sure to catch your interest?

Kawasaki: Tell us that in the last 12 months they did $1 million or more in business.

What has Kawasaki told you? Develop a plan that emphasizes your strengths (the reasons to fund it), keep it short, don't ask for too much money, and never ask potential funders to sign an NDA. Why the last point? NDAs—which bind the signer not to reveal what you show or tell him about your plan—are unenforceable in many cases, and, just as bad, a busy investor probably has heard much the same idea from multiple sources already.

On the other hand, complaints that investors sometimes steal good ideas are epidemic. Are the beefs founded? Hard to say—but a Silicon Valley legend is that when Sabeer Bhatia shopped his idea for what became Hotmail, he lied to would-be funders in initial meetings, telling them about a totally different business idea. Only when they passed some kind of test for Bhatia did he lay out his real idea. Paranoid? Bhatia became a very rich man when Microsoft bought Hotmail—proof that, at least in his case, caution pays.

Do you need to be as cautious as Bhatia? Not likely. Most entrepreneurs who take that closed-mouth route will simply strike out with funders. A better route is to tell what you need to tell to spark interest and then keep offering more details as investor interest looks ever more genuine. Besides, if you treat people sincerely and honestly, more often than not, you'll get much the same in return. Sure, there are crooks in Silicon Valley—but most folks are decent, well-meaning and well-intentioned. So play things straight, and usually you'll get the results you deserve.

> **Tip...**
>
> ### Smart Tip
> Monogamy isn't practiced by VCs. Rarely will a major VC firm act as sole funder. It seems strange, but it's a fact that a VC firm will often agree to fund if you can get another firm to fund you, too. Keep in mind: VCs like to minimize risk, and one way to do it is to share investments.

Why Financial
Angels Fund Startups

Do you believe in angels? After reading this chapter, you just might. With a little luck and lots of persistence on your part, angels—of the flesh-and-blood variety—may fund your internet venture.

Today, most dotcom companies take the following four-step funding track. Step one: The entrepreneur bootstraps the business using his own resources (usually savings and credit cards). Step two: The entrepreneur seeks angel funding from seasoned professionals, who typically put in money, plus expertise, mentoring and guidance. Step three: The business pursues venture capital. Step four: After several years of profitability, the company may go public or merge with another company.

In the fast-paced internet world of days gone by, angels may have been over-looked, as companies without any track record and no profits (nor much in the way of revenue) went public and VCs took on a mentoring role. Today, there are far fewer dotcom companies going public or getting VC funding, so angel investors are a very important part of the funding mix.

And there are many of them. According to research conducted by Jeffrey E. Sohl, director of the Center for Venture Research at the University of New Hampshire's Whittemore School of Business and Economics, there were approximately 50 formal business angel groups in the United States in 1997. He now estimates that there may be as many as 184 formal and informal organizations located throughout leading technology and business regions in the United States and Canada. Collectively, these formal angel alliances represent about 10 percent of the angel market.

Where do you find angels? Usually through personal connections because angels are generally friends of friends or parents of friends. Why do they invest? For many angels it's a thrill to get involved in a startup. Maybe they don't want to personally run one, but they are nonetheless excited about being on the periphery and offering advice in addition to capital. Of course, there is also the real possibility of hitting a major home run.

How does angel investing work? We found two angels who agreed to provide insight into what they do.

George McQuilkin is co-founder and a member of eCoast Angels Network (ecoastangels.com), a small group of angel investors in New Hampshire who offer funding on an individual basis to promising new companies as well as ongoing ventures. John May is managing partner of the New Vantage Group (new-vantagegroup.com), a Washington, DC–based company that manages next-generation early-stage venture funds for active angel investors. Their methods and approaches differ, but that's the norm: No two angels have exactly the same motivations. But if you understand who angels are and how to persuade them, you just might get one to put cash into your company.

George McQuilkin has been around the business block more than a few times. An MIT graduate, McQuilkin worked with IBM in for 16 years, left to start a company called Spartacus Computers, and ran a few other companies, including RSA Security, which sold for more than $1.5 billion.

Entrepreneur: How did you get into angel investing?

George McQuilkin: I made some money on RSA Security, and I decided to use it to invest in some venture capital funds and, at the same time, I made some direct angel investments. I was at a limited partners meeting of a venture fund in the late 1990s when I realized that I seemed to be doing better on the investment I made directly, and I also took more satisfaction out of that. I had met influential people like Mort Goulder, an angel investor who had made well over 100 investments. He was the founder of the Breakfast Club, which in this part of the country is the oldest continually running angel investor group around. I thought it would be good to start a group like that because I wanted to increase the number of deals I looked at, have the ability to spread the risk, and have the ability to bring experience to bear. When I moved back to Portsmith in 2000, I found four other like-minded individuals, and we started a group called the eCoast Angels.

Entrepreneur: How does your group operate?

McQuilkin: We started this angel group with an old-fashioned format: a group of people who come together for a common purpose. It's very Benjamin Franklin-y. We are neither a charity nor an economic development unit. We share advice and information, and we make up our own minds on each investment so there is no group fund. And we don't have a formal process, but that doesn't mean we don't have a process or we don't know what we're doing. It's just that we choose to make this decentralized so there's no administrative burden.

Entrepreneur: What's the basic difference between an angel investor and a venture capitalist?

McQuilkin: Motivation. Angels are investing their own money, and everyone has his or her own reasons for doing it. Mort Goulder said one of the key reasons he enjoyed being an angel investor is he liked to help the other guy. He said this technology and economic system had been really good to him, and he wants to give the other guy a chance to participate the same way. If you're a venture capitalist, you're actually investing somebody else's money and you have both the legal and the fiduciary responsibility to maximize their return. That doesn't mean you have to be unfair or unscrupulous, but it's harder to be an idealist with somebody else's money. An angel investor's motivation is to be part of the action, to be involved with new companies.

Most angels are entrepreneurs who started a successful business and they cashed out by selling the business or through an IPO. They don't just want to use their extra money; they want to be part of the excitement. A venture capitalist doesn't take the risks, doesn't meet the entrepreneur. If it's a tournament, you're jousting through surrogates. Some people like the hands-on feel, like the action, like being part of the technology. There is an arrogance among entrepreneurs, myself included, that causes them to want to start a business with 1 or 2 million dollars and go take on IBM or Google or Microsoft. It would be laughable if **people** hadn't been successful doing it—including Google and Microsoft. So there's

▲

the challenge, the opportunity, the matching of wits—that's a high. I think making money is lower down on the angel investor's list, though good angel investors on the whole tend to do better on returns on investment than do venture capitalists.

Entrepreneur: How many plans does your group look at in a year?

McQuilkin: We get in excess of 100 inquiries a year. I screen a lot of them myself or with someone else, and we look seriously at 20 to 25 a year. Of those, we'll probably invite 18 in to make a presentation. Sometimes we'll have a meeting without a formal presentation or sometimes I'll go to some other group's meeting. In other words, we'll meet with people without necessarily having them stand in front of the group. Of those submitted last year, we made 14 investments. Seven were new companies, and seven were follow-ups to previous investments. Not every member of the group invests every time. A typical angel in our group makes one to four investments a year.

Entrepreneur: How much can an entrepreneur expect to get from you?

McQuilkin: Last year, we invested about $6.3 million total. A very reasonable amount to ask for would be $500,000, though we could do $1 million or $2 million. We would then probably want to bring in other groups we are friendly with to share the risk. Getting an early-stage, fairly rapid investment of $300,000 to $500,000 is very realistic with our group.

Entrepreneur: How can an entrepreneur find an angel?

McQuilkin: They should talk to everyone they know, and they should use their own network. Angel groups tend to invest regionally. We have a broad experience in the group and good connections to companies, but we can't really use that for you unless you're an hour or two drive from here. Since we like to play an active role, we want to do that nearby. But if you're a serious entrepreneur and you pay attention to the business press and you can't find us, then you're not doing your job as an entrepreneur. You can also just approach us and say "I've heard of you." But again, you surely know somebody who knows us from the MIT Club, from the High Technology Council, the local high school, the community, lawyers, accountants, etc. An entrepreneur who is doing his job, which is to marshal resources in support of his vision, really ought to be able to find a better way to get to us than to just send us a generic cold e-mail. The best e-mail will say: "I met you at the meeting of the Technology Council and we talked about this and I know you might not remember me, but you had said you were interested in investments like this." Right away, I'm very receptive to that. The ones that say "to whom it may concern" are bad, very bad. If you're not willing to do a little bit of work to find us and get us information, I'm not willing to evaluate it.

Entrepreneur: What can an entrepreneur do to get a yes, and what is sure to get a no?

McQuilkin: The key is to explain why we want to invest in this business, not why your technology is a good idea. Typically entrepreneurs are in love with their business vision. That can be true if it's pizza sauce or extensive use of nanotechnology. So they'll get up, tell us all

> ### Smart Tip
>
> Practice, practice, practice. Before you go into any meetings with VCs or angels, really hone your presentation on your business—this can prove a lot more crucial than your business plan in the funding decision. Why? Investors invest in people who inspire them. Go in with a pitch that wows listeners, and you may walk out with a big check.

about their thing and run out of time, and never get around to telling us how much money they need and what they're going to do with it, and why this is good for us. They forget why they're talking to us. You'll also get turned down if you change the deal—that will get you almost thrown out. And finally, the entrepreneur has to have a realistic idea of what they're selling in terms of ownership and control. If you just say I want your money, but I'll run the business my own way and I don't need your advice or assistance, then I'm going to say then you don't need my money and you're not going to get it.

John May is not only the managing partner and co-founder of the New Vantage Group, but he has extensive experience as a venture fund manager, advisor and angel. He has been a partner or consultant to five venture funds and is also managing general partner of Seraphim Capital, a London-based venture capital firm founded in 2006. The company specializes in providing capital and assistance to emerging growth companies through noninstitutional sources. May is also co-founder (in 2004) and current chairman of the Angel Capital Association, a North American professional alliance of angel groups. This fast-growing association brings together 103 angel group leaders around the country to share best practices, to network, and to help develop data about the field of angel investing. May has spoken extensively on angel and early-stage equity investing, is a Batten Fellow at the University of Virginia's Darden School of Business, and is the co-author of a book on angel investing, *Every Business Needs an Angel* (Crown Business).

Entrepreneur: What's the difference between an angel and a VC?

John May: The main difference is that angels consider psychic reward as one of their major criteria [in deciding what to invest in]. They get an emotional, or personal, benefit from it, as opposed to venture capitalists, who get more of a financial benefit from the transaction.

Entrepreneur: What's the biggest mistake entrepreneurs make in approaching angels?

May: Being fixated on their evaluation and not being flexible. An angel might be willing to have a negotiation about their role and their money, but if entrepreneurs assume that an angel is fixated on a high rate of return only, they will be shooting themselves in the foot.

Entrepreneur: What's the one thing entrepreneurs can do to make their case stronger?

May: Network through friends and trusted advisors. Also, if you are planning to be a high-growth company and you plan to raise outside money—which not every entrepreneur plans to do—it's probably a good idea to also have sophisticated counsel, accountants and an advisory board.

Smart Tip

Don't delay. Check out NVST.com, an online private equity network. You can post and search investment opportunities, read up on the latest industry research, and browse related resources and services. If you're based in the Washington, DC, or Seattle area, check out New Vantage Group (newvantage-group.com), and see if there's anything there for you. Don't submit material too early—wait until it's polished. But once your business plan is solid, get a move on!

Entrepreneur: How many business plans come through your door monthly? How many do you think get funded by anybody?

May: We generally look at about 50 to 100 plans per month. Most entrepreneurs submit through the web; most angel groups have application forms on their websites, and entrepreneurs either fill it out there or they send an executive summary attached to an e-mail. This seems to be the dominant entry point for entrepreneurs. Out of 100 plans, 10 will most likely be presented to our group, and one or two of those may get funded. But keep in mind, there are far more angel transactions per year than venture capitalist transactions. Last year, I believe there were only 3,400 venture transactions, and there were 45,000 to 50,000 angel transactions in the United States. Sure, there may have been only $50,000 to $250,000 involved—which is a lot less than what venture transactions cost—but there are a lot of opportunities out there. There are angel investors in all 50 states, and every major metropolitan area has an angel group, while venture capital is heavily concentrated in California and New England.

Entrepreneur: What are angel investors looking for in startups?

May: Today, they are looking for mature management rather than wide-eyed ideas.

e-Chat With
Corporate Toner's Kapil Juneja

Corporate Toners Inc., which was founded in 2002 by Kapil Juneja and Mike Costache, prides itself on providing the highest-quality inkjet cartridges, refill kits, remanufactured cartridges and toner cartridges at the lowest possible prices. Its goal is to get these products to

Corporate Toners Inc. • Kapil Juneja, COO, CTO and Co-founder
Location: Canoga Park, California • Year Started: 2002

customers as quickly as possible and in the most cost-effective manner. While the company sells its goods to individuals, a majority of its sales are to businesses, organizations and schools.

Entrepreneur: What's been your biggest surprise at Corporate Toners?

Kapil Juneja: We were astonished when we found ourselves struggling to get the banks to provide us with additional credit-card processing capacity every third month as our company grew 100 percent month-on-month during the first year. We were a startup company with a short track record, run by two fresh college graduates. It was a big challenge to convince the banks that we were a legitimate business with real growth. It was like doing everything right in starting a business just to find out that you can't collect money from the banks. Finally, the banks issued a bigger credit line, and since then we created a multimillion-dollar company.

A booming business should be a cause for celebration, but at Corporate Toners, it was something of a mixed blessing. As sales increased sharply—from 150 orders per day in August 2004 to 300 per day by January 2005—we found that an old infrastructure was making it hard to manage new business. Customer records were incomplete, customer inquiries were not attended to on time, and business information was scattered across different databases. It was a less-than-ideal way to [do business and to grow a business].

With sales information stored on so many systems and so many login passwords to remember, it was hard to find customers' data when customers called us. We quickly adopted an all-in-one e-commerce CRM, and back-end technology platform provided by a San Mateo, California–based company, NetSuite Inc. NetSuite offered everything we needed—from the ability to have all data in one central location to the ability to set up customized transactions for each of our sites so we could integrate all the processes in an online platform available to all our employees at different locations.

Entrepreneur: Did you approach investors?

Juneja: We sure did. We went to various seminars and events organized by the likes of the Los Angeles Venture Association (LAVA); The Indus Entrepreneurs (TiE), a Washington, DC–based nonprofit global network of entrepreneurs and professionals, established to foster entrepreneurship and nurture entrepreneurs; and the Larta Institute, a Los Angeles–based nonprofit group that connects technology startups with funding. And we networked with alumni from our school, Pepperdine University.

We actually met an interested investor at LAVA's annual Investment Capital Conference in early 2002, and the fact that he was an alumnus of Pepperdine and had a large accounting firm and the gray hair we needed made us think we found our ideal investor.

We talked to various [other] investors, but in 2002, nobody cared to finance a

B2B startup with no proprietary technology and no real competitive advantage. Every door we opened was shut with a nice, "Come back with something more tangible 'cause I like you guys, and I see your burning desire to be entrepreneurs." But we knew that we had something going for us: We were experts in getting on the top five results in search engines through search engine optimization. This traffic cost us nothing since we understood how the search engines worked and reverse-engineered the process to beat their rules.

We were about to make a huge mistake by giving 33 percent of the company's equity for $35,000 in cash and office space for the first year in our investor/ incubator's firm [the accounting company mentioned earlier]. Luckily for us, the investor kept prolonging the negotiations, knowing that we were two young guys out of college pressured for money. We decided to stop all negotiations since we realized that it was a really bad deal for us. That was probably the best decision we've made to date.

Entrepreneur: How is building a B2B site different from building a B2C site?

Juneja: It's a completely different mentality when servicing a $20,000 repeat order from a B2B customer than a $53 one-time order from John Doe with no loyalty to your product or service. During the early phases of running an e-business, we realized that—and our research concluded the same—businesses are the biggest consumers of printer supply products. They remain loyal as long as you consistently provide them with good products and excellent service.

So we built a professional-looking B2B website while providing 100 percent quality products, money-back guarantees and good customer service. We wanted the website to be easy to navigate, quick to load and have quality content to keep the trust and loyalty of our corporate customers. In the online B2B marketplace, you compete with the companies that might be 10 to 1,000 times larger than your company. The disadvantage of being a smaller company compared with the big sharks is overcome by employing the right back-end management and sales tools. We learned it the hard way when we lost a couple of our big corporate customers as we were not able to service them accurately on time.

[That's when we integrated] NetSuite. NetSuite gives us better organization of our sales data and more information on our customers, which boosts customer service and leads to customer retention and repeat business. NetSuite offers us the tools to provide a world-class service to our B2B customers.

Entrepreneur: Is there a potentially bigger payout in B2B? Why?

Juneja: B2B has a different cash flow model where customers want competitive pricing with payment terms compared with B2C credit card transactions, where the bank provides the money in three to five days from the transaction date. Selling to well-established businesses requires that you provide them with a high level of customer service (pre- and post-sale). Price is not always the key, but service is.

An individual one-time buyer is much more price-sensitive compared with a corporate client, who may remain your customer for life as long as you consistently provide them with good products and service. Higher sales volume, repeat business and high retention rate are some of the major advantages when you deal with corporate clients. In the long run, B2B definitely is a bigger payout. As long as you keep your business customers happy, they will continue to give their business to you.

Entrepreneur: What advantage do you have over the many competitors in your space?

Juneja: We specialize in marketing our website online on various search engines where we are able to get high ranking on thousands of keywords related to our products. Of course, customer service, quality products and competitive prices all matter, but our margins are bigger than our competitors because we have a very low cost of customer acquisition.

Technology is one of the key advantages that we have over our competitors. Using NetSuite's technology with our websites, we have an all-in-one system to manage all our business processes compared with our competitors, who may use a virtual armada of stand-alone software packages: QuickBooks for accounting, Goldmine for sales calls, LivePerson for e-mail management, a customized online shopping cart, Microsoft Excel for reporting, GoToMyPC for remote access, and several proprietary databases for customer data.

> **! Beware!**
> Juneja was smart: He had a bad feeling about an investor who was stringing the company along, so he decided to stop all negotiations. The moral of the story? When it comes to money, go with your gut.

NetSuite's CRM solution provides a robust system where all our customers' inquiries are logged in their respective customer records, so anytime a customer contacts us, we look up their record and provide them an immediate response. We not only save our time and customers' time, we are able to provide a superb customer service, which is a key when dealing with corporate customers.

Since our systems and websites are based online, we also enjoy the advantages of running our inbound customer service and outbound telemarketing call center from New Delhi, India. The lower cost of running the operation in India combined with highly skilled English-speaking employees enables us to provide excellent service to our customers on time.

Finally, we have better coordination between our warehouse and our sales office in Los Angeles and our back-end customer service and support.

Cheap Tricks With

Redwagons.com's Tony Roeder

Tony Roeder is the type of entrepreneur you want to be—with a smart observation and a lot of hard work, he's built a sustainable web business. In 1998, with virtually no experience, capital, or programming skills, he launched

RedWagons.com • Tony Roeder, President and Founder
Location: River Forest, Illinois • Year Started: 1998

RedWagons.com, a site that sells a full line of Radio Flyer wagons, accessories and other products. The company, which initially enjoyed rapid growth by being a niche business, has ridden the ups and downs of the early "internet era." Ten years later, it shares a once-empty niche with Amazon.com, ToysRUs.com, Target.com, Wal-Mart.com and a whole other host of toy startups. RedWagons.com continues on, constantly changing and innovating to stay competitive in the face of stiff and powerful competition.

How did Roeder, a former handyman, get the idea to launch the site?

In 1998, he was on a customer's porch assembling a Radio Flyer wagon when he was struck by the look and feel of the wagon. He had lots of memories of Radio Flyer products growing up and started thinking about what a great company Radio Flyer was. Says Roeder, "Radio Flyer has been a part of my earliest childhood memories—from the Radio Flyer wagon we had careening down our suburban driveway to the old rusty wagon I pulled my children around in at the time I was sitting on that porch."

He was also looking for another line of work and wondered about e-tailing, since he worked regularly with a hardware store that had started selling Weber grills online. Roeder realized there was a lot of opportunity in this arena.

Then, by chance, he ran into a person who worked for Radio Flyer and had a casual conversation with the employee about putting a wagon together for one of his customers. When he learned that Radio Flyer was not selling its products online—despite its online presence—he jumped at the chance to do just that, despite the fact that he had no internet experience at the time.

Here, Roeder offers his insights into starting a successful dotcom company.

Entrepreneur: How did you start your website?

Tony Roeder: I first hired a web designer for $4,000 who worked for Radio Flyer's informational website, but he had never done an e-commerce site before and basically could not get the site up in a reasonable [amount of time]. I had to fire him. I then contacted Yahoo! and built my site on the Yahoo! Store [now called Yahoo! Merchant Solutions] system. Their costs were pay as you go, and back then, it was about $200 or $300 per month, which was less than what the designer was going to charge me for monthly maintenance.

Yahoo! made it possible for me to be my own web designer and store builder virtually overnight. The site went live in November 1998, just in time for the holiday season.

Entrepreneur: How do you handle fulfillment?

Roeder: Fulfillment is an ever-evolving process, but the key is that we make an effort to get products shipped out as soon as possible.

Entrepreneur: What are the secrets to your success?

Roeder: The combination of the Yahoo! exposure, good search engine placement and good links put us on the map.

Smart Tip

An opportunity to start a successful business can happen when you least expect it. For Tony Roeder, a chance meeting with someone from Radio Flyer, the red-wagon company, was the catalyst that prompted him to start his company, RedWagons.com. Always keep an open mind—you never know where or when a chance to start a business will pop up.

Technology has also been very important to our company. Most of our challenges have been met by judiciously applying technology to our processes.

Entrepreneur: What are your plans for the future? Your goals and objectives?

Roeder: In general, our objective is to maintain profitability and to be innovative. Our birth, growth and explosion were due to having a vision and openness for change in my life; being at the right place at the right time; and the willingness to take risks. Those particular opportunities may not exist today, but there are always new ones. You have to be able to identify them and take the necessary actions to get the business rolling. We try to stay current with what is new and what is changing in the industry and adjust appropriately. We are also constantly refining our processes, our marketing and our communication—and we try to always be aware of our competition so we can continue to grow as a company.

18

Cashing in on
Affiliate Programs

Want to generate cash, now, from your website? Even sites that aren't e-commerce-enabled—meaning they retail nothing—can put money in your pocket through the many affiliate programs found on the web. From Amazon to OfficeMax, leading online retailers are eager to pay you for driving sales their way. How? By putting their link—such as a banner or text—on your site. For every click-through

▲

that results in a sale, you will earn a commission, anywhere from 1 to 25 percent for multichannel retailers or 30 to 50 percent in the software sector. In some cases, you can get commissions on all sales that take place up to 10 days after you send someone to a site. For example, if a customer visits your site and clicks on the leading online company's banner ad and doesn't buy anything right away but purchases something a few days later, you still get credit for the sale.

In some cases, you are compensated even if the visitor doesn't buy anything, just for having driven traffic to the merchant's site. This is not as popular as the former examples, however. The affiliate's reward varies from merchant to merchant and program to program, depending on the terms of the merchant's offer.

It All Clicks

Supposedly, the idea for affiliate programs—where big merchants enlist small sites as a de facto sales force—got its start when a woman talking with Amazon.com founder Jeff Bezos at a cocktail party in 1996 asked how she might sell books about divorce on her website. Bezos noodled the idea, and a lightbulb went on. He realized the opportunities for both to benefit were great, and the upshot was the launch of Amazon's affiliate program, one of the industry's most successful.

What's the appeal of affiliate programs? "The [main] appeal lies in the fact that affiliate marketing is primarily tied to performance," says Wayne Porter, co-founder of ReveNews.com, a blogging portal for affiliate and next-generation marketing. "Marketers are not paying for relationships or placements that aren't pro-

A Touch of Class

Several years ago, the secret reason many small websites slapped on a banner from, say, Amazon was to gain a kind of legitimacy. It was hoped that the hard-won (and expensively bought) credibility of Amazon would anoint a startup with a species of classiness. Maybe it even worked—once. But if that's what you think affiliate programs will do for you now, forget it. With so many banners out there, people will think nothing more than that you took the time to copy and paste someone's HTML code into your web page.

This strategy may even backfire. Sites festooned with affiliate banners simply look cheesy, the very opposite of legitimate. The bottom line: The only valid reason to join affiliate programs is if they make sense with your content, add value for your visitors, and put cash in your pocket.

ductive. It is not without risk, nor is it always the most cost-effective in the long term, but dollar for dollar, it is usually a good investment."

How big is affiliate marketing? Although it's not as big a part of their overall sales and marketing program as paid search or e-mail, affiliate marketing is an effective strategy to build broader brand awareness and drive motivated buyers to business-to-consumer e-commerce sites, say web retailers participating in the latest Internet Retailer survey.

Most web retailers have already made a multiyear investment in affiliate marketing and count on a network of several thousand affiliates to drive visitor traffic, according to the magazine's survey. But most have pared back their programs because of unqualified traffic and fear of litigation. "There is definitely more risk, and it's difficult to manage huge groups of partners, as opposed to having a more qualified pool," explains Porter. "Also, the trend has steered away from automatic approval where anybody could become a partner. Now retailers are scrutinizing partner candidates."

For you, getting a share is not as simple as it used to be. In the recent past, you simply put a few links on your site (to any of the thousands of e-tailers that offer commissions to affiliates), and, as surfers clicked from your site to your affiliated site, you earned money. But, it's quickly becoming much more advanced. Today, you have to link to the site through a widget or data feed—it's gone way beyond simple text links.

"With the onset of 'social media,' what we call Web 2.0, we are now seeing widgets," says Porter. "For example, Amazon now has the ability to complete the entire transaction on the affiliate's site without ever leaving that site. So, in reality, there is no real linking going on. There are any number of mechanisms being used, from older style banners and text links to more advanced widgets, JavaScript, data feeds or Ajax-driven technology." But while technology has advanced, the basic idea is the same—you're getting paid for leads, a practice as old as selling that makes sense for everyone involved.

Google AdSense Makes Sense

Since 2003, one of the most significant changes in affiliate marketing has been the emergence of Google's AdSense. AdSense (google.com/adsense) allows anyone who publishes online content to display text-based Google AdWords on their website with a simple cut-and-paste format and receive a share of the pay-per-click payment. AdSense ads are similar to the AdWords ads you see on the right-hand side at Google. (For more on pay-per-click programs, see Chapter 24.)

There are many pluses to using AdSense. For example, proponents say AdSense is simple and free to join, you don't have to use different codes for various affiliate programs, and you can concentrate on providing good content because Google does the work of finding the best ads for your pages from more than 600,000 AdWords advertisers.

The payment you receive per click depends on how much advertisers are paying per click to advertise using Google's AdWords service. Advertisers can pay as little as five 5 cents per click to $10 or $12 in profitable niches, perhaps even more. You earn a share of that.

"Small affiliates now have a more acceptable way to monetize their web real estate for internet content, including RSS feeds, podcasts and video," says Porter. "In the recent past, there was a shift. Small affiliates making in the $2,000 a month range using traditional affiliate cost-per-action or cost-per-sale structures migrated to the Google AdSense model and saw revenues jump as high as $15,000 to $50,000 per month."

A key reason for the success of AdSense is its revenue model: It offered a cost-per-click model vs. a cost-per-action or cost-per-sale model. In other words, for affiliates to get paid, visitors to a site "just had to send a qualified click instead of having to complete a transaction," says Porter. "One of the reasons for the success of the cost-per-click model is it shifted the risk away from the affiliate, making it simpler. Now Google has added cost-per-action, traditional affiliate style, into the mix."

After buying out DoubleClick, the leading marketing technology service for years, affiliate marketing suddenly changed from a simple industry to a really big, important industry. The combination of Google's mountainous cash pile and the instant access to DoubleClick's big display ad client base accelerated Google's advances in online advertising. Google is planning to zero in on affiliate marketing when it sells off the search engine marketing side of DoubleClick Performics. With its focus on the affiliates marketing angle, Google will no doubt be a dominant force.

Yahoo! launched its own advertising option for small publishers in 2005 called Yahoo! Publisher Network (publisher.yahoo.com). Like Google's service, Yahoo!'s self-serve product displays text ads deemed relevant to the content of specific web pages. Advertisers pay only when a reader clicks on their ad. MSN was a latecomer to the market, having only recently launched its own service, MSN AdCenter (adcenter.microsoft.com).

There are more than text ads available now, too. You can opt in to a variety of media on Yahoo! Publisher Network or Google AdSense. Both offer banner ads in a variety of sizes and formats as well as rich text formatting to brighten up dull text with bold, italics and other fancier options.

Solid Links

AdSense aside, is it difficult to create an affiliate link? The job is simple, and you'll have it done within a minute or three. It works like this: You select the logo or link you want to show on your site. Most e-tailers offer many choices, sometimes dozens, so you can

> **Tip...**
>
> **Smart Tip**
>
> Once you've pasted in an affiliate code, always preview the revised page in all relevant browsers before going live. Often the placement won't be where you'd thought it would be (centering a logo can be downright tricky—just use trial and error), and sometimes the link is dead (usually because a tiny bit of code got cut off during copying and pasting).

get exactly the look you want. Click the logo you like, and the e-tailer will automatically generate HTML code that does two things: links to the e-tailer and includes your affiliate ID so you can earn commissions. Then you copy that code and, using your HTML editor of choice (such as CoffeeCup), paste it into the proper location on your site.

Doing all this is grunt work, not rocket science, and within a few minutes the link should look spiffy. Want to see this procedure in action? Head to Amazon's excellent resources for affiliates at affiliate-program.amazon.com. There you'll see a wide variety of customizable widgets (i.e., display options), including slide shows, videos, product previews, tag clouds and search.

No matter how spiffy your affiliate links appear and how heavy your traffic is, you won't necessarily see big profits resulting from affiliate programs. To make money, you have to follow the rules.

Rule No. 1: Don't make affiliate links your content. The advice seems obvious, but the web remains cluttered with pages that consist of nothing but banners from affiliates. Nobody is apt to buy anything from these sites. That's why a basic element in setting up a thriving affiliation deal is to strictly limit the number of programs you join. You don't want a blizzard of banners on your site.

Rule No. 2: "Do contextual placement; it's important," advises ReveNews.com's Porter. But be sparing—rarely should there be more than a single affiliate link on any page—and if you explain why you are endorsing this merchant and merchandise, you may just get visitors to check it out. A saloon owner, for instance, might recommend a cocktail recipe book; a website design firm might endorse a web hosting service. An exception to this rule might be a comparison shopping service.

Rule No. 3: Seek feedback from your site visitors. Do they find the links to affiliates useful? Distracting? Annoying? Pay attention to what they tell you—and if they're not clicking through to your affiliate merchants, that, too, tells you something. Put up different banners, try another merchant mix or placement on the real estate, or take them down altogether.

▲

The Dark Side of Banners

You've digested the warning that, on a site with modest traffic, you're unlikely to see an affiliate check in this century, but there's more bad news to consider. For starters, whenever a visitor clicks the affiliate link, he or she clicks away from your site. You may make the commission, but you'll lose the visitor. Is it worth it? That's your call, but this is an issue every site—no matter how heavy or light its traffic—has to ponder. Winning traffic just isn't easy in today's cluttered internet marketplace, and justifications have to be strong for you to willingly show a visitor the way off your site.

> ## ! Beware!
> Never forget that a bad shopping experience at an affiliate site will tarnish your reputation, too. Choose affiliates cautiously, monitor them (check into their sites), and carefully heed any feedback you get from your visitors. Better still, shop at your affiliated merchants yourself and swiftly eliminate any that don't measure up. You simply can't afford links to bad affiliates.

Then why does Amazon, one of the undisputed kingpins of e-commerce, routinely do it? The Amazon front page features links to Endless.com, a shoe and handbags site, but Endless is another Amazon brand, so the payoff is plain to see. For you, the choice is more difficult. An affiliate link might put money in your treasury, but would you make more money keeping the visitor at your site? Think hard on that.

If you choose to add a banner, remember that every banner you insert takes time to load, meaning your page will take that much longer to come into a visitor's view. Always check affiliate banners to make certain they load swiftly. Amazon banners usually pop rapidly into view, while those from lesser players sometimes can take many seconds. Ruthlessly delete slow-loading banners. You can't afford to waste your visitors' time.

And what if a site visitor clicks into an affiliated merchant and has a bad experience? Whom do you blame when your pal Joe recommends his barber, and the haircut that barber gives you makes you look old and tubby? The barber, of course—but also Joe.

When affiliate programs work, they work, but when they don't, no website owner should hesitate to take down the links and call it a noble but failed experiment. Check out affiliate programs, but don't be shy about pulling the plug if you're not seeing meaningful returns.

Want to discover more about affiliate programs? A site that offers speedy sign-up for multiple quality programs is LinkShare (linkshare.com), the wholly owned U.S. division of Rakuten Inc., the No. 1 portal in Japan for shopping, online finance and travel, and the seventh-largest internet company in the world. LinkShare offers deals with Dell Computer, 1-800-Flowers.com, Foot Locker and plenty more. Another leading company is Commission Junction, a ValueClick company (cj.com).

Crave more obscure programs for your site? You'll find them at ClicksLink (clickslink.com), which provides a searchable directory, plus tools for signing up with everyone from astrology services to watchmakers.

New Alliances

The old-fashioned approach to affiliate relationships—and still the web's most prevalent way—is to pop some HTML code onto one of your pages and hope that produces a ringing cash register for your affiliated merchant. But the drawbacks to doing e-commerce this way have prompted the creation of new styles of programs.

Working the System

Is joining an affiliate program an instant way to get yourself discounts on the stuff you intend to buy anyway? It might seem that way. Put up an Amazon logo and, bingo, whenever you buy a book, you get a 10 percent commission (or discount, since it's you shopping).

But affiliate program owners aren't that stupid. Read the fine print: In most programs, there's a clause that says you won't get a commission on your own purchases. End of story? Maybe not: Whispers in the industry are that few affiliate program operators enforce that exclusion. Sources insist that although the program operators know it's you when you're buying—cookies make your identity known—they pay the commission anyway because they don't want to alienate affiliates and, furthermore, are fearful of driving business to competitors.

For example, some savvy merchants are giving private-label sites to their partners or finding more innovative ways to integrate them. Here are some examples, provided by Porter:

- RegNow's (regnow.com) affiliates can add targeted software products to their shopping carts and define style sheets so product purchases appear to be seamless on their sites.
- Most affiliate network systems like My Affiliate Program (myaffiliateprogram. com) allow affiliates to pick up web pages or a web catalog with products and host them in their own databases.

- Flexible tools like Website.Machine (web-sitemachine.com) allow merchants to produce private-label sites that cannot only do commission splitting but also actual profit sharing.

Smart Tip *Tip...*

Find more information on affiliate programs at AssociatePrograms.com or Refer-It.com.

Teaming Up With
Big Brick-and-Mortar Companies

Forming alliances with major corporations has become a common strategy for dotcom companies seeking to carve out a niche for themselves in an ever more brutally competitive marketplace. Why? Nowadays branding is crucial—it takes a name and a sizable chunk of consumer mind share to win eyeballs, and getting there is an expensive proposition.

The days when a little startup could go it alone the way Yahoo! and Amazon did are waning, and a new philosophy is taking hold. "If you're a small dotcom, you have to build alliances with bigger companies," says Phil Anderson, a professor of entrepreneurship at INSEAD, an international graduate business school in Fontainebleau, France. "You have no choice. You need to build share, fast, and that means you have to leverage more resources than you can get your mitts on by yourself."

Align with a big partner and you instantly get multiple pluses: cash, deep management expertise and—when it benefits you—a name you can use to help open doors. Those are very real, very substantial benefits, and that's why partnering is epidemic (in the best possible sense of the word) among dotcoms.

A good example of a dotcom company partnering successfully with a big brick-and-mortar company is The Knot Inc. (theknot.com). This New York–based life-stage media company offers products and services for couples in the five-year span from proposal to pregnancy. Before the network expanded to this five-year period, The Knot got its start in weddings and formed a strategic alliance with The May Department Stores Co., based in St. Louis.

In 2002, the two companies launched a strategic marketing alliance linking theknot.com to the wedding-gift registry sites of May's department stores. With a $5 million investment, May purchased a 19.5 percent interest in The Knot and was given a place on The Knot's board of directors. The alliance is still going strong, despite the fact that May has become part of the Federated Department Stores retail empire and now operates as Macy's.

Under the terms of the alliance, May and The Knot launched a marketing campaign to promote May's department store wedding registry services to The Knot's audience of engaged couples and wedding guests on the web and in stores. The promotions included online advertising and in-store promotions, direct-mail and e-mail campaigns, and advertisements in The Knot's publications.

The Knot has formed other partnerships as well. In November 2004, The Knot and Michael C. Fina, a New York City-based specialty retailer of fine home goods and jewelry, signed an agreement making Michael C. Fina the exclusive provider of china, crystal and silver to The Knot's Gift Registry. In addition, in April 2005, the Target Club Wedd gift registry announced that it formed a partnership with The Knot. Under the agreement,

> **Tip...**
>
> ## Smart Tip
> Don't use just any lawyer to consult with when a tech marriage looms. Find one in a tech center—Silicon Valley; San Francisco; New York City; Austin, Texas—with prior experience in doing deals, and be prepared to pay fees that start upward of $500 per hour. Look at that money as an investment in your future, because that's exactly what it is.

Target Club Wedd was The Knot's premier registry provider and was featured prominently in The Knot's Gift Registry Center.

The partnerships with Michael C. Fina and Target have since expired and been replaced, largely due to the monumental acquisition of WeddingChannel.com—the leading wedding registry resource—by The Knot in 2006.

WeddingChannel.com hosts the online registry service for Macy's and Bloomingdale's on co-branded sites (macysweddingchannel.com and bloomingdales.weddingchannel.com), and each company has responsibilities for marketing the joint service, both online and in the stores.

In addition, WeddingChannel.com has registry partnerships with 18 other leading retailers in the United States, forming the largest aggregated registry service on the internet. WeddingChannel has a patent on registry aggregation and currently has more than 2.2 million registries searchable for prospective gift givers in its registry finder.

This is just one example of how one site can have a number of successful alliances. And there are plenty more examples out there, and many different kinds. For example, some stores turn to dotcom players because building a viable in-house dotcom operation has proven tough for old-style companies, and an alliance with a brash, youthful dotcom is a fast answer to the question "How will you succeed tomorrow?"

Risky Business

Good as some of the news is about the partnerships that are proliferating throughout the dotcom world, there's also a dark side. For example, big companies often put up their money but are unprepared to offer anything more. Another trouble spot is pointed out by INSEAD's Anderson: "Almost by definition, you're taking the larger brand where it hasn't been before. That's a recipe for conflict." Chew on that, because it's at the paradoxical core of small-big alliances. The big company wants the little partner for its creativity, its innovation and its ability to plunge into terrain previously unexplored by the big fellow. But once the deal is done, the risk aversion that is at the heart of virtually all megacorporations kicks in—and suddenly the partner is counseling caution and slow forward motion.

Another problem is that today it is more difficult for young technology companies to find willing deep-pocketed partners, says Christopher O'Leary, a vice president with The Concours Group, a management consulting, research and education firm based in Kingwood, Texas. He points to several reasons for this, including the increasing scarcity of capital, the equivocal success of past alliances, and simply the fact that there are more Cinderellas looking for a ticket to the ball.

Another worry to gnaw on is that a big company may acquire effective control of a little company, meaning that although a straightforward acquisition hasn't been done, by taking command of key functions—accounting, say—or by assuming multiple board seats, the big company has simply grabbed control. As a result, you absolutely need a third party to assist you in creating a fair deal.

Ken Burke, founder and CEO of Petaluma, California–based MarketLive, an e-commerce tool developer that in 1998 brought in publisher R.R. Donnelly as a sizable partner, seconds that recommendation. It took eight months to negotiate the deal—which, according to Burke, left him still controlling the vast majority of the company's ownership. "Donnelly has no real decision-making power," he says. But, he says, a key for

Beware!

Are you concerned about simply being acquired—and losing all effective control? Before making any partnership deal, do research that tells you how many small companies the big company that's courting you has swallowed in the past few years. If the number is high, that's not necessarily an indication that you need to back away from the deal. But it does mean you need to be aware of the possible outcomes.

him was hiring good lawyers. "They found many things in the deal we had to get revised or deleted. You don't want to negotiate this sort of thing alone."

Don't pop the cork to celebrate a business alliance too soon—60 percent of alliances fall apart within three and a half years, says Larraine Segil, author of *FastAlliances: Power Your E-Business* (John Wiley & Sons) and *Partnering: The New Face of Leadership* (AMACOM). Just why do these marriages unravel? Incompatible corporate cultures were cited by a majority of the executives Segil surveyed. Seventy-three percent pointed to incompatible management cultures, 63 percent referred to incompatible management personalities, and 55 percent said that different business priorities contributed to the falling out. A majority of the companies surveyed felt that all three factors contributed, but some felt that one or two contributed more than others.

That's why Segil tells small companies to ask themselves: If this marriage ends in divorce, do I have the resources to recover? If you don't, get moving on developing a separation strategy. Maybe it will never be deployed, but with more than half of corporate marriages ending in quickie divorces, prudence dictates concocting a scenario for survival without the larger partner.

There are other things companies can do to help the alliance succeed. "In order for partnerships to work, it is important that the courtship be more deliberate and involve deeper investigation than may have been required in the past," says The Concours Group's O'Leary. He explains that enterprise strategies and operating models should be compared for compatibility and consistency.

Also crucial is the development of a mutually acceptable exit strategy to protect the companies if the intended success proves elusive. In general, "a dedication of

Beware!

Toysmart, the now-defunct online toy store, thought it had a primo deal when Disney acquired it in 1999 for an undisclosed amount. Those hopes turned to dust in mid-2000, when Disney simply unplugged Toysmart, shutting down the site to stop its losses. Big companies may have deep pockets, but they may also have shallow patience—and that's a real pitfall. The cruel fact is, just as they have the resources to quickly make substantial investments in a little dotcom, they can also—without a shudder or even any hesitation—afford to write off all that money and walk away.

resources to alliances and the adoption of best practices are crucial to successful alliances," says Bill Lundberg, founding president and executive director of the Association of Strategic Alliance Professionals Inc. (ASAP) in Wellesley, Massachusetts.

What are some of these best practices? "Alliances formed must be driven from the business development objectives that the company has," says Lundberg.

Which companies would be preferred partners? Lundberg says asking where the value is migrating in the market, what resources you need to deliver that are valuable to the customer, which of those resources you have, and which you need to bring in from the outside will give you the profile of preferred partners.

Then, Lundberg says, "You have to make sure that the alliance is built around a compelling value proposition, both for each of the alliance partners and for the customer. If it is not compelling and doesn't add substantial value, it's not worth doing."

Lundberg says you also need a clear operations plan for the alliance, clear metrics to measure the value being created, clear commitments of resources to drive performance of the alliance, clear commitment by senior management of each partner, and champions driving the daily performance of the alliance.

For more information about these best practices and other information about strategic alliances, visit ASAP's website at strategic-alliances.org.

Forging Ahead

Know that it won't be easy to create a partnership with a big company—no matter how good your dotcom is. How tough will it be? Here's a true story that ends with success, but the going was tough along the way.

Picture this: You have a great idea for a dotcom. You'll sell gift certificates that can be redeemed at many major retailers, and you'll make a little bit on every transaction. Sounds terrific, except there's a problem: How do you talk retailers into letting you sell their gift certificates?

▲

Jonas Lee, former CEO of GiftCertificates.com (giftcertificates.com) knows—and he also knows how hard it was to do the persuading. Currently, the company has hundreds of major retailers, but "we knocked on many doors before we signed the first deals," he says. Why? Startups are potentially pathways to wealth, but they may also be fly-by-night concerns. Major established businesses don't want to risk tarnishing their brand by partnering with a startup that goes bust.

Eventually Lee got his initial commitments from a couple of name-brand shops—Barnes & Noble and The Sharper Image. "It took me two or three months of persistent calling and explaining," he says. "You may have a good idea, but you have to also convince people you are a good businessperson, and that takes time." The broader point: Partnerships can be wonderful, but persuading partners to ally with you is about as hard as building a winning website in the first place.

Getting Hitched

Want to pursue alliances? Make up a list of potential partners, and make very sure that you see the deal from their perspective as well as yours. Then put yourself in those potential partners' faces. Talk to them at trade shows, for instance, and take every step that comes to mind that will increase their awareness of you. But let them make the first move.

In every instance of successful partnerships I've heard about, the big company made the initial suggestion. Maybe there's no jinx involved in taking a direct approach, but maybe there is. So wait to be wooed.

e-Chat
With eBags.com's Peter Cobb

Eliot and Peter Cobb, Frank Steed, Andy Young and Jon Nordmark all joined forces in spring 1998 to build a major store for shoes and accessories out of bytes, not bricks, and boy, have they pulled it off. Currently, eBags is the self-proclaimed world's largest online retailer of bags and

eBags.com • Peter Cobb, Co-founder,
Senior Vice President of Marketing and Merchandising
Location: Greenwood Village, Colorado • Year Started: 1998

accessories, and it has sold more than 7 million bags and accessories since the site launched in March 1999.

eBags has grown 30 percent per month since its launch, and in July 2007, it announced its fourth straight profitable year. The company also has launched eBags in Europe and has seen strong sales in the United Kingdom. Eliot, Frank and Andy are no longer involved in the business, but Peter and Jon are as active as ever.

To start the company in early 1998, each of the five founders—who collectively had more than 60 years of bag and retail experience in companies like Samsonite USA, American Tourister and The Wherehouse—came up with a significant amount of cash and worked without pay for eight months. Then eBags raised $8 million from angel investors, friends and family. The company then decided it wanted to get venture capital funding, too, so to make room for the capital infusion, eBags cut its angel funding by 50 percent (to $4 million) and sent checks back to all its angels. In 1999, financial relief came from VC firm Benchmark Capital. Other investors have followed, allowing eBags to continually invest in people and technology. To date, the company has raised $30 million in VC funding.

A key to the company's success? It does not overspend. For example, executives don't have golden parachutes or big bonuses. In fact, no one at the company, including its executives, makes a six-figure salary. And after 9/11, all employees, including the executives, took a 10 percent pay cut without complaint. This kind of frugal approach is one reason eBags.com is still around when so many other dotcoms aren't.

Another success secret? eBags maintains little or no inventory of its own. Instead, it relies on manufacturers to drop-ship products directly to customers.

For example, the majority of the 500 brands eBags sells are drop-shipped, including High Sierra Sport Co., Samsonite and Kipling. The practice has turned eBags into a luggage category killer, offering a selection of more than 33,000 items that dwarfs the several hundred products carried by the average specialty baggage store. Company executives believe their lack of inventory is one of the primary reasons eBags has survived.

Here, Peter Cobb discusses some other secrets to eBags' success.

Entrepreneur: What made you decide to launch eBags.com?

Peter Cobb: In May 1998, we saw what was going on with people starting companies selling books and music online, and there was a product we knew and loved—bags—that we knew would be a great fit for the internet. We knew from our research that many people were buying bags through catalogs, so people didn't need to feel and touch the product to make a purchase decision. They were comfortable buying bags from Orvis, L.L. Bean, Lands' End and Eddie Bauer catalogs. Bags and accessories weren't like clothes or shoes, where people really needed to see the color, the size and the materials. Also, people don't really get excited about going to the mall Saturday afternoon to pick out some luggage or a backpack

> ## Smart Tip
>
> Tip...
>
> Is there a niche out there that you are familiar with that isn't on the web yet—and you just know it could be a perfect fit? Then what are you waiting for? As eBags' success shows, if you have the right niche product and you do e-tailing right, you will find success on the internet.

for their son. So with three, four or five photographs nicely done for a product, you can really get the point across.

Another key reason we started was because the retail bag market was very fragmented. If you wanted luggage, you'd probably go to a travel goods specialty store. If you wanted a ladies' handbag, you'd probably go to a department store. And if you were looking for backpacks, you'd go to a sporting goods store. There was no "Bags R Us." Because of this fragmentation, we knew there'd be a great opportunity. And there happened to be nice margins on the product—markups [average] 50 percent.

The other important thing is that in the brick-and-mortar retail world, when inventory comes in, it's there for 180 days. If somebody buys a bag, the store orders another one. What's more, these stores are limited to about 250 products because of physical space.

Because we do business on the internet, however, we can offer more than 33,000 products, and when we take an order, we pass it on to Samsonite, for example, and Samsonite ships it to the customer. We get the sale and then, 30 to 90 days later, we pay the brand.

Entrepreneur: How long did it take to go from idea to funding to launch?

Cobb: Idea to funding was about eight months; idea to launch was 10 months.

Entrepreneur: What's been the biggest surprise you've had in building eBags?

Cobb: There have been a few of them. The biggest surprise is how we've been able to gain such fantastic momentum. We've shipped 7 million bags.

Another one probably has been watching the flame-out of all the e-tailers that took in many times more money than we did and somehow spent it all. It's been a huge surprise to see companies that I thought were pretty solid companies fail—like Planet RX, Garden.com and MotherNature.com, sites I shopped on and had great shopping experiences with. What you don't know, however, is what is going on behind the scenes. These companies were spending tens of millions of dollars on inventory in their warehouses, which we didn't have to do. They were also spending money on TV advertising, which we never really did. We have a saying at eBags: "Too much money makes you stupid." We just kept seeing that over and over again. We didn't raise nearly as much money as these guys did, and we always understood that the money we were dealing with was our money—money we put into the company with some investors' help. Every decision we made was "This is our money; how should we spend it?" as opposed to

▲

"Boy, we've got $80 million in the bank, so who cares if we spend $1 million on Super Bowl ads?"

Another surprise has been how much internet retailing has taken hold with a large percentage of the population. I think it has mainstreamed. The growth of broadband has [also] made online shopping faster and more enjoyable. I think that says good things for the future of internet retailing for those who are doing it right.

Entrepreneur: What's been your biggest challenge?

Cobb: I think the biggest challenge is managing your cash properly while continuing to grow.

Entrepreneur: How many VCs did you meet with before you got a funding commitment?

Cobb: We met with well over 100 VC firms.

Entrepreneur: What's your strategy in coming out ahead of competitors?

Cobb: Our competition is really brick-and-mortar stores. Online shopping isn't for everybody. Some people want to feel and touch and taste and smell before they buy a product, and that's OK. But a large majority of shoppers value convenience and selection, and that's why online shopping is experiencing explosive growth. Bags and accessories is a $40 billion market. Our strategy is just to continue to offer the ultimate shopping experience on eBags.com.

Cheap Tricks
With Blinds.com's Jay Steinfeld

Who likes buying window coverings? Probably nobody, a fact that Jay Steinfeld—founder and CEO of Blinds.com—has turned into a thriving web-based business that was started with just $3,000 and has been profitable from day one. Steinfeld tells his story here:

Blinds.com • Jay Steinfeld, CEO and Founder
Location: Houston, Texas • Year Started: 1996

▲

The Name of the Game

A good domain name is essential to creating your internet presence. The name needs to be memorable, marketable, and easy to remember and type in. And the shorter the better, as Jay Steinfeld learned. What happens if you come up with a better idea later or changes in your business make the name less relevant in a few years? You can switch to a new URL any time—if it's available. Websites like Ajaxwhois.com make it super easy to determine availability of a domain name. But don't be surprised if the name you want is taken. With 15,000-plus ".com" registrations each week, it's getting harder to snag the domain name of your dreams. But don't give up. Go Daddy, one of thousands of dealers in the domain name aftermarket, keeps track of domain names going up for sale. Don't want to wait? Have Go Daddy track down the current owner and negotiate a deal for you to buy it.

Entrepreneur: Where did you get the idea for the site? When did the site go live?

Jay Steinfeld: My wife and I owned a full-service brick-and-mortar window coverings store [in Houston]. We owned the store for about 14 years, so we knew the window coverings business inside and out. But we wanted to expand into a different niche—the price-sensitive, do-it-yourself market. In June 1996, we launched our first website, and then in March 2001, we went full time online. With the internet, I have a website working 24 hours a day. I'm able to do so much more volume online than what I could have done in a 1,000-square-foot store. Sales have increased every year since then and now we're the largest online seller of blinds in the world. Why? Because people are becoming more comfortable with the internet, and even in a bad economy, people are trying to get good deals, and they naturally associate the internet with a good deal. We also make the whole process simple and allow people to buy confidently.

I've been selling online now for 12 years, which is two years longer than the web has been a proven entity. We figured if we hustled and used the same service-first, high-touch philosophy; kept our personality present on the site; and made it fun, then customers would react favorably.

We wanted to make it easy, too—a no-brainer. So we called our first site NoBrainerBlinds.com. That name occurred to me in about two minutes. As soon as I said it, I knew it would work. It made sense, it's descriptive of our mission, and people get it. We later launched our flagship site, Blinds.com, based on everything we learned from our NoBrainerBlinds.com site—and its sales have soared. The site has more products, better help, is faster, and has better navigational experiences than the NoBrainerBlinds.com site.

Entrepreneur: Have you sought outside funding?

Steinfeld: We did get some financing from some local angel investors in February 2001, and it enabled us to buy our then-biggest competitor, Blindswholesale.com. This was a fantastic acquisition, and it let us have access to the technology we needed to expand our business. This acquisition tripled the size of our business, and we've grown tenfold since then.

There are some blinds factories and many investors that have made offers to buy us, so who knows…maybe one day we'll sell. This is my baby, so it would be hard to sell. On the other hand, I suppose everything is for sale.

Entrepreneur: How do you attract visitors to your site?

Steinfeld: We use all the guerrilla tactics—newsgroups, link building and search engine optimization. We have about 12,000 sites linking to us. We also encourage our existing customers to tell their friends by providing them with an experience that exceeds their expectations. These days, 45 percent of our volume is either repeat customers or referrals. We also do paid advertising, such as keyword buys. For Blinds.com, we also intend to advertise on radio and TV, because our name is so easy to remember.

Entrepreneur: What's your look-to-buy ratio?

Steinfeld: About 5 to 10 percent.

Entrepreneur: How big is the average purchase?

Steinfeld: When we were just NoBrainerBlinds.com, the average order size was about $460, but now it's about $350 because we added lower-priced products for those customers who just want a no-frills, quality blind at the lowest price possible. We attracted many more customers, but we attracted customers who buy at lower levels. That's fine, because they are so happy to tell all their friends about what a great deal they got with Blinds.com. That yields a lot more sales. That $350 is still over two times the industry average, which is $150.

Entrepreneur: For the consumer, what's the advantage of buying online?

Steinfeld: They save a bunch of money, and they can read up on the options/products at their own pace—no pressure. They can also read thousands of actual reviews written by consumers so they can tell which products others like to help them make an informed decision. We have created our own private-label product line, accounting for more than two-thirds of our products sold. Those products are custom-made by the well known manufactures, but without their labels—and all have lifetime warranties. Plus, all our products have a money-back satisfaction guarantee.

Entrepreneur: What challenge do you face in making this site grow?

Steinfeld: Our challenge right now is to make sure that our success doesn't cause us to implode. We now have to start looking at the company in a different way. We have to start thinking of systems, procedures, control and—God forbid—coming up with an organizational chart. We will have to write memos now and then and have meetings. We're going to have to get organized. Hiring the right people and getting them trained into the best positions to help us grow smart will be the key.

In April 2008, we launch yet another site, Blinds.ca, which we believe will be the Canadian equivalent of Blinds.com. This new site should greatly increase our revenue and be our first step internationally.

Website Traffic Builders

H ere's the bad news: There are currently some-
where between 15 and 30 billion web pages and well over 100 million websites. Wow! That's a lot of websites out there competing for
attention. You've done your best to build a great site that users will
want to visit again and again, but the tough reality is that no matter
how great your site is, chances are slim that a customer will randomly happen on to your site. It's imperative that you use a variety

▲

of strategies to get your website noticed by the billion-plus people who now surf the web.

"Putting up a website is just like opening an antiques store down a country road," says Larry Chase, publisher of Web Digest for Marketers (wdfm.com), a weekly e-mail newsletter with reviews of marketing-oriented websites. "Unless you tack up signs on better-traveled routes, you won't get any visitors."

What's more, traditional marketing campaigns don't necessarily produce results for websites, warns Mark DiMassimo, CEO of DiMassimo Brand Advertising, an agency that has handled many dotcom clients. "The only offline medium that works is TV," says DiMassimo. "In fact, the complaint of many dotcoms is that they can't find other forms of offline media to compete with TV. That's a scary place to be because you don't want to be overdependent on any one advertising medium."

Baiting Your Hook

What will lure visitors to a site? Although heavily funded internet companies can make seven- and eight-figure deals to buy prime advertising real estate on the major internet portals and online services like Yahoo! and AOL, you're likely to be priced out of that race. So winning visitors becomes a matter of creative, persistent marketing. And the good news is that it's still the little things that will bring plenty of traffic your way.

There are fundamental steps that too many businesses neglect. For instance? "You should always put your URL and a reason to visit your website on your business cards," says Chase. "I call this cyber-bait. For example, you should mention what people will get when they visit the site, such as a newsletter or a list of 'Top 10 Tips' or

something. That substantially increases visitors and eventually customers or subscribers."

Several years ago, Chase says, "you could get away with just putting a URL on your business card because the novelty of that URL was enough to draw people to the site. Nowadays it's just like putting up a fax number. People are not going to fax you just to see how your fax machine works." An e-mail signature is also an especially powerful—and absolutely free—tool. Create a signature with a link to your website in it and have it automatically attached to every one of your outgo-

> **! Beware!**
> A strong bias against overt advertising remains on the net's newsgroups. Sigs are OK with postings, but be careful to use a sig that's informational. "Best parrot seeds on the net" is out. "Seeds for parrots" is fine. The lines seem blurry? They are. But if you cross them, hostile postings from anti-ad folks will tell you the difference.

126

Snazzy Signatures

Pretty much every e-mail program offers the ability to include a signature that goes out with every e-mail. Think of a signature—"sig" in tech-speak—as a teaser, a fast ad for your website. How do you create a signature? In Microsoft Outlook Express, for example, go to "Tools/Options/Signatures." Some advice: Shorter is better than longer with signatures. Rarely should you use more than six short lines, and three or four are better.

What to include? If your website sells foreign language tapes, for instance, you might use this sig:

John Smith
President, TapesRUs.com
"Learn Languages by Tape"
Tapesrus.com

Once you've set it up, that signature will appear on every e-mail you send out (unless you override the default). If you send out 20 e-mails in a day, that's 20 repetitions of a fast ad message. It's one of the net's best marketing bargains.

ing e-mails. If your e-mail recipients click on the link, they'll be taken to your site. It takes only a few seconds to create an e-mail signature, and it may bring in visitors to your site every day.

Another low-cost traffic builder: "Get active in online discussion groups and chats, and, where appropriate, give out your URL," says Shannon Kinnard, author of *Marketing With E-mail* (Maximum Press). Sell bird toys? Scout out the many groups that focus on birds and get active. A good place to find groups is at Google Groups (http://groups.google.com), which archives discussion lists. Getting active in these groups spreads the word about you and your site. "You'll get traffic coming to you," says Kinnard.

Similar advice can be given for social networking sites like Facebook, MySpace, and Flickr. You'll want to create a profile for your business, get active in the groups that cater to your web audience, and befriend other like-minded businesses and people. Like any community-oriented activity online, you don't want to cross the line into spam. Only "friend" people when it makes sense. And keep your profiles updated—if you'll be participating in real-world events with your business, put that in your "events" section on MySpace, for example. If you've updated a section of your site, broadcast that on your Facebook profile.

The Most Bang for Your Buck

Another big-time traffic builder for any website that retails is posting items for sale on the major auction sites, such as eBay, Yahoo!and Amazon. Those sites let you identify yourself to viewers, and a few dollars spent on putting out merchandise to bid may just bring in lots of traffic from surfers seeking more information. Many small e-tailers tell me their entire advertising budget consists of less than $100 monthly spent on eBay, but they nonetheless are seeing traffic counts above 500 daily, with most of those viewers coming via eBay. My advice: Put up a few items for bid on each of the leading auction sites and then track traffic. Even if you sell the auctioned goods at no profit, the traffic jams your site may experience could well justify your efforts.

Classified ads offer more possibilities for traffic generation on the cheap. Sites like Oodle.com and Sell.com offer low-cost classified ads. For example, on Sell.com, 30-day ads have a $1 to $3 insertion fee. Extra services, like a bolded or highlighted list, are available for additional fees. Listing is simple—just follow the steps on the site.

If you have a real-world component to your business, be sure to try out Craigslist (craigslist.org). All ads on Craigslist are free, except for job ads in a handful of cities and brokered apartment listings in

Budget Watcher

Worried that your copy won't be up to snuff? You may be right. A sure way to make a site look amateurish is to post stuff that's riddled with misspellings, bad grammar and worse. The good news: The leading word processing application (Microsoft Word) will meticulously check your copy. Link-checking site Keynote NetMechanic (netmechanic.com) also offers spell check. Use these tools! Doing so takes a few minutes, but the improvements in writing are well worth the time.

New York City. It takes just a few minutes to post an ad, so it's worth your time to see if anyone bites. And with 9 billion page views each month, 450 local sites in the United States and abroad, and more than 25 million U.S. users, you know people will see your ad—and hopefully answer it.

For my money, classified ads—at least the freebies—represent one of the very top ways to generate no-cost traffic. And classified ads are becoming a major online advertising category, with revenues reported to be $3.1 billion annually, outpacing all predictions for growth.

Should you buy ads on other websites? That depends on your budget and the type of results you're seeking. The key is to stay away from companies that offer to put your ad on thousands of websites for very little money. Instead, work with a banner ad network that will help you build long-lasting, profitable relationships with your target audience. For example, check out BannerSpace (bannerspace.com). There you can choose to advertise on premium sites—high-traffic destinations, portals and directories with well-known brands. Or, save money with channel advertising by placing your banners on sites that have specific content related to your offer. Costs will vary either way. The cost of advertising on premium sites averages about $50 for 100 guaranteed visitors, or $500 for 1,000. Is that money well spent? If you have a quality banner ad and a large number of exposures on premium sites, you may see a traffic jump.

There are also ad networks that specifically target bloggers, which may be worthwhile if you have a very narrowly targeted niche—say kayaks or knitting supplies—and want to focus on places where such hobbyists gather. For example, you can buy a wide skyscraper ad that will run one week and gather 110,000 impressions on the fifth-most popular blog (according to Technorati.com) BoingBoing.net for $36. A small, square button costs only $7 for the same period of time and 220,000 impressions. More narrowly targeted (and less popular) blogs will probably be less expensive. You can also buy ads based on audience profile ("hip parents," "tech innovators"), rather than by specific site. FederatedMedia.net, where these price examples came from, and BlogAds.com are two places to explore these types of ads.

Budget Watcher

Want more pointers about traffic building and promotion on the cheap? Check out *101 Ways to Promote Your Web Site* (Maximum Press) by Susan Sweeney. The book provides entrepreneurs with information on proven techniques such as using e-mail, links and online advertising to increase the number of initial users and repeat visitors. Or you could do a quick Google search for things like "How to Drive Traffic to Your Website Cheaply." You'll be surprised at how much information pops up. Understand, however, that there are no magic formulas. No-money promotion can work if you stay at it, and that means consistent, solid effort. Do that, and you'll see the results in a rising daily visitor count.

With any ad campaign you purchase, closely monitor results. Renew only the deals that are generating traffic to your site, and know that net advertisers have a big plus over advertisers in offline media, such as magazines, because on the net it is very easy to track—via your log files (see Chapter 33)—which ads are producing which results. That takes the guesswork out of decisions to renew media buys.

What's a fair payback? If small businesses goof, it's in wildly overestimating the results they can anticipate from a media purchase. If you spend $100 on ads that bring in sales that produce $110 in revenue, consider it money well spent. Expecting more than that is just fantasy.

When it comes to offline advertising, expert opinion is mixed. Some pros advocate big investments in traditional media, while others tell you to fish where the fish are, and that means advertising online to promote an online store. I split the difference here, and my advice is to incorporate your URL prominently into all offline advertising you're doing—never overlook a chance to plug your website—but don't launch an offline campaign for an online-only property. Sure, many of the big guys, such as Priceline.com (priceline.com), Go Daddy (godaddy.com) and Overstock.com (overstock.com) extensively advertise in offline media, but these are businesses with heavy venture capital backing and the dollars to experiment with. When money is tighter, go where you know you'll find surfers—and that means hunting online.

A Direct Approach

For many businesses, direct mail—good old e-mail—may be the surest and certainly the cheapest tool for building traffic. And it gets results: Customized e-mail can generate response rates upward of 6 percent—sometimes as high as 30 percent, but that kind of response is rare even for an in-house list.

What's more, according to a recent Direct Marketing Association (DMA) report, 15 percent of Americans in 2006 made a purchase in response to a commercial e-mail in the previous 12-month period.

News Flash

What's the best way to get people to respond to e-mail? First, follow the law.

The Controlling the Assault of Non-Solicited Pornography and Marketing Act (or the CAN-SPAM Act of 2003) became effective on January 1, 2004. The law requires commercial e-mail messages to be labeled and to include opt-out instructions as well as the sender's physical address. It also prohibits the use of deceptive subject lines and false headers. (For more information on this subject, see Chapter 33.) A good way to get folks to opt in to your e-mail list—which, of course, they will have the option of opting out of—is to offer a free monthly e-mail newsletter.

About what? Content is wide open, but effective newsletters usually mix news about trends in your field with tips and

> **Tip...**
>
> **Smart Tip**
> Always give e-mail recipients an easy way to opt out of future mailings—and whenever anybody asks to be removed from your list, honor that request immediately.

updates on sales or special pricing. "Whatever you do, keep it short," says author Kinnard. How short? About 600 words is probably the maximum length. Says Kinnard, "The rule is, the shorter, the better." Another key: Include hyperlinks so that interested readers can, with a single mouse click, go directly to your site and find out more about a topic of interest.

Socializing for Fun and Profit

If you want to draw attention to your website, go where online crowds converge: MySpace, Facebook and YouTube. Whether you're marketing to other businesses or to consumers, social networks must be in your marketing mix. In fact, social network marketing is fast on the rise and is currently the second most popular online marketing tactic (search engine marketing is first). Start by creating a free profile, but be careful—your profile shouldn't be a blatant advertisement. Instead, make it similar to a blog that allows you to share your knowledge on a particular subject. Then create a group or network where people can join the discussion. For example, if you have a landscaping company, you would set up a gardening network. And of course, you would be the expert moderator. It's a great form of viral marketing, especially if you get a lot of people joining the group.

Which social networking site should you use? There are dozens to choose from, but the 1,000-pound gorilla is still MySpace. According to Hitwise, the online research service, more than 3 out of 4 social network visits went to MySpace in 2007. By February 2008, MySpace had more than 110 million active monthly users. That's a lot of potential customers!

How often should you mail? Often enough to build a relationship with your readers, but not so frequently you become a pest. "Monthly works for most mailing lists," says Kinnard, but she notes that every other week is OK for some businesses.

Daily updates are a big mistake, and weekly ones are probably ill-advised, too. The reason: Recipients will ask to be deleted from the list or, worse, they'll simply delete each of your e-mails, unread, as soon as they come in.

Some mailing list drawbacks: Maintaining a list can be time-consuming. Worse, most ISPs put limits on the size of outgoing mailings (a maximum of 50 recipients is common) to keep spammers away, so mailing to a large list can be an aggravation involving the use of many small lists. When I recently mailed to a charity's list of 1,000 as a do-good deed, I had to break the master list into about 25 minilists. When I tried to use more than, say, 50 names at a crack, the server rejected the whole mailing.

Special Delivery

A solution to these common mailing hassles is to use a mailing service, says Kinnard. Three good choices? Topica (topica.com), Constant Contact (constantcontact.com) and ExactTarget (exacttarget.com). These services maintain mailing lists and, on your schedule, send out the mailings you provide.

A lot of the grunt work involved in mailings is handled by these services, including handling your opt-outs in a timely fashion and helping you measure your e-mail newsletter results, which leaves you free to focus on the fun part: your message. Keep it simple, keep it sharp, and always use e-mail to drive traffic to your site. Don't make the big mistake of trying to cram your website's entire message into every e-mail. Nobody has the patience for that. E-mail should stick to "headline news," with the full story residing on your website. (For more effective e-mail practices, see "Best Bets" on the next page.)

Is your list succeeding? There's no reason to guess at the answer. Just track site-traffic for a few days before a mailing and a few days afterward. Effective e-mail ought to produce a sharp upward spike in visitors. How big a spike? That answer hinges on your usual traffic, the size of your list and your personal goals. A good target, though, is a 6 percent response rate.

If you don't see an increase in traffic, take a hard look at what you're mailing. Is it succinct? Focused? Does it encourage readers to click through for more information? If not, odds are you need to hone your message to encourage recipients to click through.

Another possible reason for less-than-desirable results: Your mailing list is bad. Send a vegan mailing to a list of self-proclaimed steak lovers, and you're knocking on the wrong door.

The best way to build a targeted mailing list is to make it simple for site visitors to sign up to receive it. Ask customers each time they complete a transaction on your site if they'd like to receive a newsletter. Leave the "yes" box unchecked, though, so you're not accidentally opting in those who don't want to receive it. Also include an easy-to-find newsletter sign-up box or link prominently throughout your site. You may even want to offer a special coupon or free article for those who sign up.

Stick It to Me

"Sticky" is the dream that keeps website builders going. When your site is sticky, visitors hang around, and that means they're reading and buying—and the time a surfer sticks to your site translates into greater brand awareness for you. Whether you're in a mall or your site is stand-alone, sticky is the Holy Grail—but making your site

Best Bets

How can e-mail help you be a more effective marketer? In a report titled "Actionable Insights Into Email Marketing," the DMA offers some practical advice for marketers on how to be more successful at reaching current and potential customers or donors through focused e-mail messages. "The e-mail marketing channel offers fantastic opportunities for reaching customers efficiently," says Sue Geramian, the DMA's senior vice president for interactive and emerging media. "However, legitimate marketers must continue to monitor the evolving delivery landscape, especially emerging technologies that are helping to distinguish legitimate e-mail communications from fraudulent efforts."

These best practices are intended to improve the likelihood of permission-based e-mail being delivered to the inbox and read by the intended recipient. The recommendations suggest that e-mail marketers:

- **Encourage customers and prospects to add the marketer's legitimate sending address to their personal "approved list/address book"** and provide upfront instructions on how to do so in registration pages. Benefits vary by mailbox provider but may include special icon designation, full image content/link rendering, and no lost e-mails in the spam folder. Being an "approved" sender yields higher response rates and generates fewer complaints and blocking issues.

- **Carefully consider the content and presentation of marketing messages,** as recipients are increasingly labeling any e-mail communication that's not relevant or looks suspicious as spam. In addition, marketers are encouraged to create messages that strike a balance between images and text, as many mailbox providers now routinely "hide" images in default settings.

- **Follow established protocols such as authentication and white-listing criteria** to ensure that e-mail messages "pass muster" with mailbox providers. A growing number of ISPs use spam-filtering software to eliminate junk mail. This technology uses algorithms to determine whether incoming messages qualify as junk e-mail and filters them out before they get to an end user's inbox. In addition, marketers should register for all mailbox-provider feedback loops. In general, marketers should aim to keep complaint rates (total complaints divided by total delivered e-mail) below 0.1 percent to avoid temporary or long-term blocks.

- **Adopt good list-hygiene and monitoring practices** that help facilitate message delivery. Monitoring campaign delivery, open and click-through

(continued on the next page)

> rates is essential because a low open rate or high bounce rate may indicate a delivery problem.
>
> • **Educate consumers and other stakeholders about anti-spam tools, technologies, laws, and industry programs** developed to separate legitimate communications from fraudulent messaging.

sticky doesn't have to be that elusive. The key is to offer information—that is, content—that will interest your visitors.

For a measuring stick, just look at the following statistics: Netratings, a firm that offers internet audience measurement and analysis, published a chart called "Top 25 Stickiest Web Brands" in December 2007 that measured, among other things, how many hours people spent on different websites during that month. The No. 1 site that month? FullTiltPoker.com, which had people spending nearly 11 hours on its site. In second place was EA.com (Electronic Arts Online), where people spent nearly eight hours that month playing fantasy sports.

So what do the winning sites have in common? Good content. In both cases, people actually play on the site—and the sites are easy to navigate. Of course, content is lots easier to say than it is to deliver. The following are concrete building blocks for making any site stickier:

- *Fast loading time:* Surfers are impatient. Force them to watch a stagnant screen as dense images or fancy Java applets load, and they will be out of there before your cool bells and whistles ever come into sight. It's tempting to use these gizmos—you might think they'd increase your visitor stays because just watching them load eats up minutes—but in most cases, forget it. When you force surfers to wait until

On File

Using e-mail services isn't the only way to go when sending out e-mail marketing messages. Some small e-tailers swear by FileMaker Pro 9 database software to manage and execute their e-mail marketing efforts. The software includes an e-mail campaign management solution that allows you to easily deploy e-mail marketing from within the system to targeted customer groups. The software is especially great for monthly newsletters and staying in touch with customers and prospects. FileMaker Pro 9 also lets you track e-mail campaigns by printing individualized bar or promotional codes in e-mails and then placing detailed notes in each customer's file so you can create reports on current and past campaigns. Best of all, FileMaker Pro starts at only $299, which is a pretty good deal. For more information, visit filemaker.com.

meaningful stuff happens, they won't. They will simply leave—often in a huff—and that means they won't be bookmarking your site for future visits. True, more and more people are using broadband services to access the internet, which means they can get a faster connection. But it's still important that you don't overload your site with too much "stuff."

- *Good copy:* "The web is still about text, words," says Motley Fool (motley-fool.com) co-founder David Gardner, and he's spot on. You're not a writer? That doesn't necessarily matter—not when you stick to your field of expertise. Are you a criminal lawyer? Put up a list of the "10 Dumbest Mistakes Defendants Make." An accountant could do likewise. An electrician could

> ## ⚠ Beware!
> While encouraging more frequent shopping with a loyalty program for existing customers is a smart strategy, promoting loyalty on the web does pose some challenges. For example, establishing loyalty online tends to be difficult, given the nature of the web environment and its one-click access to competitors. So what is an online merchant to do? You need to speak to shoppers' uniqueness, not require the user to jump through hoops to participate, and provide a simple reward structure and clear value for information given.

put up a list of dangerous goofs made by do-it-yourselfers. Think snappy and useful, and try to provide info readers can't easily find at thousands of other websites.

- *Loyalty programs:* Another way to get targeted customers coming back for more is by using online incentive marketing, such as setting up loyalty programs on your site. In fact, 60 percent of the top 100 e-merchants surveyed by Chicago-based consulting firm The e-Tailing Group reported in a recent survey that they reward shoppers for frequent purchases and other activity. Why? Acquiring customers isn't as easy as it used to be—so if you have regular customers, it is wise to do something to keep them coming back for more.

There are numerous such programs out there. You could do something as simple as offering customers the ability to earn gifts—like T-shirts emblazoned with your logo—if they buy enough merchandise on your site. Or you could go with the most popular option, known as a frequent-buyer or points program. This choice gives customers the opportunity to receive discounts or points toward the purchase of merchandise by buying products on your site. The more your customers spend—which can also mean the more times they come back to your site—the bigger the discounts or the more points they receive.

- *Easy navigation:* Every pro webmaster has a few favorite awful sites that offer great content but that nobody will ever see because they're too hard to navigate. Simplicity has to be a byword for any site builder, because the price of boring or confusing a visitor is that surfer's quick exit.

e-Chat
With GiftTree's Craig Bowen

Sometimes e-tailers find taking a step backward technologically—into the world of print catalogs—is a big step forward for their business. Craig Bowen, CEO and co-founder (with his wife, Esther Diez) of GiftTree (gifttree.com), is a successful e-tailer who found that mail

GiftTree.com • Craig Bowen, CEO and Co-founder
Location: Vancouver, Washington • Year Started: 1997

▲

order was the best growth option for his business.

In business since 1997, GiftTree is a premier gift services provider. Its clients include many large multinational and U.S. corporations as well as individuals. Its products include handcrafted gift baskets, as well as new-baby gifts, balloon bouquets, thank-you gifts, get-well gifts, wedding gifts and business gifts.

In 2003, the online merchant decided to add a catalog to its e-tailing business. Why? Because catalogs keep e-tailers "top of mind" with customers and ultimately encourage those customers to come back for more, Bowen says. The company now makes its catalog a key part of its marketing plan. Here's a closer look at Bowen's mail order experience.

Entrepreneur: Tell me about your company. Where and when was the company founded?

Craig Bowen: Our company was started in 1997 by myself and my wife in our studio apartment in Key West, Florida. My wife is from Spain, and our dream was to build an internet company, sell it, and move back to Spain (where we met). We're still working on the "move back to Spain" part.

Entrepreneur: Why did you decide to start the company?

Bowen: We felt the internet was the perfect medium for busy people to buy and send gifts. I really liked the idea of jumping into the internet revolution to see how we'd do running our own business.

Entrepreneur: When did you decide to add a mail order or catalog component to your company?

Bowen: Our first catalog went out in 2003. It was sent to a small group of very specific clients during the holiday season, and it worked very well: We saw a lift in sales. We were encouraged by its success and began to grow our catalog distribution. We sent another during the holiday season in 2004 and then sent two out in 2005—one in the fall and one around holiday time. We expanded our distribution to five catalogs in 2007.

Entrepreneur: How did you go about launching the catalog? How expensive was it?

Bowen: GiftTree decided to create and design its catalog in-house. Employees took photographs of GiftTree's products in the company's own photo studio. We hired a printer to print the catalogs and then mailed the catalogs through the U.S. Postal Service.

Since the catalog was launched in tandem with other fliers—and since GiftTree used in-house employees for the work—it's hard for me to give an answer as to how much the whole project cost. However, taking on this kind of project is definitely not cheap. It can cost at least $100,000 once you factor in the costs of hiring an agency to produce it, printing, mailing, and perhaps buying or renting a prospect list. Basically, it is as expensive as you'd like it to be. Also, we have exceptional technological capability for a company our size, so most of these things are costing us far less than other companies our size.

Entrepreneur: What types of changes did you have to make on the back end to support the catalog?

Bowen: Initially, very few. Launching the catalog was a logical channel for GiftTree to explore. The company's fulfillment system was already in place, ready to take orders. And GiftTree had already collected the names and addresses of customers to whom it could send catalogs. Now that we are trying to gather more data and increase our catalog's distribution, we are finding that adding and changing technologies is extremely important. For example, we have started to use Matchback software to make sure the information we have on people in our sales data and mailing list match up properly. We also have added a much better profiling system to help us identify and target our customers.

Beware!
While Craig Bowen has had success with his catalog, keep in mind that a nice-looking catalog that works is usually a very expensive proposition. And once you're in it, you're in it for the long haul. So before you decide to launch a catalog, make sure you have exhausted all the other ways to promote your products—such as pay-per-click advertising and e-mail marketing.

Entrepreneur: In general, was adding a mail order component to your company difficult to do?

Bowen: It's time-consuming, and mistakes and missteps can be costly. There is a lot of knowledge available on the subject, and time spent on research will make things easier, or at least reduce some anxieties you might feel when creating your first catalog. For those who can afford it, a website and a catalog make the perfect marriage. There's a reason people do catalogs: They work. If you make a very beautiful catalog, and it's got what consumers want, they are far more likely to order from you than if you didn't send them something.

Entrepreneur: What types of challenges did you face?

Bowen: Making our product "appear" more like a catalog product. There is a difference between web and print. Catalogs are not interactive, and that was new for us. Print is also very unforgiving; once you make a decision, you can't undo it with a few keystrokes.

Entrepreneur: Has the catalog side of your business helped the growth of your company?

Bowen: Yes, and we expect it to add more as we move forward.

Entrepreneur: How successful is your company?

Bowen: I think we are very successful. We're still a bit of a diamond in the rough, but we've done most of the hard work already.

Entrepreneur: What are your secrets to success?

Bowen: Never give up. Never surrender.

Secrets of
Search Engines

Search engines have become a crucial part of the online experience of internet users. According to a recent report from the Pew Internet & American Life Project—which produces reports that explore the impact of the internet—the number of American adults using search engines on an average day jumped from roughly 59 million to 86 million over a one-year period—an increase of about 45 percent.

Smart Tip

Usually, the "Add URL" or "Submit Your Site" button is at the bottom of the page, sometimes in tiny print. A few engines hide theirs. At Google, for instance, it's under "About Google." Some engines don't offer this option and instead rely on their own spiders (search tools that automatically move from site to site, following all available links) to add listings. Find out more about spiders in "Spider Webs" on page 146. Keep in mind, however, that following Help links will usually bring up submission details.

"Most people think of the internet as a vast library, and they increasingly depend on search engines to help them find everything from information about the people who interest them to transactions they want to conduct, organizations they need to deal with, and interesting factoids that help them settle bar bets and backyard arguments," says Lee Rainie, director of the Pew Internet & American Life Project.

Search engine marketing is also a rapidly growing and profitable segment of the internet. Overall, the online advertising market has grown to more than $40 billion in 2007 and is expected reach nearly $80 billion by 2010, far outpacing all prior predictions. According to online market research firm eMarketer, annual spending on sponsored ads alone is predicted to exceed $11 billion in 2010. Google, so far, is king. eMarketer estimated that in 2007, Google received 75 percent of the U.S. $8.6 billion paid search advertising market. Yahoo!, in second place, received 9 percent, and the rest of the crowd split the final 16 percent.

While search engines are great marketing tools, getting your site listed where consumers are sure to see it isn't always easy. With roughly 30 billion pages on the web, how do you win a high ranking in search engine results? The inside scoop is that many engines use algorithms—mathematical formulas—to rank sites. Not only do

Express Delivery

You want a listing in Yahoo! now? Pay $299, and you'll qualify for Yahoo! Express. The hitch is, payment doesn't guarantee entry into the index. What your money buys is priority handling: Yahoo! guarantees you'll hear a verdict within seven business days of filing. Get more information at docs.yahoo.com/info/suggest/busexpress.html.

Is this a good deal? If you get into the directory, yes, because you'll be weeks ahead of the game (in many cases, perfectly good sites simply get overlooked in the crush of applicants). But it's a risk—you may not get in and will have wasted the money.

they all use different algorithms, but they don't reveal them, and, worse still, they change frequently. Should you just shrug your shoulders and give up? You can't. Experts agree that search engines have to figure largely in any website's marketing plan because they are where users hunt for the information they want. So hunker down and follow these steps.

Getting Listed

Just about every search engine provides tools for easy submission of new sites. Just look for an "Add URL" or "Submit Your Site" button, and then follow the directions (ordinarily no more complex than typing in the address and hitting "Send").

There are hundreds of search engines to choose from. For-hire site registration services typically say they submit to more than 100 engines. But there's little value in being on an index no one uses, which is why e-tailers should focus on a handful of high-traffic engines.

Which search engines are the most popular? The latest statistics from comScore Media Metrix show that Google was the most heavily used search engine in December 2007 (5.6 billion core searches), followed by Yahoo! Search (2.2 billion recorded searches). Next in line was Microsoft Sites (MSN Search) with 940 million, Time Warner Network (AOL Search) with 442 million, and finally, Ask Network (formerly Ask Jeeves) with 415 million searches.

Do you use Dogpile (dogpile.com) or Mamma (mamma.com), which calls itself "the Mother of All Search Engines"? Don't try to list with them. These are "parallel engines" (also known as meta engines) that query various search engines with your question. They don't index sites; they aggregate information from other sites. Dogpile, for instance, queries the internet's top search engines, including Google, Yahoo! Search, Live Search and Ask. These parallel engines are handy to use when searching, but put them out of mind when seeking to get listed.

Engine Trouble

One hitch in the listing process: Don't expect immediate results. It can take a month or so for the major crawlers to index your pages. Engines list new sites in their own time frames, and because they're constantly hit with a tsunami of new web pages, queues of "to be added" sites have grown long. Yahoo!, however, offers an expedited entry option. (For more on this option, see "Express Delivery" on the previous page.) What's more, paid inclusion programs can speed up the process, while paid placement programs will even guarantee that you are listed for a particular word. (For more about these types of programs, read on.)

▲

Smart Tip

Tip...

There are two terms you should know—search engine optimization (SEO) and search engine marketing (SEM). While both are forms of online marketing, they are very different. SEM is an umbrella term that includes things like SEO, paid listings, and other search engine-related activities that could increase exposure and traffic to your website. SEO refers to techniques that use the content on your site to help it appear higher in a list of search engine results. SEO is important because most people find sites through search engines. The higher a web page "ranks," the more searchers will visit that site.

Rank and File

Getting listed is the easy part. Getting a high position in the search engines is another story, but that's also where the money gets made. It does little good to be the 212th business plan writer in Yahoo!'s search listings. Who will wade through 21 screens to find you? Nobody is likely to read that many pages of information. Most searchers only look at perhaps 30 results from a given search, in rare cases as many as 50 or 100 if the query is proving elusive. Patience runs only so deep, and a surfer's attention span isn't infinite.

Can you do some of this yourself? You bet. The best way to score high in search engines is to have good, solid content, especially with regard to the terms that you want to be found for. Experts say it is also important to continually add new content to your site.

According to Danny Sullivan, editor-in-chief of SearchEngineLand.com, a website about all things relating to search engines, good page titles are extremely helpful. As for meta tags, he recommends using the meta description tag as a way to help hint to search engines how you'd like to have your page listed. What's a meta description tag? It's a line placed in the header of a web page that provides a short description of the contents of the page. Invisible to the anyone browsing your site, some search engines use the meta description tag to describe the page in search results.

The title of your page is also crucial. It's not technically considered meta data, but rather HTML. However, it's also used in the same way as meta information. It's the text that shows up in the top bar of your browser when you visit a site. When someone bookmarks your site, it's also the

Beware!

While meta tags give website owners the ability to control, to some degree, how their web pages are described by some search engines—and offer the ability to prevent pages from being indexed at all—don't think they're a magic solution to get a top ranking in search engines. To achieve a top ranking, you need to do more than simply add a few magical "meta tags" to your web pages.

text that pops up as the link in the bookmarks folder. And when your site shows up in a search engine, it's going to be the text that is hyperlinked to your site. SearchEngineWatch.com offers a good tutorial on meta descriptions, page titles and meta keywords: searchenginewatch.com/showPage.html?page=2167931.

Another good tip from Sullivan: If you have links to your site from good sites about topics you wish to be found for, that can help you rank better.

Directory Assistance

There's another way to get your site in front of users' eyes: directories at Yahoo! or the Open Directory Project (ODP) (dmoz.org). They're not search engines but rather directories compiled by human editors. ODP, which launched in June 1998 under the name NewHoo, uses more than 70,000 volunteer editors to catalog the web.

Should you submit your site to these types of directories? By all means. When you submit your site to these indexes, keep in mind that the tweaks the pros use to maximize search engine placement will not work with these human-edited directories. What's especially important about getting listed here? Good, relevant content and design are the secrets with the human-edited directories.

How do you get listed in a human-edited directory? You can go to the sites and—as with search engines—look for an "Add URL" or "Submit Your Site" tab. Then cross your fingers, and you just may show up in that directory. "Getting listed in these directories provides important links that may help you rank better with crawlers," says SearchEngineLand's Sullivan.

Paid Placement

What are paid placement and paid inclusion programs? Paid placement—also known as sponsored search or pay-per-click—offers the ability to place your site in the top results of search engines for the terms you are interested in within a day or less. Basically, every major search engine accepts paid listings, and they are usually marked as "Sponsored Links" on the websites.

The leaders in paid search right now are Yahoo! Search Engine Marketing (sem.smallbusiness.yahoo.com/searchenginemarketing) and Google (adwords.google.com). Both allow sites to bid on the keywords for which they wish to appear and then pay a certain amount each time someone clicks on their listings.

Tip...

Smart Tip
Want to learn even more about Google AdWords? Check out Howie Jacobson's AdWords for Dummies. Jacobson, a Google AdWords expert, shares tips, tricks and strategies he's learned while working with clients on their Google AdWords campaigns.

▲

Spider Webs

User submissions aren't the only—or even the main—way search engines compile their indexes. A popular tool used by the engines in scoping out the lay of the web are spiders—also called crawlers—which meander from site to site, following links and reporting findings back to the search engine.

Yahoo!'s spider is called Yahoo! Slurp. It collects documents from the web to build a searchable index. These documents are discovered and crawled because other web pages contain links directing to these documents.

Has your website been spidered? Check your log file (see Chapter 33 for more on logs), and you'll easily see a spider's trail. A sure tip-off that a spider has come is when the log file reveals a request for the "robots.txt" file—a file that tells a visiting spider what parts of a website are off-limits.

As part of its crawling effort, the Yahoo! Slurp crawler takes robots.txt standards into account to ensure it doesn't crawl and index content from pages whose content someone doesn't want included in Yahoo! Search. If a page is disallowed to be crawled by robots.txt standards, Yahoo! will not read or use the contents of that page. The URL of a protected page may be included in Yahoo! Search as a "thin" document with no text content. Links and reference text from other public web pages provide identifiable information about a URL and may be indexed as part of web search coverage.

Do you need a robots.txt file? Some say no. Why? Because if you have nothing that's meant to be strictly private stored on your website—and you shouldn't, because if a file is on the web, it's in the public domain—there's no need to tell a spider "hands off." What's more, a downside to having a robots.txt file is that a spider may miss key pages. If this happens, resubmit those pages to the search engine. Maybe the engine already knows them; maybe it doesn't. Either way, resubmitting is always a good policy.

For example, if you wanted to appear in the top listings for "clocks," you might agree to pay a maximum of 25 cents per click. If no one agrees to pay more than this, then you would be in the No. 1 spot. If someone later decides to pay 26 cents, then you fall into the No. 2 position. You could then bid 27 cents and move back on top if you wanted to.

With Yahoo! Search Engine Marketing, there are two ways to create an account: Through a self-service online channel that requires a small deposit (this deposit will be applied to your click-throughs) or through a service called Fast Track, which has a one-time service fee of $199 and includes a custom proposal with suggested keywords, bidding

Smart Tip

Want to know more about search engines and rankings in general? Head to SearchEngineWatch.com (searchenginewatch.com), where all the ins and outs are explored. Another site worth a look is Search Engine Showdown (searchengineshowdown.com).

recommendations and more. Yahoo!'s minimum bid requirement is 10 cents.

In the Google AdWords program, Google sells paid listings that appear above and to the side of its regular results, as well as on its partner sites. Since it may take time for a new site to appear within Google, "these advertising opportunities offer a fast way to get listed with the service," says Sullivan.

In the Google AdWords program, the cost of your campaigns really depends on you—how much you're willing to pay and how well you know your audience. It all boils down to knowing your own goals and letting Google know what they are.

There is a nominal, one-time activation fee for Google AdWords of $5. After that, you pay only for clicks on your keyword-targeted AdWords ads, or for impressions on your site-targeted AdWords ads. You can control your costs by telling Google how much you are willing to pay per click or per impression and by setting a daily budget for spending.

For example, a new advertiser can activate his or her AdWords account with $5 and then choose a maximum cost-per-click from 1 cent to $100.

Daily budgets start as low as 1 cent up to whatever limit the advertiser is comfortable spending. Site-targeted ads, which let AdWords advertisers choose individual sites in the Google content network where they'd like their ads to appear, require a maximum CPM (cost per thousand) price of 25 cents.

While there are myriad choices out there and the concepts may seem confusing, many small businesses swear by paid search programs. As long as you plan your campaigns carefully, budget properly and read the fine print, they can really help you improve your reach.

e-Chat With
Drugstore.com's Dawn Lepore

Since its inception in 1998, drugstore.com has been a leading retail force on the web—and it is continuing to be popular, thanks to its recently appointed president, CEO and chairman of the board, Dawn Lepore.

Drugstore.com • Dawn Lepore, President,
CEO, and Chairman of the Board
Location: Bellevue, Washington • Year Started: 1998

▲

After a 21-year career at discount brokerage Charles Schwab, Lepore—who had risen to vice chairman of technology, operations and administration and was responsible for moving Schwab onto the internet in 1995—moved with her family in October 2004 from the San Francisco Bay Area to Bellevue, Washington, to run drugstore.com. Listen up as Lepore explains what prompted her to head up drugstore.com and what she believes it will take to succeed in the online drugstore space.

Entrepreneur: Why did you join drugstore.com?

Dawn Lepore: I love retail businesses, and I am a firm believer that the internet is at the beginning of its evolution. I believe in what drugstore.com is offering, which can make a difference in customers' lives. Also, the company is not a technology company, but technology plays a huge role [in its success], and that was attractive to me. I met so many happy customers and really loved the passion of the employees—so the combination of that, along with the investors and the board members, all made it a great opportunity from my perspective.

Entrepreneur: Can you elaborate on how drugstore.com can make a difference in customers' lives?

Lepore: There are two pieces to this. One is that you can't pick up a newspaper today without hearing about affordable prescriptions for Americans, and of course we all know that many people are going outside of the country and buying things from pharmacies that maybe are less regulated, and there might be some kind of risk associated with that. We, however, are a fully licensed U.S. pharmacy, our prices are up to 70 percent lower for generics and up to 30 percent lower for brand-name drugs when compared with traditional brick-and-mortar pharmacies. We have less overhead because we are not operating a lot of drugstores—we just operate through our website.

Another way drugstore.com can make a difference in customers' lives is our breadth of product—more than 30,000 over-the-counter (OTC) products in addition to our pharmacy. We focus on men and women, but our demographic happens to be predominantly female. I have very young children, so I know what it's like when it's 10 o'clock at night before you really have time to think about doing the errands you need to do for your family or for yourself. I've heard from so many women who sit down at 10 o'clock at night, log on to the site and get diapers for their children, shampoo, their favorite face cream, and their husband's favorite products all at one sitting. They just love the convenience, they love the service, and they love the breadth of our offering.

Entrepreneur: How big is the drugstore category? How big will it become?

Lepore: This market is huge, although I'm not sure anybody knows exactly what it is. I think it is probably close to around $300 billion, but I still think the internet penetration in this category is very low—so there is a lot of upside for us.

Entrepreneur: Who is your major competition?

Lepore: Competition is a lot about people's habits, such as stopping at the drugstore on their way home from work. We have to continually remind them to come online. It takes time to change customer behavior, but I think we are at the beginning of the trend of people moving these types of purchases online and that we will be the beneficiary of that.

Besides the brick-and-mortar stores, we also compete with some niche players in different categories, such as Sephora [a makeup company] and MotherNature.com [an online retailer that primarily sells vitamins]. But what our customers tell us they love about us is that they can get Maybelline mascara, Philosophy face cream and vitamins. You can't do that at Sephora, you can't do that at MotherNature.com, and you can't do that in almost any other place. We are unique in that capability, and I think it's a good differentiator.

Entrepreneur: Hasn't the online drugstore space taken off more slowly than many expected?

Lepore: I do think this category is a little bit slower to adapt online, and I think that it has to do with the fact that it takes a while to change customer behavior. There are so many brick-and-mortar stores out there, but the problem is, people don't like the customer experience in a brick-and-mortar store, and they can't find all the products they want. [And] sometimes people run out of their shampoo or deodorant or toothpaste. And what we need to do is train people to order a few days before they are going to run out.

Entrepreneur: Do you think it will grow?

Lepore: I do think the online drugstore space will continue to grow. e-commerce in general is growing at about 20 percent a year right now, so looking at that alone shows me that we have potential for continued growth.

Entrepreneur: How will you beat competitors?

Lepore: It's the breadth of product, our prices—which are very, very competitive— our offers, and our free shipping if you spend $49. We also have special offers where you can get free shipping when you spend $25. Our convenience, service

Smart Tip

How do you persuade wary consumers to buy? For drugstore.com, the answer is information—and that's an area where the net can excel. For example, drugstore.com's website has customer reviews. Here, people can write reviews about products they use and post them on the site. The site also offers FAQs on prescription drugs. And keep in mind that on the web, an e-tailer can offer this kind of information at very little cost, while gaining a leg up on traditional retailers.

and customer experience [will also help us beat the competition]. We make it very easy for our customers to order and reorder. For example, we will send you "your list," and you just click on what you want. All these things add to our competitive advantage.

Entrepreneur: Where will your profits come from—prescription drugs or other merchandise?

Lepore: Our OTC category—which includes prestige beauty products in our Beauty.com web store—is our fastest-growing and highest-margin category. That's where most of our profitability comes from. The prescription part of our business is important, but it is not the growth engine for the company. Certainly our customers appreciate the fact that we carry prescriptions.

Entrepreneur: Critics say online drug-stores will sell drugs to kids—is this a worry?

Lepore: We absolutely have to have a valid prescription—we verify the prescription with doctors—so there is no way that you can get a drug that you don't have a valid prescription for. We take lots of information, and we do insurance claims, etc. And then, from a quality perspective, we check, double-check and triple-check those prescriptions going out of our distribution center. We are very, very confident in the quality and the legality of our prescription business.

Entrepreneur: In your opinion, what will e-commerce look like in a few years?

Lepore: I definitely think e-commerce's growth will continue, and there are certain categories where that growth will accelerate. I think people will do more and more on the internet, and I think there will be a number of new business models that will continue to emerge.

Cheap Tricks
With eHolster.com's Scott Quarterman

Who hasn't lost a PalmPilot or a cell phone? There's never anyplace to comfortably tuck them, and that is why they are so easy to leave behind in restaurants, airplane seats and such. But that also meant a big business

eHolster.com • Scott Quarterman, Owner and Co-founder
Location: Norcross, Georgia • Year Started: 2000

▲

opportunity for Scott Quarterman, co-founder of eHolster.com, where the product is a shoulder holster for personal electronics gadgets. E-Holster cases are unique because they are modular by design and can be worn on a shoulder harness one day and then easily moved to your belt or across your chest another day. The costs range from less than $20 to $123, depending on the number of cases you purchase and the material of the cases.

The web is ideal for launching an innovative product because there aren't dozens of other sites all selling essentially the same product. You can find a broad audience online and don't have to fight to get your product on big-box retail shelves. On the other hand, it takes work, time, money and even luck to build public awareness that this new gizmo exists. As Quarterman learned, it can be done, but it's not enough to simply come up with a clever product idea.

Here, Quarterman tells how he designed the product, arranged for its manufacture and built his website—all on a thin budget.

Entrepreneur: What were your startup costs?

Scott Quarterman: Total costs amounted to roughly $25,000 to develop the e-Holster product, create the electronic storefront, and complete the trademark searches and the LLC, etc. We earned those startup costs back within the first three months of opening our online "doors." The business has been profitable ever since.

Entrepreneur: How long did it take to build the site?

Quarterman: First, we needed to fully design the product, which took about nine months. Then it was on to the website, which took another six months.

Entrepreneur: What are you doing now to bring in new site visitors?

Quarterman: We still have the e-Holster branding label on all our harnesses, which helps get the brand out there. However, the bulk of our traffic and sales come from word-of-mouth advertising from our long list of very satisfied customers. Many of our new customers are referred to us from friends who have owned our products and have been very happy with them. We also purchase keywords on Google and Yahoo! to help drive customers to the site. Our website is optimized for the search engines and ranks very high (usually in the top three spots) in Google's organic listings for keywords like "cellphone holster" and "PDA holster." This helps drive a good percentage of the traffic to our website.

27

Accepting Credit Cards

The number-one question on the minds of most new website builders—whether they are "doing it themselves" or using a hosted e-commerce provider—is "How do I arrange to accept credit cards for payment?" Only a few years ago, getting merchant account status for an online storefront was tough because credit card companies were suspicious about vendors who lacked brick-and-mortar storefronts. No more.

▲

Bankers have awakened to the reality that the net has created a revolution in how commercial transactions are completed, and credit card issuers nowadays truly "get it"—they understand that the net is a legitimate retail channel, and they are rushing to set up merchant accounts with online stores.

But that doesn't mean it's suddenly easy. Issuers still want proof that yours is a real business and not a fly-by-night con game. Patiently answer all their questions and show the requested documents, and you're likely to get the status you crave.

Taking Credit

If you want to accept credit cards for real-time online payments, there are two things you will most likely need: an internet merchant account and a payment gateway.

An internet merchant account gives you the ability to process credit cards, and can be obtained through a bank. An internet merchant account is viewed by the bank as a line of credit that is extended to you. You must apply for this, just like you would any loan.

A good place to start your search for a merchant account is your own bank. Most issue credit cards, and if you have a long-term relationship with the institution, that's a big plus. What if your bank says no? Try a few other local banks—offer to move all your accounts there—and you just may be rewarded with merchant status.

You can also log on to Google or Yahoo! and search for credit card processing. You'll find dozens of outfits, large and small, that are on the prowl for startups seeking merchant accounts.

You will also probably need a payment gateway account, which is an online credit card processor or transaction handler that is capable of hooking into credit card accounts belonging to the online shopper and your internet merchant account. The payment gateway handles verification and transfer requests. It interacts with the card issuer's bank to authorize the credit card in real time when a purchase is made on a website.

Leading providers of payment gateway accounts targeting smaller merchants include:

- *PayPal*, paypal.com (owned by eBay)
- *Authorize.Net*, authorize.net
- *Cybersource*, cybersource.com
- *Verisign*, verisign.com (owned by eBay)

If you don't have a merchant account, these providers can help you set one up and offer a payment gateway in one convenient package.

Credit cards aren't processed cheaply, at least not for a startup. A typical fee schedule for a small-volume account (fewer than 1,000 transactions monthly) would include monthly processing fees ranging from $10 to $100, plus transaction fees of about 3 to 5 percent per transaction. Some providers also charge startup fees as high as $400, but shop around—in many cases the startup fee will be waived if you ask.

Small-Business Pal

Founded in 1998, PayPal enables any individual or business with an e-mail address to securely, easily and quickly send and receive payments online. PayPal's service builds on the existing financial infrastructure of bank accounts and credit cards, and uses advanced proprietary fraud-prevention systems to create a safe, global, real-time payment solution.

Beware!
Plenty of shady outfits are bent on getting rich offering bogus merchant accounts to gullible online beginners. Before shelling out any cash, make sure you're setting up an account that will handle industry-standard cards (such as MasterCard and Visa, not "Big Bob's Lollapalooza Credit Card" or some specialty card). It's a good idea to stop at the Better Business Bureau (bbbonline.com) before inking any costly deal with an unknown vendor.

PayPal has quickly become a global leader in online payment solutions with 164 million account members worldwide. Available in 190 markets and 17 currencies around the world, online and traditional offline businesses use PayPal.

The two major PayPal offerings for merchants are:

- *PayPal Website Payments Standard:* This is an easy, quick way to start accepting credit cards online. A simple integration into your shopping cart allows your customers to pay securely and easily. (PayPal seamlessly integrates with hundreds of compatible carts or custom-built storefronts.) If you don't have a shopping cart, the free PayPal Shopping Cart can be set up quickly and easily as well.

    After setting up the system on your website—which takes just a few minutes—you will be able to accept all major credit cards, debit cards and bank transfers. Website Payments Standard is secure, and you don't need a separate merchant account or gateway. Your customers don't need a PayPal account. The price is right, too—there are no monthly fees, no setup fees, no cancellation fees, and the transaction fees are 1.9 to 2.9 percent, plus 30 cents.

- *PayPal Website Payments Pro:* This all-in-one solution gives you features comparable to merchant accounts and gateways—through a single provider and at a lower cost. There are also no setup fees, no cancellation fees, and the transaction fees are 1.9 to 2.9 percent plus 30 cents. However, there is a $30 monthly fee.

    With this service, customers paying by credit card stay on your website for the entire transaction; PayPal is invisible. Website Payments Pro is already integrated into many popular shopping carts, or it can be easily added to a custom-built shopping cart.

▲

PayPal Website Payments Pro includes a Virtual Terminal, which allows you to process payments for phone, fax and mail orders. The secure solution offers comprehensive online reports to help you measure sales easily, and allows PayPal account holders to check out quickly with saved information.

Secure Horizons

The one must-have for online credit card processing is secure, encrypted connections. You've seen this many times yourself. Go to virtually any major e-tailer, commence a purchase, and you are put into a "secure server" environment, where transaction data is scrambled to provide a measure of safety against hackers. Truth is, worries about credit card theft from nonsecure sites are generally unfounded—the odds of a hacker grabbing an unencrypted credit card number from a nonsecure website are pretty slender—but buyers by now expect a site to be secure, and that means you need to provide it.

Is this a technical hassle for you? It shouldn't be. Whatever vendor sells you your credit card processing services should also, as part of the package, provide a secure transaction environment. If they don't, look elsewhere.

It may sound daunting to arrange for online credit-card processing, a secure server, etc., but nowadays, you can have all of this in place in a matter of minutes—especially if you use a hosted e-commerce solution. Sign up with Yahoo! Merchant Solutions, for instance, and it's simple to tack on an application for credit card processing through Chase Paymentech or PayPal Website Payments Pro. Yahoo! then charges a transaction fee for all sales by its merchants, and the fee varies depending

---

You'd Better Shop Around

My hunt for online credit card processing services revealed wide variations in fees and pricing menus. Startup fees ranged from free to more than $500, with monthly fees ranging from free to more than $100. Volume is a key factor—sites anticipating fewer than 1,000 transactions monthly can often arrange low-cost credit card deals—but a lot of this seems to be Wild West pricing.

Should you go with the lowest price? Not necessarily. My advice is to go with companies you trust. If there's a premium involved, pay it if you can. Always do business with your local bank, if it will accept you as a customer, even if the rate schedules are higher than those charged by online credit card processing specialists. There have been many, many crooked operators, and caution in this realm can pay off big time.

on the level of Merchant Solutions package you choose (Starter, Standard, Professional). It also varies by payment method used, such as credit card, PayPal, etc.

The Yahoo! Merchant Solutions program also doesn't charge extra fees for online processing; those fees are included in the regular monthly fees. That's a pretty good deal—especially since it takes only one to three business days to process your application, and if your application is accepted, that's all you have to do. Your new merchant account will be automatically hooked up to your store, and you'll be ready to process orders online.

Once approved, you're set to take credit and debit cards—nothing more has to happen. You may hear how hard and time-consuming setting up an online merchant account is, but that was yesteryear. Now it's one of the easiest parts of setting up your dotcom.

e-Chat With
Newegg.com's Bernard Luthi

ave you ever heard of Newegg.com? If you're interested in hardware or software products, you probably have.

Founded in 2001, Newegg.com is an online e-commerce company that has created a powerful channel for manufacturers

Newegg.com • Bernard Luthi, Vice President of Merchandising
Location: City of Industry, California • Year Started: 2001

of computer hardware and software, consumer electronics and communications products to reach do-it-yourselfers, hard-core gamers, students, small to midsize businesses, IT professionals and resellers. Today, Newegg.com is the second-largest online-only retailer in the United States, posting close to $1.9 billion in revenue in 2007, according to Bernard Luthi, vice president of merchandising at Newegg.com.

At Newegg.com, consumers can find the latest technology parts and products, along with product information, pictures, how-tos, customer product reviews and opportunities to interact with other members of the technology and game enthusiast community.

Newegg.com has more than 8.7 million registered customers and 1,800 employees globally and is repeatedly ranked as one of the best websites by consumers. Why? Probably because Newegg.com is built on the philosophy that every customer is a customer for life.

To get an inside look at Newegg.com, we chatted with Bernard Luthi, vice president of merchandising.

Entrepreneur: Tell me about Newegg. When was it started? Why?

Bernard Luthi: Newegg.com was founded by our CEO and chairman, Fred Chang, on January 1, 2001. The predecessor to Newegg was ABS Computer Technologies Inc., a systems integrator that made build-to-order PCs. ABS was founded by Fred in 1990 and specialized in high-end gaming PCs. During the late '90s, we started to recognize an emerging market in the DIY space. Since ABS had many customers from years past, many of them began to inquire if ABS could help them with upgrade parts for their existing systems. The answer was no, since ABS could only sell a complete system. This is how we recognized this emerging market of tech-savvy customers who were not afraid to crack open the case and upgrade or build their systems themselves.

Entrepreneur: What were your startup costs?

Luthi: Newegg was founded with only $100,000, and grew to be just about a $1 billion revenue company within four years.

Entrepreneur: What types of marketing do you do?

Luthi: At Newegg, we believe our best advertisers are our customers. We owe our success primarily to word-of-mouth and customer loyalty. We also use print, online banners, search engine marketing as well as billboards, radio and TV advertising.

Entrepreneur: What was your goal when starting? Have you achieved that goal?

Luthi: Our goal was to provide the best online shopping experience. To accomplish this, we needed to go above and beyond customers' expectations, thus establishing Newegg's three pillars of excellence, each of which helps ensure unsurpassed customer satisfaction.

First, we strived to offer the best value to the customer, combining selection and competitive pricing. Anybody can make a website and sell products; however, we differentiated ourselves by becoming the most efficient solution between supply and demand. Today Newegg provides not only a myriad of tech products, but also an abundance of relevant information and product reviews. By doing this, we not only better serve the customer, but also help our vendors reach and educate consumers on their products. The result is a stronger partnership between Newegg and vendors, which leads to better support and pricing for the customer. Since IT was our background and expertise, we have one of the deepest selections of cutting-edge technology components with the best prices.

Our second pillar is state-of-the-art logistics. In early 2001, our sales orders were climbing quickly. The executive vice president at the time, Ken Lam, commissioned the design and implementation of a state-of-the-art logistics center. I remember before Newegg was hatched, I would order from the internet and if the item was in stock, it would take several days to process the order. If it was not in stock, it sometimes took weeks to ship. Then it was another week or more for the item to arrive at my doorstep. You would be lucky to receive your order within two weeks.

To change that, Newegg set out to establish a new standard in online order processing: ship same day and deliver next day. We created a custom logistics system that today allows us to ship over 98 percent of approved orders within one business day. Whether a customer buys a single item, like a video card, or 30 different items to build a system from scratch, we can pick, pack and load for shipping within two to four hours with over 99 percent accuracy. This speed and precision of delivery without any extra premium was key to helping grow Newegg in the early days.

Our last, but not least, pillar is our commitment to excellent customer service. Back in 1999 to 2000, online companies were notorious for having poor customer service. In the absence of an opportunity to build a relationship with the customer through face-to-face interaction, we sought other ways to earn the customers' trust and respect. We established a customer-centric business model aiming to become the most loved and trusted company on the web. This strategy has paid off earning Newegg consistent number-one customer satisfaction ratings in the computer/ electronics segment several years in a row.

Having the number-one customer satisfaction rating in our industry, fastest logistics, and best selection/pricing value have been the keys to our success. I would say we are happy with our accomplishments toward the goals set forth at the time the company was established, but never satisfied. We continue to seek new ways to ensure the best online shopping experience.

Entrepreneur: Why have you decided to keep your company private? Have you thought about going public? Have you been approached to do so?

▲

Luthi: We are currently a private company and do not foresee that changing in the near future.

Entrepreneur: What advice do you have for entrepreneurs thinking about starting an online company today?

Luthi: Never forget that business success begins and ends with satisfying customers. Find out what the customer wants and provide it. The online world is extremely competitive and fast-changing. Therefore, it is crucial that you understand your customers and bring added value to them. There's very little margin for error in a retail environment where a competitor is a mouse click away—that is why Newegg has, since day one, tried to treat every customer as our only customer.

Entrepreneur: What are some best practices in online retailing in your opinion?

Luthi: Being customer-centric is a must. The beauty of the internet is that many aspects can be tracked and boiled down to a science. Best practices include having a good analytics tool to help generate the metrics and reports you need to make good business decisions.

Another must have is usability and effectiveness of online communication. Since Newegg does not have brick-and-mortar locations, our website is the only interface we have with the customer. Therefore we constantly strive to improve it.

Entrepreneur: Who do you perceive as your biggest competitors today?

Luthi: I would say our biggest competitors today would be players like Best Buy, Circuit City, Dell, Tiger Direct and a host of other smaller online companies.

Cheap Tricks With

BowlingConnection. com's Gary Forrester

Turned on by pink retro bowling shirts? How about bowling jackets and T-shirts? If bowling is your passion, you want to know about BowlingConnection, where pretty much everything a bowler craves is on sale.

BowlingConnection.com • Gary Forrester, Owner
Location: Sahuarita, Arizona • Year Started: 1999

Site owner Gary Forrester has implemented many changes over the course of his business, some because of technology and others because of the products he was carrying. After starting BowlingConnection.com for "just about zero" using an e-business solution, he quickly launched two more sites: southwest-gifts.com and usatiles.com. In 2001, he combined BowlingConnection.com with another one of his sites, RockinRetro.com, and renamed it Creative Productions (cpstore.com). A year later, he combined his tile site and southwestern gift site into TeissedreDesigns.com.

He had several reasons for making those changes: He moved to a new, faster server that could handle more products, and he found that some of his products crossed over to multiple sites.

By 2005, however, he made BowlingConnection independent from CPstore again. "The bowling shirts that we sold on the Bowling Connection website from the start of our business in 1999 were only those of the '50s retro style," says Forrester. "The costumes that we sold on the Creative Productions website were also only from the '50s. So basically, everything we were selling was from the 1950s era," says Forrester. "[In 2005,] we decided to add modern-style bowling shirts and costumes from other eras. We didn't want to overload one website with too many categories or products. We gave this a lot of thought before separating the websites because we knew that it was going to take time, and it was going to cost money. Besides using our own shopping experiences, we talked to friends and customers about theirs. What our unofficial research showed was that people enjoy shopping on a website that isn't cluttered. Hence, the separation occurred."

Now, Forrester has branched out into more products. Creative Productions still sells vintage-style '50s wear, and Teissedre Designs still sells southwestern gifts and tiles. A new site is The Pool Rack (thepoolrack.com), which sells pool- and billiard-related clothing, and Forrester sells car racing apparel via his BowlingConnection.com site.

Entrepreneur: What were your startup costs?

Gary Forrester: My startup costs were almost zero. I already owned the computer, and US West Sitematic made it so easy to build the website, I didn't have to employ any outside sources at all. One of my websites cost $49.95 per month, and the other two sites are $79.95 per month because the catalogs are bigger. I look at that cost as my "rent" payment. Where can you have a store that is open to the world 24 hours a day, and you don't even have to pay employees to take care of your customers? You actually make money while you sleep.

Entrepreneur: What is your monthly revenue?

Forrester: The monthly revenue has leveled off, but we are still very comfortable. My partner, Connie (who is also my wife), and I have had many opportunities to take our business to the next level, but we decided that we like it the way it is. We don't want to rent office or warehouse space. Instead, we bought a four-and-a-half-

Way to Grow

J. Peterman built a hugely successful business starting from one item—a duster-type raincoat that he happened to discover in the West. It was a cool coat, different, and he began running little ads selling it. Orders came in, and he expanded. Yes, he eventually filed for bankruptcy, but that doesn't mean there wasn't a good business in that duster, or in Forrester's retro bowling shirts. Think about it: It cost Peterman big bucks to buy even little ads in places like *The New York Times*. A website's cost is mere pennies by comparison. What cool products can you build a site around? Think unusual, easy to ship, and good profit margins. For every product you can think of, there's a thriving web business that's waiting to happen.

acre ranch with a nice home, and we built a detached 400-square-foot office, a stockroom and an additional 250-square-foot building for more stock.

Entrepreneur: What has been the biggest surprise?

Forrester: The first [1999] Christmas season was our biggest surprise. I expected business to pick up a little more than usual. I didn't expect it to get crazy. We worked day, night and weekends to fill the orders. It was a challenge, but we did it— all our customers received their orders by Christmas.

Entrepreneur: Has your business continued to stay seasonal, like that first year?

Forrester: Overall, our bowling shirt sales have continued to increase each year. Not only have we added new shirts to our online catalog, but our custom screen-printing and embroidery services continue to grow. So now, our busy season starts in the middle of August because people are buying bowling shirts for their winter leagues, which usually start on Labor Day. Then we go from the bowling shirt season right into Halloween with our costume sales. After Halloween, people start buying Christmas presents from TeissedreDesigns.

ThePoolRack is our site that brings in sales throughout the year—any time there's a national pool tournament coming up. When things slow down (typically between January and July), we usually go on vacation, take in a few trade shows to see new products and work on the websites, still filling orders to keep the revenue coming in.

Entrepreneur: How do you promote the site?

Forrester: There is a helpful site called selfpromotion.com that makes it easy to list your site with all the search engines. When we started, we promoted our BowlingConnection website by passing out fliers at bowling tournaments. We promoted our other three websites by opening a temporary gift store in Las Vegas. We passed out a lot of fliers and business cards to tourists from all over the world.

We no longer pass out fliers and business cards, and we don't promote our website [by posting auctions] on eBay anymore. In fact, eBay no longer allows you to promote your own website. Because of that, very seldom do we put anything up for auction on eBay. Now, the only form of paid advertising that we use is the pay-per-click search engines—Yahoo! and Google—and we find this is our best way to advertise. The cost is reasonable, and we have complete control over how we advertise each individual product. Of course, we do get repeat business, and word-of-mouth is still the cheapest form of advertising. We have sold to Bon Jovi, Campbell's Soup, Merrill Lynch, PricewaterhouseCoopers, Disneyland and many more.

Entrepreneur: How do you handle online purchasing?

Forrester: Our website is still very secure, and customers can feel confident when they order from us. We do not sell, trade or give away any information about any of our customers whatsoever. Due to changes in our product line and because our customers have "must have" dates, 25 percent of the orders are made by phone. If they need their order by a certain date because of a company event, they feel more confident talking to a real person instead of just sending the order through the website. We don't mind at all when our customers call on the phone. Imagine sitting in your home office talking on the telephone to Bon Jovi's marketing manager.

We are going into our eighth year in business, and we are still enjoying it tremendously. We are really in our element. The busy season, August to December, can get a little rough sometimes, though, working some long hours just to keep up. Connie and I were working late one night catching up on getting the orders processed. It was about 3 a.m. I was at the shipping table packing orders, and she was at the computer typing up invoices. I happened to look over where she was sitting and she had fallen asleep at the keyboard. I spoke a little louder than normal to get her attention, and I said, "Hey, honey, do you want to go to Jamaica this year?" She looked up, finished the invoices, and we jammed out some more orders.

30

Tapping International Markets

One of the lures of the web is that once your site is up, you are open for business around the world 24 hours a day. But don't be too quick to take the hype at face value. Yep, you are open 24/7, but international sales may prove elusive, and even when you land orders from abroad, you may wonder if they're worth the bother.

▲

There are excellent reasons for many e-tailers to aggressively pursue global business, but before you let yourself get dazzled by the upside, chew on the negatives. Then, once you have seen that foreign customers represent their own hassles but you still want them, you will find the information you need to grab plenty of international sales.

Foreign Affairs

Here's the root of the problem with selling internationally: Whenever you ship abroad, you enter into a complicated maze of the other country's laws. Let's assume you're in the United States. You know Uncle Sam's laws, and you know that one neat thing about doing business in the United States is that barriers against interstate commerce are few. For a Nevada e-tailer to ship to California is no more complicated than putting the gizmo in a box and dropping it off at the post office. With some exceptions, few e-tailers collect sales tax on interstate sales.

Sell abroad, however, and it's a quick step into a maze of complexities, including customs, for instance. Generally, it's up to the buyer (not you) to pay any customs owed, but make sure your buyers know that additional charges—imposed by their home countries and payable directly to them—may be owed. You can pick up the forms you'll need at any U.S. post office.

Some countries also charge a national sales tax, or a value-added tax (ranging from 15 to 25 percent on many items in European countries). Again, as a small foreign retailer, you can pretty safely not worry about collecting these monies, but your buyers may (and probably will) be asked to pay, and they need to understand this is not a charge on your end.

⚠ Beware!

It's tempting: Declare that an item is an unsolicited gift, and the recipient often doesn't have to pay any customs charges. The amount that can be exempted varies from country to country; usually, it's $50 to $100. But don't make that declaration even if a buyer requests it (and savvy ones frequently will)—they are asking you to break the law.

Mailing costs, too, escalate for foreign shipments. Airmail is the best way to go for just about any package, and that gets pricey. A 1-pound first-class shipment to Europe costs more than $10, for instance. Insurance, too, is a must for most shipments abroad, mainly because the more miles a package travels, the more chance of damage or loss. To get insurance for international mail, you must step up from first-class mail to priority mail. The insurance is free, but the cost of mailing doubles, adding to the charges you've got to pass on to the customer. Add up the many fees—customs, value-added taxes, postage, getting insurance—and what might initially seem a bargain price to a buyer can easily be nudged into the stratosphere.

Getting authorization on foreign credit cards can also be time-consuming. Although many major U.S. cards are well-entrenched abroad (especially American Express and Diner's Club), and validating them for a foreign cardholder is frequently not difficult, as a rule, this process is fraught with risks for the merchant, so be careful.

All Aboard

If you're still not discouraged, do one more reality check to make sure international sales make sense for you. Is what you are selling readily available outside your country? Will what you sell ship

Budget Watcher

Want a no-cost translation of your site? Offer a link to PROMT-Online (translation2.paralink.com), a free online translation service. Before putting this up, however, ask friends—or pay an expert—to take a look at the translation. These types of services usually offer excellent work, but you don't want your site's translation to be the embarrassing exception. Google has a slick (and free) translation tool, too. Google Translate (google.com/translate_t) works by typing in your web page's URL and clicking on the desired language. The page instantly pops up with all the text translated.

reasonably easily and at a favorable price? Even with the costs of shipping factored in, will buying from you rather than from domestic sellers be a benefit to your customers? If you pass these tests, you are ready to get down to business.

Step one in getting more global business is to make your site as friendly as possible to foreign customers. Does this mean you need to offer the site in multiple languages? For very large companies, yes. (American Express, for instance, has more than 70 worldwide sites accessible at americanexpress.com, and many of them are written in different languages.) But the costs of doing a good translation are steep and, worse, whenever you modify pages—which ought to be regularly—you'll need to get the new material translated, too.

Small sites can usually get away with using English only and still be able to prosper abroad. Consider this: Search for homes for sale on Greek islands, and you'll find as many sites in English as in Greek. Why English? Because it's an international language. A merchant in Athens will probably know English because it lets him talk with French, German, Dutch, Turkish and Italian customers. An English-only website will find fluent readers in many nations. (But keep the English on your site as simple and as traditional as possible. The latest slang may not have made its way to English speakers in Istanbul or Tokyo.)

Still, it's important to recognize that more than 65 percent of web users speak a language other than English. Providing the means of translating your English content

▲

to another language will go a long way toward building good customer relationships with people outside the United States. Your multilingual website becomes more accessible and popular if users can translate your website content into their native language.

One way to make this possible is to provide one of the free web-based language translation tools offered by AltaVista Babelfish (babelfish.altavista.com/) or Google Translate (google.com/translate_t). Both work similarly. For Bablefish, all you have to do is cut and paste some simple code, and web audiences who speak Chinese (traditional and simplified), Dutch, English, French, German, Greek, Italian, Japanese, Korean, Portuguese, Russian or Spanish will be able to translate websites into their native language with one click. The code creates a box on each page (wherever you've put the code) that says "to translate this page, click a flag." The visitor clicks on his or her country flag and—voilá—your web page is in the visitor's chosen language.

At the very least, you should make your site more friendly to foreign customers by creating a page—clearly marked—filled with tips especially for them. If you have the budget, get this one page translated into various key languages. (A local college student might do a one-page translation for around $20 or you can explore a solution like Elance.com, where you can hire a freelance translator.) Use this space to explain the complexities involved in buying abroad. Cover many of the hassles we just discussed, but rephrase the material so that it looks at matters through the buyer's eyes. By all means, include the benefits, too, but don't leave anything out, because the more clear a customer's thinking before pressing the "Buy" button, the more likely he is to complete the transaction.

In the meantime, routinely scan your log files in a hunt for any patterns of international activity. If you notice that, say, Norway is producing a stream of visitors and no orders, that may prompt you to search for ways to coax Norwegians into buying. Try including a daily special "for Norwegian mailing addresses only" or perhaps running a poll directed at Norwegians.

Clues about foreign visitors will also help you select places to advertise your site. While an ad campaign on Yahoo! may be beyond your budget, it's entirely realistic to explore, say, ads on Yahoo! Sweden. If you notice an increase in visitors (or buyers!) from a specific country, explore the cost of mounting a marketing campaign that explicitly targets them.

> **(Tip...)**
>
> ## Smart Tip
>
> When is a foreign customer not a foreign customer? When he or she wants you to ship to a U.S. address (perhaps an Edinburgh father sending a birthday gift to his daughter at a Boston college) or when the customer is an American in the military or diplomatic corps (shipping to their address is no different from mailing to a domestic one). Don't judge an e-mail address by its domain. The address may end in "it" (Italy) or "de" (Germany), but it can still be a U.S. order.

At the end of the day, whether or not you reap substantial foreign orders is up to you. If you want them, they can be grabbed, because the promise of the web is true in the sense that it wipes out time zones, borders and other barriers to commerce. That doesn't mean these transactions are easy—they can be challenging, as you've seen—but for the e-tailer determined to sell globally, there is no better tool than the web.

e-Chat
With ProFlowers'
Jared Polis

When Jared Polis launched ProFlowers
(proflowers.com) in 1998, his vision for the venture was to provide customers with a fast, easy, reliable way to send the
freshest-quality cut flowers and plants—shipped directly from

ProFlowers • Jared Polis, Founder
Location: San Diego • Year Started: 1998

growers—at a competitive price to and from anywhere in the world.

Over the years, the company has undergone a number of changes. In 2003, ProFlowers was renamed Provide Commerce Inc., reflecting the company's broader mission to be the leading e-commerce marketplace for the delivery of perishable products direct from supplier to customer. That same year, Provide launched two new websites: Uptown Prime (uptownprime.com) for premium meat and Cherry Moon Farms (cherrymoonfarms.com) for fruit and gift baskets. Secret Spoon (secretspoon.com), a high-end sweets e-commerce site, was launched in 2005. Provide Commerce was purchased in 2006 by Liberty Media Corp. for $477 million in cash and is now a wholly owned subsidiary.

ProFlowers, however, is still around, focusing on its core mission. Valentine's Day 2008 marked 10 years of "growth" for ProFlowers. History tells the tale of ProFlowers' success: On February 14, 1998, ProFlowers delivered its first 500 bouquets of roses shipped direct from a single farm in California. For Valentine's Day 2008, the company served more than 1 million customers with 185 different varieties of fresh-cut flowers shipped from eight different countries around the world.

Clearly, Polis knows a little something about growing a business: Since its launch, ProFlowers has become the largest domestic direct-from-the-grower internet flower company. Other dotcoms have come and gone while ProFlowers has experienced consistent growth over the past 10 years from zero to almost $300 million in annual revenue. Here, we offer a look back at ProFlowers' early days—and a peek into its future.

Entrepreneur: Why did you decide to focus on flowers on the internet?

Jared Polis: I had been involved in several internet businesses before [Polis founded, funded and/or ran several high-tech startups, including BlueMountain.com, American Information Systems Inc., Onesage.com, Dan's Chocolates, Lucidity Inc. and FrogMagic Inc.], and what excites me the most is introducing new efficiencies into the economy. The way that flowers were sent to people was obsolete. Most retail floral companies buy their flowers through wholesalers and distributors, so the companies not only incur overhead along the way, but by the time they were delivered, they were much older flowers. So I saw the opportunity to use new technology to disintermediate the supply chain to get better flowers at better prices. ProFlowers ships direct from suppliers to the end consumer.

ProFlowers has also developed a technology that allows us to electronically interact with the customer, shipper and supplier within minutes after a customer places an order. Without any human intervention, the system automatically transmits a shipping label, packing slip and customer-generated gift message to the supplier. Through our automated link to FedEx's and UPS' shipping and billing data, e-mail notifications are sent to customers when orders are confirmed, shipped and delivered. The system is entirely automated, expediting the order and delivery process and allowing us to deliver superior customer service in a cost-effective manner.

Entrepreneur: Do you ever have problems with your growers where they're not able to provide what your customers want?

Polis: Actually, that's another competitive advantage of our business model. We can guarantee what each bouquet consists of. The legacy model used by companies such as FTD.com and 1-800-Flowers relies on whatever a local florist has in inventory. For example, they can say that they have a spring bouquet, but they cannot say that it has three mums, two tulips and one red rose in it, for example, because it depends on what the local florist has. We can tell our customers exactly what each bouquet consists of because we get the flowers from the source, and we design the bouquets ourselves so we know what goes in them.

Entrepreneur: How did you fund the company?

Polis: In a variety of ways. We bootstrapped it for a while, and then I sold one of my companies—American Information Systems—and I put some of that money back into ProFlowers. We also raised the minimum amount of money that we thought we could to build the company. We didn't raise significant outside capital. Among our many investors, there were some venture capital firms that offered small amounts, but I'm not a big fan of venture capital, so we tried to avoid venture capital wherever possible. We haven't raised any capital since 1999, and we don't have any plans to get more funding to expand. We generate cash flow from our business to expand.

Entrepreneur: Tell me about your marketing techniques.

Polis: Flowers are a very marketing-intense category, so we do a variety of marketing. The key metric we look at is cost of customer acquisition. So we look at the cost of acquiring a customer across different channels like radio, TV, print, online, etc. With any [advertising or marketing] deal where we can acquire customers at the right price, we will take it.

Entrepreneur: How do you ensure good customer service, which is essential with gift items like flowers?

▲

Polis: Maintaining the quality of product is a key part of our long-term success. Every week, we survey hundreds of recipients so we can quickly identify which bouquets—and which growers—are delivering the best value to our customers. And because our flowers come directly to the consumer from the fields, we deliver the freshest flowers possible. We also give our customers a seven-day freshness guarantee. And that means your flowers are guaranteed to last seven days, or you receive a replacement bouquet or full refund.

Cheap Tricks
With FridgeDoor's Chris Gwynn

Fridgedoor Inc. (fridgedoor.com) has one primary goal: to be the single largest stop for all things magnetic.

The company, founded in May 1997 and located outside Boston, is a retailer of novelty magnets for consumers, custom magnets for businesses, and magnetic supplies for consumers

Fridgedoor Inc. • Chris Gwynn, President and Founder
Location: Quincy, Massachusetts • Year Started: 1997

and businesses. The items are purchased at wholesale from more than 100 suppliers around the world. The company stocks close to 3,500 items for immediate shipment. Visit fridgedoor.com and you're greeted by lists of dozens and dozens of magnets—everything from Superman magnets to increasingly popular magnets for cars. Products include humorous magnets sets, such as the popular Cat Butts set, custom-imprinted business-card-size magnets, attractive magnetic bulletin boards, and sheets of magnet material.

Fridgedoor was founded and is operated by Chris Gwynn, whose online experience dates from early 1994 and encompasses marketing and e-commerce positions with Ziff-Davis' ZDNet, the AT&T Business Network, and Industry.net, and as a B2B internet commerce analyst for the Yankee Group. Gwynn started Fridgedoor as a part-time endeavor in May 1997 while employed as the product marketing manager for Industry.net. Revenue had reached a point by the end of 1999 that Gwynn felt comfortable enough about the company's future to quit his day job.

Entrepreneur: What were your startup costs?

Chris Gwynn: The startup costs came to approximately $20,000. The most significant expenses were inventory and a software program to handle all back-end order processing, credit card payments and inventory management functions. Smaller expenses, such as hosting fees, domain name registration, telephones, etc., collectively get expensive.

Entrepreneur: Is this do-it-yourself, or did you hire a programmer?

Gwynn: I created the site myself using a template-based store builder and hosting solution designed for nontechnical users like myself. I wanted to avoid a situation where I was beholden to a programmer to make changes and maintain the site. Creating a basic site took less than a day. The time-consuming part is determining the products you want to offer, and creating product images and descriptive copy. Creating the site is the easy part.

Budget Watcher

Do you make something unique or special? Put up a website, submit the URL to all the main search engines, and see if traffic comes in. Chris Gwynn suggests building traffic on the cheap. His is not the kind of site that's likely to become a gazillion-dollar business, but it's a site that can easily generate a nice, steady cash flow, month in and month out.

Entrepreneur: What are your monthly revenues?

Gwynn: Our monthly revenues are in the six figures.

Entrepreneur: What are your monthly visitor counts?

Gwynn: Fridgedoor [has] approximately 125,000 unique visitors per month.

Entrepreneur: Where did you get the idea for the site?

Gwynn: I had always wanted to start my own businesses and thought the web was a unique opportunity for someone with a limited budget. I also felt I had an understanding of how people buy online that I developed by working in marketing for an online service and later at web-based companies. I looked for a "low touch" product that was easily displayed online, easy to ship and relatively hard to find, all in a fragmented market. I hit on magnets, which I personally like, and decided to give it a try. Luckily, it worked.

Entrepreneur: How do you attract visitors?

Gwynn: We rely heavily on search engines, word-of-mouth and press [coverage]. Since we've been around for a while, we're extensively indexed by the search engines. Our market is very fragmented, making it difficult to profitably attract customers through traditional print advertising. Creating positive word-of-mouth by handling customers properly is our best advertisement.

Knowing Your
Customers

Know thy customer. If there's a first commandment of business, that's it. Run a brick-and-mortar store, and knowing customers is easy. Talk to them, size up their clothing, note if they have kids in tow, check out their car when they head to the parking lot—and in a matter of seconds, a traditional storefront owner knows a lot about who's stopping in. But the question for companies doing business on the web is "How do we know customers when all they amount to is a wispy cybervisitor?"

This is a key issue because knowing your visitors can help you more precisely target your website. Suddenly notice a flood of visitors from, say, Japan, and that could lead to a decision to edit certain sections of a website to make them more friendly for those users. See that you're a hit on a particular college campus or in a government agency, and you can post a special deal just for those people. Observe that you're getting a lot of traffic from Puerto Rico, and that's a clear signal to market there. Not making an effort to get to know your customers makes as much sense as golfing in the dark.

Log Rolling

The good news: Every website visitor leaves a trail that, when properly analyzed, will tell you the country of origin, the browser and platform used (Windows Vista or XP, Mac, Unix, etc.), the ISP, and more. This data is ordinarily collected by web hosting services in a "log file," but only hard-core techies could ever have the patience to scroll through a log because it contains a mind-numbing avalanche of details.

There are smarter ways to measure traffic.

Analyze This

If you're curious about your logs, go to your web hosting service and look for a directory called "Logs." Download the most recent file and have a look (any text editor should open the file). Your web hosting service probably provides—free of charge— a basic analysis of those logs. The log is run through interpretive software, and the output is tucked in a folder that's usually called "Stats." Open that folder and look at recent files.

What will you see? The date, followed by the time of day, amount of time spent on the web page, and the web page (or other web element, such as Java buttons) viewed.

The free stats file reports are good, but even better analysis is easy to come by when you use third-party software tools

> **Tip...**
>
> **Smart Tip**
> Most stats folders include a file that details the search phrases used by visitors in finding your site. Check it out regularly. Know what visitors want to find, and give them more of it.

designed to dissect log files and automatically produce spiffy, usable reports that will tell you not only which countries are producing visitors but also their ISPs and more. The products and services available today also allow you to do things like website optimization, which lets you track how people behave on your site and then, using that information, optimize it in the best way possible.

Top choices among traffic-analysis tools and services include:

- *WebTrends Analytics 8 On Demand/WebTrends Analytics 8 Software:* WebTrends has a service and a software package, both of which allow clients to optimize different areas of their site and then track how well their websites are performing. Customers can use either the service or the software, depending on their needs. Pricing is based on the number of page views you receive in a year. Basic pricing for WebTrends Analytics 8 On Demand starts at $1,500 per year (can be billed monthly), and WebTrends Analytics 8 software starts at $699 for a one-time license fee, plus $140 yearly maintenance. For more information, visit webtrendslive.com.

- *Unica NetTracker:* NetTracker includes clickstream analysis, custom reporting, content analysis, campaign reporting and more. It costs $995, but you can try it for free before you buy. For more information, visit netinsight.unica.com.

- *SiteMeter:* This self-service solution requires no hardware or software and provides real-time website visitor analysis to help improve your online business. Get dozens of reports, including how visitors are getting to your site, what pages they look at, and whether your site is gaining in popularity. All the data is collected in real time and made available on demand through a convenient web browser interface. One click and you see it all. The service starts at $6.95 per month for up to 25,000 page views. Those who sign a one-year contract get a discount rate of $59 per year. You can also try out the basic version of SiteMeter for free. For more information, visit sitemeter.com.

Just the Stats

The building block for site analysis is the log file—but what if you don't have one? Users of free web space may not, but don't despair. Sign up with Counted! (statsview.com), a free web-based service that lets you track many facts about visitors, including referrer stats, unique hits, browsers used and more. Just register with Counted!, paste some HTML code (provided by Counted!) into your pages, and you're in business.

The downside? You have to put Counted! buttons on your pages, and that means not only more clutter, but the buttons can slow page loading. But when a log file isn't readily had, this is the way to go. A twist provided by this service is that it also lets visitors vote on your pages and provides you with user ratings for design, speed and content. Painful as these votes can be to read, they're invaluable when it comes to modifying a site to maximize user-friendliness.

Go Google

Google also offers a free web analytics service (google.com/analytics) that measures the effectiveness of websites and online marketing campaigns. Google Analytics allows users of its AdWords service to see exactly how visitors interact with their website and how their advertising campaigns are faring. The hosted service is available in English and 25 other languages, and uses technology from San Diego–based Urchin, which Google acquired in 2005.

Website owners can see exactly where visitors come from, which links on the site are getting the most traffic, which pages visitors are viewing, how long people stay on the site, which products on merchant sites are being sold and where people give up in multi-step checkout processes.

Marketers can also use the service to track banner, e-mail, nonpaid and paid search advertising campaigns from other ad service providers. That service is free even if companies do not advertise with AdWords, as long as their users do not view more than 5 million web pages in a given month.

Budget Watcher

Find plenty more free analysis tools and hit counters at TheFreeSite.com, a page devoted to linking with just about every tool around (the-freesite.com/Webmaster_Freebies/Free_counters_and_trackers/).

Which should you use? The Google offering sounds promising, but you can also try the free version of SiteMeter. In addition, NetTracker offers personalized one-on-one demos for business professionals.

Put these programs through their paces and see what you like best. Also, before deciding to buy, ask yourself if you really need this level of analysis. Many low-traffic sites don't, and for them, the free stats files provided by the server may be sufficient. When traffic increases to the point where you need more fine-tuned analysis, buy a sophisticated tool—but certainly wait until the traffic increases to more than 100 visitors daily.

Getting to Know You

Logs provide a step toward knowing your customer, but more can be done. Here, the big guys can clue you in on strategies you can use.

Survey Says

In this morning's e-mail came a discount coupon from Amazon, with a string attached. If I answered a half-dozen multiple-choice questions, I would earn a $15 credit good on any electronics item sold by Amazon. Through highly specific questions about competitors and Amazon's own product offerings, prices and service, Amazon picks up valuable insight into the thinking of a customer and its competition.

Strip this down, and what Amazon is doing is taking its customers' e-mail addresses, firing off a survey and, to sweeten the pot and up the percentage of respondents, offering a discount if you answer the survey. The discount isn't so hefty that it would obliterate margins; it's exactly what it seems to be—a small "thank you."

Don't wait: Do a survey right now. Keep it short, and offer a tangible reward. You don't have Amazon's many millions of people to survey, so randomly choose 10 or 100 customers. Then—and this is

Smart Tip

A must in website customer service is to include a phone number on your website. Different folks like different channels. Some thrive on e-mail, but others still need the reassurance of a human voice before placing a large order. I've done it myself. On the L.L. Bean website (llbean.com), I found furniture I liked—but rather than click the "Buy" button, I called the 800 number, and the friendly voice that answered the phone helped win a big order. The web changes many, many things—but it won't soon eliminate the need to pick up the phone.

Beware!

Never assume your online activities are private. With court orders in hand, law enforcement can track virtually all surfers in a matter of minutes. That may be no big deal to most of us, but if you're doing stuff you want kept private, think about it. One way to avoid the scrutiny is to head to a public internet cafe and pay cash for a surfing session. You might do that simply to keep competitors from knowing you're checking out their sites. Another option: Go to Anonymizer (anonymizer.com), which allows anonymous surfing, starting at $29.95 per year.

crucial—read every answer that comes in. Trust me: Jeff Bezos isn't doing this surveying to fill slow days. The CEO of Amazon honestly wants to know what's on his customers' minds and, for sure, every response is logged. Odds are, Bezos—a notoriously hands-on boss—personally puts in time eyeballing survey data because he knows what every CEO needs to know: If you want to find out ways to run your business better, look at it as customers do.

Surveys are also sweeping the web as "pop-ups"—screens that jump up when you surf onto a site. Pop-up windows may be popular (I've seen maybe 10 in the past week), but I don't recommend them. Surfers don't like them; complaints about pop-ups are epidemic because they often cause system crashes. They're also technically tricky to put into place—probably beyond your budget and technical know-how. Don't feel left out just because your site lacks pop-ups. Instead, rejoice!

Creating a survey is easy with tools like SurveyMonkey (surveymonkey.com). In a matter of minutes, you can customize and publish a survey, then view the results graphically and in real time. There's a free version of SurveyMonkey, but the professional version is a modest $19.95 a month. Both are online tools, so there's no software to install.

Going to the Polls

What tools should you use besides e-mail? Online polls can be tailored to serve many ends, and you'll find many variations. For example, check out Sparklit (sparklit.com). Here you'll find a free option that lets you sign up for advertising-supported web polls, or for $9.95 per month, plus $5 per month per poll, receive "Gold Web Polls," including advanced features, improved integration and no advertising. You can also try Pollwizard (pollwizard.com), which offers free polling.

These tools may cost you next to nothing, but, used intelligently, they can be powerful. "Making Your Own Poll: Easier Than Ever," says Pollwizard's front page, and these resources live up to that promise. How good will the data you collect be? As good as the polls you create and as good as the tools you use for analyzing your responses.

Don't just put up a poll as a plaything for visitors. Oh, sometimes that's useful— polls are fun and we all like completing them, at least when they're short (never

> **Tip...**
>
> **Smart Tip**
>
> Want to wow your customers? Respond to all e-mail the same day—and offer answers that are truly responsive to what the customers are writing about. One sure way for a small business to excel is with a personal touch, and e-mail gives you a powerful weapon. Use it.

go over 10 questions in a poll—five or fewer questions is ideal). But the real payoffs come when you carefully construct polls to target highly specific concerns. Do customers like your website's speed? Your product selection? Pricing? Ask them, and watch out—they'll love telling you their answers. Big corporations pay megabucks to marketing wizards to examine customers and their motivations, but the truth is, you can get most of the payoffs from this work, free of charge, just by using the tools that are readily at hand.

And one last thing: Read and respond to as much customer e-mail as possible, because it, too, is a real window to customers and their motivations. Strangely, many small businesses, when asked, will mumble and admit that they don't read e-mail and certainly don't respond to it, but there is no faster way to make yourself obsolete than to stay aloof from customers. Sure, nine customers will write with complaints for every one who has good things to say about you, but read it, absorb it—and stay alert to trends. If one person complains about your packaging materials, big deal. If 10 do and you only sent out 12 orders last week, you have a problem—and the great thing is that now you also have the opportunity to fix it.

Private Eyes

Now that you're excited about gathering information on your customers, know this: It all has to be done gently, respectfully and cautiously. The web is a powerful tool for gathering information, and while that's useful as a business owner, it makes privacy a very big concern for consumers. Web snooping is a touchy topic—and sensitivities are increasing as more users realize exactly how detailed a trail they leave behind when visiting websites.

Beware!
Get another eyeful at BrowserSpy (gemal.dk/browser-spy). Exactly how much this web-site knows about you, instantly, is frightening. Check it out!

But there is a remedy—one that will let you gather the information you need while also reassuring visitors. It's simple: Develop a privacy policy. If you don't, this lack just may cost you big bucks.

Why? Because by not winning trust—and by not safeguarding visitor privacy—you just may be inadvertently pushing would-be customers toward the exits before the cash registers ring.

Too Close for Comfort

In America, proof of consumers' sensitivity to this issue are the PR nightmares suffered several years back by RealPlayer, Alexa and numerous other net companies that were found to surreptitiously collect information on users. The companies claimed no harm was done—that the information (mainly pertaining to a user's viewing habits) was collected so that user needs might better be served—but for a time, dark clouds hung over many net companies as users fretted about invasion of privacy. And these controversies are still brewing: Facebook faced a backlash late in 2007 after launching a service that allowed users to share their activity on outside partner sites with their Facebook network. The company was quickly criticized for sharing too much information with these partner sites and for making the service an automatic "opt-in," therefore requiring users to take steps not to participate.

A study conducted by in March 2008 by TNS, a global market information group, found that there's a high level of awareness that internet activities are being tracked for purposes of target advertising, and there's an equally high level of concern associated with that tracking. The study found that more than 70 percent of online

▲

Can the Spam

The ability to reach millions of people instantly has proved too seductive for some unscrupulous and shortsighted people. These are the advertisers who spread spam on the internet.

Spam is the internet term for unsolicited e-mail (e-mail you didn't ask for). Think of it as junk mail—only it's sent via e-mail instead of the USPS. In practice, spam is utterly undifferentiated advertising that's sent to millions of people daily, offering instant riches, high-quality sex talk, lucrative investment opportunities and other suckers-only come-ons.

The problem is so prevalent that the Controlling the Assault of Non-Solicited Pornography and Marketing Act (or CAN-SPAM Act) was passed into law and went into effect in 2004. The law requires commercial e-mail messages to be labeled and to include opt-out instructions as well as the sender's physical address. It also prohibits the use of deceptive subject lines and false headers.

So follow the law—don't spam. Your customers will thank you for it.

consumers are aware that their browsing information may be collected for advertising purposes, and nearly 60 percent say they are not comfortable with that.

Why do websites want this information in the first place? Mainly because it's a marketer's dream. In an era when "knowing thy customer" is seen as a path to riches, it's hard to resist collecting vast stores of customer data that tumble into your lap when you create a website. Know where a visitor has been before—which sites he's visited earlier in this internet session, for instance—and an alert marketer can use that insight into the surfer's interests to tweak offerings to more closely match the surfer's wants.

That's so tempting that some sites dramatically up the ante by overtly collecting more detailed and personal information from visitors. Usually that occurs in tandem with an offer the visitor accepts. This is common, and experienced web surfers have come to expect a trade-off of personal information for freebies—except the savviest surfers long ago stopped giving out accurate information. Many maintain a separate e-mail box just for use in connection with freebies and simply lie when filling out the forms.

Another dose of bad news is that, in some cases, information collected in your "cookies" has been transmitted to third-party sites—and that can strike fear in just about everybody. A cookie is a bit of information about you that's written to your hard drive while visiting a website that will let that website identify you as a repeat visitor in the future. This is how some sites greet you with "Welcome Back, Fragonard" (or whatever your name is) when you return. Cookies, their architects argue, save users time and make the surfing process more efficient. Who could complain? Well, cookies by them-

> **⚠ Beware!**
>
> Not getting the response you thought you would from an e-marketing campaign? The problem may be with the major e-mail service providers and ISPs that block e-mail via their spam filters. AOL, Gmail and Hotmail are notorious for over-filtering incoming e-mail. What do these filters look for? Use of large or colored fonts and ALL CAPS; use of words such as "free," "special" or "click here"; language in a subject line that says something like "urgent assistance needed"; and incorrect or old date stamps. Check your own ISP, too. Some ISPs will also block based on volume. If they see an IP address that's blasting a bunch of e-mail messages, they may block it or shut it down to investigate or simply block any outgoing e-mail that's being sent to more than 200 people. The message won't get to anyone on the list, and you might not find out for days.

selves don't pose a serious security threat. You just need to understand what information is being stored in them and how it's being used. For example, you should never allow a website to store financial information in a cookie. Likewise, you shouldn't allow a site to use a cookie to log you in automatically if the site contains sensitive personal or financial information (like online banking), because it could be accessed by anyone with access to your computer, like a co-worker or a hacker.

A last privacy breach is that, wherever you go on the net, you leave a trail. Very good hackers can hide their trails, but 99.9 percent of us leave tracks that are easy to follow. That is no big deal to most of us. But it means that your feeling of anonymity on the net is a false one: Your movements can be cataloged and associated with you.

Added up, the situation is this: Experienced surfers do their best to mock the system, while comparative newcomers—fearing privacy violations—avoid making purchases to protect their identities. This is not good for you, and it's not good for web users, either, because it is limiting their use of the medium.

Confidence Boosters

What should you do to reassure visitors? As a rule, mainstream websites openly explain their privacy policy. At the Entrepreneur.com site, for instance, at the bottom of every page is a link that says "Privacy Policy." Click it, and you are delivered to a clear, concise statement of what information is collected from visitors, what's done with it, and if it's made available to other companies. (The answer in this case is no— "Unless you otherwise agree, the information you give us or that we collect about you will not be shared with any third party," says the Entrepreneur.com statement.)

Most other leading U.S. sites you'll visit will explain their privacy policy somewhere on their sites in much the same way. They may vary in how easy it is to find the

▲

Wireless Dangers

Are you using high-speed net access via a wireless connection? If you are, you're enjoying the best web access around, but you're also exposing yourself to invasion by hackers.

Theoretically, a hacker could penetrate your system when you're connected to the net with a dial-up connection, but the likelihood isn't high. Why? Usually when you're connected, you're sitting at the computer. If suddenly you see that you're opening Quicken financial files—and in fact you're not—you'd know a hacker was there, and poof, you'd shut down. End of threat.

Wireless connections raise different worries. Even when your computer isn't on, your cable connection is wide open to invasion. But the antidote is free and simple—set up password protection. That way, only you (and anyone you give the access number to) will be able to use your connection.

link and how clear the statement is, but poke around and you'll probably find a policy.

Another trend: privacy promises made by third parties, such as by the Better Business Bureau OnLine Privacy Program (bbbonline.org/privacy) and TRUSTe (truste.com). Program mechanics vary a bit, but the essence is that a business site meets certain basic privacy requirements, pays a fee, and then gets to display a button on the website touting that it fulfills the program's requirements. Some users grumble that these programs don't truly guarantee privacy so much as they promise disclosure of what happens to information surfers reveal, but pretty much everybody agrees that such programs are a step in the right direction. Should you join? Since the cheapest TRUSTe membership started at $649 annually in a recent look, it may not be the shrewdest use of sparse cash in a startup. My advice: Keep the money in your pocket and look for do-it-yourself tactics to up visitor security.

To sum up, the steps you should take are to post a link to your privacy policy in a prominent place on your site. In that policy, be clear, simple and direct. A good strategy is to say: "We sell no information that we collect about you. Never. To anybody." Don't ask questions about visitors' kids—unless there's a compelling and obvious reason to do so. And if you offer visitors free sign-up to e-mail newsletters or sales notices, be quick to remove anybody who asks—preferably on the very day you receive the request. Users grumble a lot about spam, and an easy way to win visitor confidence is to promptly remove anybody from any list upon request.

Winning—and keeping—visitor trust really isn't, and shouldn't be, rocket science. Lots of the same hurdles were overcome years ago by direct mail and catalog sellers. In the case of the net, plenty of credit card issuers (American Express,

Citibank, etc.) are working overtime to encourage their cardholders to make online purchases with the full assurance that the card will protect them from fraud. And in probably the broadest, most objective look at net privacy issues, the FTC remains reluctant to intervene to offer more assurances of privacy and thinks that, on balance, the industry is doing a satisfactory job. For most site operators, this means don't screw up, and you'll be able to develop trust on the part of visitors. And once they trust you, they will buy.

Customer Service
for Success

E-tailers used to be innocents who thought that with web-based retailing, all customer service would be a thing of the past because the entire sales and service process would be neatly (and oh-so-inexpensively) automated. Ha! If there's a mantra for e-commerce players, it's this: Customers may be virtual, but their dollars are real.

Nowadays, consumers expect a high level of service from online retailers. How can you use customer service as a competitive advantage? Just follow the leaders:

- *Anticipate questions.* Many e-tailers anticipate questions and then answer them in their FAQs. This will save you and your customers time. Of course, sometimes customers will e-mail you with questions, and this can be a good thing. Get lots of e-mail complaining about a certain feature that the customer has simply misunderstood or bemoaning the lack of a particular product that you know is in stock, and you are learning important things about how your site is failing to communicate to visitors. As e-mail comes in, don't ever look for how the e-mailers are wrong. Look for ways to reshape your site to eliminate user problems (even the ones they only imagine they have).

- *Stay in touch.* At the HP Home & Home Office Store (shopping.hp.com), every customer is asked if he or she would recommend shopping.hp.com to friends, and 85 percent say they would, according to Cindi Zelanis, director of customer delivery for HP Home & Home Office Store. But the small percentage who say "no" aren't forgotten. "We often get back to these customers individually or through telephone surveys to ask how we can satisfy them," says Zelanis, who feels that this closed-loop approach is important. "Contacting them can win customers back and also generate ideas for new features on our site."

  Hewlett-Packard's way is cheap. Why aren't you doing likewise? A week or two after any order is filled, e-mail the customer and ask if they would recommend your shop. "No" answers will hurt, but follow up on every one because these are the people who will tell you what you need to do to build a winning website. Given how awesomely powerful this simple tool is, it's stunning that more e-tailers haven't jumped on it. Don't make the same mistake!

- *Turn feedback into action.* Hewlett-Packard's Zelanis says, "To win these 'no' customers, keeping in touch is just one piece of the puzzle. We evaluate and prioritize the collected customer feedback to address key customer needs, and then implement new features to the website that improve the online shopping experience for customers."

- *Respond quickly.* The web is an instant medium—except when it comes to getting responses from many businesses, which seem to route incoming e-mail into a folder labeled "Ignore Forever." Smart e-tailers know better. To keep in touch instantly, try free, easy-to-use, messaging services, such as AOL's Instant Messenger (aim.com), Yahoo! Messenger (messenger.yahoo.com), Google Talk (google.com/talk) or MSN Messenger (webmessenger.msn.com). The more accessible you are, the more sales you are likely to log.

  Smart companies are always raising the bar, with responses within four hours emerging as the new goal of many. What's right for you? With a smaller staff (and probably no overnight staff), you might find a 24-hour standard to be enough of a challenge. But monitor customers. If they demand faster response, somehow you have to find a way to meet their needs.

- *Hold their hands.* "Online, not every customer knows how to shop, and you have to be ready to help them buy," says Anne Marie Blaire, former director of internet brand development at Limited Brands, where she oversaw the successful launch of VictoriasSecret.com and the continued growth of the Victoria's Secret brand online. No brick-and-mortar retailer has to teach customers how to buy, but online, that remains a thorny problem. Every day thousands of shoppers log on for the first time, and these newbies genuinely crave handholding as they make purchases. Understand that and be ready to help. Be patient, too. Only a very ignorant e-tailer complains about how stupid his newbie customers are. They can, in fact, become your best customers, because they will shop only where they feel comfortable—and if your site makes it on that shortlist, watch the orders tumble in.

> **Tip...**
>
> **Smart Tip**
>
> You'll blow customers away when you send instant responses. Maybe that's not a realistic goal for you to set, but if you happen to be online when an e-mail comes in, try answering it right then—and know you're really impressing the customer who gets an instant and personalized response.

- *Use cut and paste.* Canned responses—cut-and-paste scripts—are used by all the leading sites, which track questions, hunt for the most asked, and produce templates for their representatives. You can do likewise. As you answer customer questions, file away your responses. Odds are, you will be asked the same question within the week, and it's a great labor saver to have an answer ready.

> **Tip...**
>
> **Smart Tip**
>
> Do it now: Create a place for FAQs on your site. View your FAQs as a work in progress. You'll continually update and expand them as more customer concerns and needs come to light.

- *Stay sensitive.* A worry with e-mail: It's easy to seem cold and unresponsive in the formality of the written word. Read and reread your responses before they go out. You want to be—and appear—interested in the customer's issues and eager to find solutions.

- *Aim higher.* In the online space, the service bar is being lifted ever higher. "Good service is expected these days for online retailers," says Steve Jarmon, a spokesperson for 1-800-Flowers.com, a leading gift retailer and an online pioneer going back to 1992. "Only truly outstanding service will get your company noticed. And the term 'service' has been greatly expanded. At a minimum, you must have 24/7 phone support, as well as functionality like real-time chat and

Smart Tip

Take a tactic used by the slick catalog companies, and when you haven't heard from a customer in a while, drop him or her an e-mail: "Have we disappointed you in any way? We would really value your feedback." Maybe the customer is indeed irked with you; maybe not. Either way, this e-mail will remind the customer that you are a site that cares.

personalization that enables you to better meet your customers' needs."

Office Depot is another company that has gone beyond providing great customer service. For example, its website (officedepot.com) offers a free online "Business Resource Center" featuring expert advice, downloadable templates and forms, and a free online *Small Business Handbook* full of useful business information on basic bookkeeping, recruiting and hiring, writing a business plan, and more.

These steps will get you started delivering better customer service, but they are not enough. Successful entrepreneurs say that the only way to do online service right is to have the right attitude, really believe the customer is king, and make sure that every one of their customer service reps knows it. Many fail on this score, but when you've made customer service your top and continuing priority, success is within reach. Don't get seduced by the notion that the websites with the best technology will inevitably win. Usable, reliable technology is a must, but where the real e-tailing battlefield will be is in service. That's the irony about e-tailing: At the end, what prevails online is what prevails off—and that's consistent, respectful, considerate service.

e-Chat
With Netflix's Reed Hastings

Netflix (netflix.com), the world's largest online DVD movie rental service, is a true e-business success story.

Founder and CEO Reed Hastings and his colleagues formed

Netflix Inc. • Reed Hastings, CEO and Founder
Location: Los Gatos, California • Year Started: 1997

Netflix in 1997 and launched a subscription service in 1999 with the goal of becoming the world's largest and most influential movie supplier.

The company wanted to use the DVD format and the internet to make it easier for people to find and get movies they would appreciate. As a result, they could reliably discover and enjoy lesser-known titles and watch more films, and at the same time, filmmakers could reach a larger audience and produce more new films.

Hastings is no stranger to successful startups. He founded his first company, Pure Software, in 1991, took it public in 1995, completed several acquisitions, and made it one of the 50 largest public software companies in the world by 1997. Pure was acquired in 1997 by Rational Software.

Here's how Netflix works: For $16.99 a month, members rent as many DVDs as they want (with three out at a time) and keep them as long as they want. It's this "no late fees, no due dates" online movie rental model that has eliminated the hassle involved in choosing, renting and returning movies. Netflix also has eight other price plans, starting as low as $4.99 per month, for unlimited rentals with one DVD out at a time.

Members also enjoy free shipping both ways, and currently more than 95 percent of Netflix's members receive next-day service. Netflix also operates 50 shipping centers—a key to providing overnight delivery—and plans to open more throughout the country.

Members are also encouraged to rate movies, allowing Netflix to customize its site based on a member's movie tastes. Netflix says this helps to make the more than 90,000 film titles it offers relevant and accessible. The Netflix Community section allows members to see their friends' film queues and ratings, as well as send messages, adding a social networking component to the rental process. The company, which is now a cash-flow-positive public company traded on Nasdaq, had total revenues of $1.2 billion for the fiscal year 2007, up 21 percent from $997 million for fiscal 2006. It also ended 2007 with 7.5 million subscribers, an 18 percent increase over the previous year.

The company has weathered competition from some heavyweights. In the spring of 2005, Wal-Mart closed its online DVD rental business and, in a joint announcement with Netflix, referred its online customers to Netflix. Blockbuster, meanwhile, has started an online DVD rental service, but it has not affected Netflix's growth.

> **Tip...**
>
> ## Smart Tip
>
> The essence of Netflix is both very simple and very complex. Its founder, Reed Hastings, realized that the web was the perfect tool for a no-hassle, subscription-based DVD movie rental service with no late fees and free delivery. Tomorrow's billionaires are likely to come from the ranks of creative thinkers who get out of the box and see new ways to put the web to use. What new ways can you think of?

Can Netflix stand up to the competition? Netflix thinks so. Here, Hastings offers some secrets to his success.

Entrepreneur: Why did you decide to start an internet company focusing on DVD movie rentals?

Reed Hastings: It was a growth opportunity to improve the movie experience for consumers using the internet. An internet store can offer a very broad selection and free home delivery, and I believed there was a need for something like this—there was nothing else like this out there.

On a broad scale, the idea stemmed from the fact that consumers in general dislike the late fees, the due date and the limited selection of the store-based video rental model.

The idea also stemmed partly from personal frustration. I had a very large late fee one day—approximately $40—and it was all my fault because I had not returned a movie that I had rented from a little independent movie rental store. After that experience, I started thinking that one could do video rental on a subscription basis with no late fee.

Entrepreneur: How was Netflix funded?

Hastings: We raised a little over $100 million in venture capital from Technology Crossover Ventures and Foundation Capital. We received our first round of funding in 1997.

Entrepreneur: In your opinion, what was it about your company that attracted that kind of cash from VCs?

Hastings: A lot of companies attracted that kind of cash back then, but it's not the case today. They saw great potential.

Entrepreneur: What is your marketing philosophy?

Hastings: Early on, we had very lean marketing. We did a deal back in late 1997 with Sony and Toshiba where they put a "try Netflix for free" offer in their DVD players. We did some online banners, and we did the search listings—both paid and regular search—on Google. But our biggest source of marketing early on was word-of-mouth, which has grown over time as we've gotten a better reputation. We recently have expanded our marketing to include TV and radio advertising, direct mail, more online advertising, and events and promotions, but word-of-mouth continues to be extremely effective for us.

Entrepreneur: What's the biggest surprise you've had in building Netflix?

Hastings: How complicated the logistics are. We ship about 1.8 million packages on a typical day, and it is very complicated dealing with large volumes. There are [many] things that can go wrong, such as performance issues, mail ability—just the complexity of the whole process.

▲

Entrepreneur: What has been your biggest challenge?

Hastings: We've grown so rapidly. Scaling our operations systems to be able to ship more and more movies has been very challenging.

Entrepreneur: Who is your competition?

Hastings: Blockbuster remains a competitor, but Netflix has demonstrated its ability to grow in the face of tough competition.

Entrepreneur: What is your market objective over the next five years, and how will you go about reaching that goal?

Hastings: Just improve every aspect of the business. Continue to improve our service and the website while we expand our streaming option. We've added the option to stream movies to the PC and we'll get that to TV in the second half of 2008 through various partnerships with consumer electronics companies. We believe that DVDs have a long life, but we're expanding with streaming movies so that when it's all digital, we'll be there, continuing to lead.

Entrepreneur: What are your secrets to success?

Hastings: We focus on a simple, core proposition and doing that really well, and not getting distracted by 100 gimmicks or extensions on the business model. Instead, we focus on doing the core model very, very well.

Cheap Tricks With
FrugalFun.com's Shel Horowitz

Want to see a simple site that also makes money? Check out FrugalFun.com and its sister sites—FrugalMarketing.com and PrincipledProfit.com. No doubt about it: They are frugal—really cheap, in fact—but their developer and owner, Shel Horowitz, says the sites produce a

FrugalFun.com • Shel Horowitz, Owner and Founder
Location: Hadley, Massachusetts • Year Started: 1996

steady stream of income, mainly from sales of his books, among them *Grassroots Marketing: Getting Noticed in a Noisy World* (Chelsea Green Publishing), but also from ads, consulting/speaking services and affiliate links. To keep the traffic flowing, Horowitz serves up generous portions of freebies—tip sheets on frugal living and inexpensive travel tips on the FrugalFun.com site, and reams of low-cost marketing tips on FrugalMarketing.com.

PrincipledProfit.com is a business ethics website that highlights another book Horowitz has written called *Principled Profit: Marketing That Puts People First* (AWM Books). Horowitz has two additional sites, ShelHorowitz.com, which directs visitors to the most appropriate of his websites, and AccurateWriting.com, which promotes Shel's marketing and copywriting services. Read on to find out more about why his sites are successful.

Entrepreneur: What were your startup costs?

Shel Horowitz: I went online in 1994 with an AOL account. When I set up FrugalFun in 1996, I registered a domain name [$70 for two years] and started with a $45-per-month account covering e-mail, web hosting, web surfing and site updating, then switched to an $18-per-month ISP/web host. Several years ago, I outgrew that host and separated hosting from my internet access. Since I went online, I have spent $60 on ads hawking the site. My first two site designs [for FrugalFun] cost me nothing—the first version was done by an intern, and the second was a barter. The site was up for over three years before I paid anything for site design. Oh, yes, and I had to renew my domain name when the time was up. I am currently operating nine domains; most of them are hosted by httpme (httpme.com). Three of the domains—FrugalFun, PrincipledProfit and Accurate-Writing—are hosted by a company called Bluehost (Bluehost.com) at a total cost of $192 per year. I also spend another $50 per month through the local cable company for high-speed internet access. I pay $8 or $9 per year each to register the domains with Go Daddy (godaddy.com).

Entrepreneur: Where did you get the idea for the FrugalFun site?

Horowitz: People started telling me in early 1995 that I needed a website. In my field, marketing, I was shooting myself in the foot not having one. I thought for several months about what the site would contain, did a lot of preplanning, and found an intern who wanted to learn HTML. She coded the first 40 pages, which went up in April 1996. She also taught me what she'd learned. A year later, I bartered with a website designer for the template I used for the next three years. That design, dating from 1997, became somewhat tired. In 1999, I paid a high school student to redesign the page, but it was left unfinished. So, in 2000, I hired a woman I'm still working with, who has redesigned FrugalFun twice and created FrugalMarketing using a similar design. PrincipledProfits uses a template model. I couldn't achieve the look I wanted, but a friend set up a better template for me.

Entrepreneur: How do you attract visitors and market the site?

Horowitz: I have done quite a bit to market the site. I participate actively in many discussion lists, and my sig [e-mail signature] draws people to the site. I use some 30 different sigs, depending on what I want to emphasize. I do radio talk shows as a guest about 20 times a year, and I always mention the URL and a reason to visit. For example, [I'll say], "On my site at FrugalFun.com, you can find out how to have a wedding for $300," or "One of my tip sheets has a really good article on trade shows. You'll find the back issues archived at FrugalMarketing.com. These days I also promote through blogs (my own and others'), social networks and, of course, my speaking and writing.

> ## Smart Tip
>
> Listen up when Shel Horowitz tells you how he markets his site on the cheap. Maybe you don't have books that will win reviews, but you do have e-mail. Are you using your "sig" (signature) for maximum impact? Keep it short—four to six lines is optimal. Then, as Horowitz says, get busy scouting out internet chat groups and discussion lists where visitors who might find your site useful hang out. Put up your posts, sig included, and watch the traffic come in.

Also, for the book *Principled Profit*, I'm starting a reseller program, which should spread my reach to many other sites. I am hoping that resellers will account for a high percentage of sales for that title and perhaps with some spillover to sales of another one of my titles—*Grassroots Marketing: Getting Noticed in a Noisy World*.

I've also started attracting significant attention to the book through an international Business Ethics Pledge campaign, with a goal of changing the world by getting 25,000 business leaders to run their businesses according to the values in the book. This has resulted in some very good press, excellent contacts and a higher caliber of client projects.

Also, I actively solicit book reviews and editorial coverage, and most mention the URL. Search engines draw a fair amount of visitors, but they're mostly in to see a particular page of the rather diverse content. They'll find one article that interests them, and then they move on. If they're looking for marketing info, they stay a while. I've been averaging 45,000 to 55,000 visitors a month—with spikes as high as 110,000 for FrugalFun.com lately. The other [sites] are much less heavily trafficked, something I'll be working to change in the coming months.

Entrepreneur: What's your look-to-buy ratio?

Horowitz: Low—but I am not real concerned about that, because the people who need what I have seek me out.

Entrepreneur: How big is the average purchase?

Horowitz: I have two kinds of buyers: those who buy books, who spend $8.50 up to

▲

$120 or so, and those who buy marketing services, who spend between $155 and several thousand dollars over time. Because of the integrated nature of my business, it's hard to separate revenues. It's not an uncommon pattern, for instance, to have someone visit the site to order my marketing book and then some weeks or months later come back to look over the pages about my marketing services—and then they buy.

Entrepreneur: Is your site profitable?

Horowitz: This site, while not bringing in megabucks, achieves a very high return on investment, in my estimation. I sell a fair number of books directly from the sites, and I secure a number of lucrative marketing clients from the sites. I also now have more than 12,000 subscribers to three tip sheets—Frugal Fun Tips, Frugal Marketing Tips and Positive Power of Principled Profit—so I have a way of marketing to my visitors.

How's that for a cheap, effective website? Of course, I've written three books on cheap marketing and one on cheap fun, so I am a very good shopper—but pretty much anyone could duplicate my success.

Security Holes,
Fraud and
More Bad Stuff

I t seems too simple: Put up a website, and you're on the road to riches. Guess what? There are plenty of potholes in that road. Experts are eager to acknowledge the dark side of the web—the many ways it is easy to go wrong, often before you even suspect there's a problem.

According to Wally Bock, author of *How to Create a Profit-Building Web Site* and a consultant on business in the

▲

digital age, "Today, many websites are bad. They don't answer the questions or solve the problems that visitors have. They are hard to use, and many simply don't work the way they should." Bock says that even though there are still plenty of problems, the overall picture is not as gloomy as it once was. "Dotcom companies over the past few years have gotten the message and made the necessary improvements to avoid failure."

Fledgling e-tailers need to know the problems this industry faces, from visitors who look but never buy to wholesale theft of your most sensitive information. Keep reading, and you'll discover the obstacles e-businesses face on the way to the top.

- *Security:* Experts say that security fraud and theft is still a big issue today. How can that be, when most web browsers and e-business server computers use encryption technology that scrambles a customer's credit card information when it's moving through the internet? Because one of the biggest problems is hackers who break into the websites' computers and steal the whole credit card database. It can happen to the largest of companies. The cure? Work with security experts. Usually, inexpensive solutions can be implemented that safeguard data.

In a survey by Webroot Software, 70 percent of online shoppers said they are quite comfortable with entering their credit card numbers on an internet site. So far, that's a giant improvement over the past few years. In a November 2004 survey, about 6 in 10 consumers said they were so concerned with identity theft that they might reduce their online shopping during the holiday season that year. Despite the improvement in attitude, 1 in 7 of the Webroot survey respondents also say that they have been a victim of some form of online fraud or identity theft. Apparently, people either don't know or don't care how fragile they are online—until they become victims. But by then, it's too late.

Cases of identity theft, credit card fraud and phishing—where impostors lure victims into submitting personal information—are all too common. Don't delay: Start improving your site's security features today.

> **Tip...**
>
> **Smart Tip**
>
> Well-funded e-tailers install system-wide redundancy—if the whole Amazon setup were to collapse, for example, a carbon copy is ready to stand in and do the job. You probably don't want to incur those expenses, but you need to back up all your files. No need to get fancy here. Backups on Zip disks that are kept off-site will do. Why off-site? Losing your backup files as well as your originals in a fire, flood or hurricane is a nightmare you'll want to avoid. If off-site storage is too much of a hassle, use a fireproof and waterproof safe. You can also look into online storage solutions as a way of triple-proofing your redundancy.

A Lose-Lose Situation

According to the ninth annual CyberSource fraud survey conducted by the Mountain View, California–based provider of electronic payment and risk management solutions, fraudsters took $3.6 billion out of e-commerce in 2007—a 17 percent increase over the year before. The study also found that international e-commerce continues to be a far higher risk. It found that orders originating outside the United States and Canada tend to carry a particularly high risk of fraud. Merchants that accept international orders say they decline 11.1 percent of them on suspicion of fraud—on average, two and a half times the overall rejection rate of 4.2 percent. The portion of those international orders accepted that later turn out to be fraudulent is 3.6 percent.

The good news: In the 2007 survey, smaller merchants see improvements when they use two common fraud detection tools: Address Verification Service (AVS) and Card Verification Number (CVN). AVS is a check built into the payment authorization request that compares the address on file at the credit card issuer with the billing address provided by the cardholder. The service is available only for customers in the United States and Canada, though, which may at least partially account for the higher percentage of fraud from international sales. CVN is a check of three additional digits printed on the back of a credit card.

Merchants with e-commerce revenues below $25 million were able to reduce fraud loss 80 percent of the time by using these two tools to verify a customer's home address and prove that the card being used did indeed belong to the person using it online.

The study also said that "chargebacks" may understate actual fraud loss. Traditionally, fraud losses are reported based on fraud-coded "chargebacks"—the value of charges reversed by the issuing banks based on disputes initiated by cardholders claiming unauthorized charges against their accounts. But this metric may be capturing only a portion of actual fraud losses. The survey asked merchants to count not only orders that were identified by the banks as fraudulent but also to specify any charges merchants reversed as a result of calls directly from the cardholders to the merchants claiming fraudulent use of their cards. According to the survey, bank-identified fraud chargebacks accounted for less than half (50 percent) of total fraudulent orders.

- *No buyers:* Industry publications report a 52 percent average shopping cart abandonment rate for the majority of retailers. Since, on average, websites convert visitors to sales at a rate of 1 to 2 percent, that means 98 to 99 percent of the visitors to your website leave without purchasing! In other words, fight hard to get traffic, and that might not matter at all. A site can be full of visitors, but the cash register may never ring.

Beware!
What's your vulnerability to hackers? Create a vulnerability scorecard to pinpoint exactly where your weaknesses are. One common solution: Keep credit card and customer databases on a separate computer from the one connected to the internet. This isn't the only security issue, however, so ask yourself what you would do if you were a hacker, then find ways to fend off that line of attack.

- *Outages:* eBay has had them, and so have many of the online stock brokerages. The inevitable result is a flood of bad publicity as daily newspapers rush to slam a faltering web business. Sometimes outages are flukes—bugs that surface in software or during a site upgrade, an unexpected server outage or even a

hacker—but often the problem stems from poor planning at the beginning.

More troubling still is the fact that outages often happen exactly when a website begins to catch on. For example, a site that works fine when there are 100 visitors a day may show strains at 1,000 and go into meltdown at 10,000 visitors because the sites' server cannot handle that much traffic. Sites need to be built to scale as traffic increases and, frankly, doing that requires nothing more than planning. Always ask, "If traffic goes up tenfold, how will we handle it?" If you don't know the answer, make sure your technical consultants do and that your servers are up to snuff. And if you can, address the issue before launch—because when a website catches fire, it often becomes a wildfire.

- *Fraud:* What better place to use stolen credit cards than under the relative anonymity afforded by the internet? Most e-tailers flatly refuse to talk on the record about their losses from fraud, but know that every site has had to battle with crooks.

What are some things to look out for? Experts say you should watch out for orders with different "bill to" and "ship to" addresses, as well as orders coming from countries with high cyberfraud rates, such as Bulgaria, Egypt, Indonesia, Israel, Lithuania, Malaysia, Pakistan, Romania, Russia, Turkey, the Ukraine and Yugoslavia.

For a comprehensive list of things you can do to reduce credit card fraud, check out scambusters.org. ScamBusters.org is a website and a free electronic newsletter designed to help people protect themselves from internet scams, misinformation and hype.

- *Fighting off the big dogs:* Larry Cuneo, the CEO of Minneapolis-based CarSoup, knew he had big problems from the day he launched in 1998. The space he coveted—selling cars through dealers and connecting auto buyers with auto sellers on the net—had already been staked out by very big companies, including Microsoft (with CarPoint, now called MSN Autos) and Autobytel.com. But Cuneo thought he had a unique twist—his site would be local, targeted strictly at nearby dealers and car buyers. Sounds good, doesn't it? "[But] we had considerable difficulty gaining credibility," says Cuneo. "That's lowered our recognition—and our revenues—from advertisers and e-commerce partners."

> ## ⚠ Beware!
>
> When it comes to preventing credit card fraud, the e-tailer conundrum is that you don't want to lose a sale to a valid customer due to cumbersome security clearances, but you also can't afford to get ripped off. Instead think about it like this: It's better to lose a sale than it is to become a victim. Always look for ways to improve your security as well as the customer's shopping experience, but keep an eye firmly on the till at all times.

Small might sometimes be beautiful, but on the web, it's rarely a distinct advantage. Cuneo didn't quit, though. For one thing, he had budgeted about 50 percent of gross revenues for marketing and promotion, he says. He also invested substantial time in coming up with local promotions the big boys couldn't rival. "We'll sponsor cars in parades and little local events," says Cuneo. The upshot: Today, his site, CarSoup.com, holds a genuine lead in its market over the national rivals. "We are the dominant automotive website in Minnesota over all the big national companies," says Cuneo. "We have now expanded to 54 markets, with more on the way. There is no road map to being successful on the web, but so far, so good. David can compete with Goliath."

Is this dark side of the web so gloomy that you should rethink your enthusiasm for this business venue? Nope, because the upside is the potential of fantastic wealth—the payoffs scored by the founders of, say, Amazon, Yahoo! and eBay.

A Tour of
the Web

Sam Walton, the legendary founder of Wal-Mart, loved to shop—especially in competitors' stores. He did not necessarily buy anything, but he delighted in roaming the aisles, noting prices and observing unique, eye-catching ways to display merchandise. Why? Every shopping trip turned into an exercise in competitive intelligence, and whenever Walton caught a competitor doing something right, he looked for ways to do it better in his Wal-Mart stores.

You would be wise to do the same, and that means routinely surfing the web, visiting pace-setting e-tailers, and learning everything you can about what people are doing right. Don't think of surfing as goofing off. When you are doing it so that you can become a better e-tailer, it's some of the best work you can do. Jeff Bezos, founder of Amazon, is known to keep his Tuesdays and Thursdays open whenever possible to give himself time to surf the web in search of cool ideas.

Here's a yardstick: You are doing valuable work when, after every surfing session, you have specific, concrete ideas for improving your site. If you're not getting ideas, you're surfing the wrong sites or not thinking hard enough. And neither will get you ahead in the competitive world of e-commerce.

Want to know how to look at websites? On the following pages, many name-brand websites are critiqued. Some win generous praise, but throughout, the emphasis is on what we can learn from these sites. And next time you put in a surfing session, ask yourself the kinds of questions you'll see in these site critiques.

RIVER OF DREAMS
Amazon.com Inc.
amazon.com

Amazon founder Jeff Bezos named his website "Amazon" because that river is bigger than any other river on earth—or so the story goes. And Bezos' aim from the get-go was to build the web's biggest store.

Bezos came up with the idea when, as an employee of a New York financial firm, he was asked to run numbers on various possible web businesses. When he hit upon books, all the lights went on—Bezos knew he had a winner. Just a couple distributors stock pretty much every book in print, and it seemed simple to set up a business that amounted to a website with no inventory. As orders came in, books could be bought from distributors, and whoosh—profits would roll in. Bezos took the numbers to his bosses and asked them to join in funding a startup, but the verdict was no way. So Bezos quit, moved to Seattle, and began building what just may rank as the web's crowning e-tailing achievement.

In an April 2007 tally of the top 50 internet properties by total unique web

> **Beware!**
> Amazon has filed patents on various bits of its site operation, and although nobody is clear about what Amazon intends to do to assert its rights, wary site designers are treading softly when it comes to closely imitating Amazon. This will not likely be a worry for you, both because your operation will be small and your technology will not be nearly as robust as Amazon's, but if you find yourself exactly duplicating the "1-Click" purchase tool, back up a few steps and try another approach.

visitors from comScore Media Metrix, Amazon's sites, including its international sites, ranked eighth. Why is Amazon so successful? In part because its pages and tools are brilliantly executed, and throughout the site the emphasis is on making it as easy as possible for the buyer to make a purchase.

Case in point: "1-Click" buying. Like a book? A registered Amazon user can, with a single mouse click, buy it. It's that fast and that simple (so much so that tests showed users didn't believe it could be so easy—so afterward a screen pops up that says the deal has been done). It doesn't work only on books, however. Anything Amazon sells can be bought with a single click, and nowadays that includes TV sets, videos, CDs, power saws, toys and more. Doesn't Bezos risk diluting Amazon's message by expanding into so many diverse product lines? Remember the company's name—Bezos envisioned expanding into other product lines from the start.

Amazon also offers free shipping. While free shipping has been used as an online promotional tool since the internet's earliest days, the idea really picked up steam in 2002 when Amazon began experimenting with it as a full-time service. Initially, the company offered free shipping to customers whose purchases totaled $99 or more. The company later lowered the minimum to $49 and then to $25, which it currently offers. (There are some exceptions to free shipping, however, including oversize items, e-books and e-documents, software downloads, music downloads, gift certificates, and items from other sellers using Amazon's system.) In 2005, Amazon launched its Prime service; customers pay $79 per year for unlimited express shipping and discounted overnight shipping with no minimum purchase. While it may be difficult for a small company to offer these types of promotions, it is something to think about.

What else is cool about Amazon.com? Notice how fast the home page loads. The look is fresh and clean but is primarily text-based, with plentiful use of white space to make the page easy on the eyes. With its treasury, Amazon could well afford to put up the glitziest tech tools imaginable, but it doesn't. Cool tools—Java applets, sound effects and so on—gobble up bandwidth and really bloat page-loading times. And Bezos from the start has put a primacy on making it easy for a customer to buy what he or she needs, fast.

Keep looking at the home page, and you'll notice that if you've bought from Amazon in the past, the page is personalized in keeping with your prior purchases. Books, music and videos are recommended in line with an educated guess about what you'll like. Although personalization is hard for a low-budget site builder to incor-

Smart Tip

Always compare your site with competitors', and do this ruthlessly and without an iota of favoritism. What do your competitors do better? If you cannot list a dozen things, go back and look at their sites more closely until you come up with a dozen. The only way to make your site the best it can be is to study competitors, see what they are doing well, and then do it better.

porate, any site builder can insert "Today's Deals," just as Amazon does.

One exceptionally clever feature is called "Creating a Wish List for a Nonprofit Organization." This feature lets representatives of nonprofits create a Wish List for their organizations—and Amazon.com shoppers can buy the items they need.

The Wish List works like a wedding registry. The Wish List administrator creates an Amazon.com account for the organization and then shops in any area of the store to select the items the organization needs. Donors can visit the site and help the organization by purchasing those items. Wish List administrators can make the list searchable and add a description of their organization to help potential donors find their Wish List. For more information, visit amazon.com, click on the "Help" link and then click "Wish Lists," or go directly to amazon.com/gp/help/customer/display.html?ie=UTF8&nodeId=13837531.

IN FULL BLOOM
1-800-Flowers.com Inc.
1800flowers.com

1-800-Flowers.com Inc., a leading florist and multichannel retailer of gifts for all occasions, has had its share of ups and downs. The company reported losses in several quarters from 2003 to 2005, yet managed to end each year in the black. It has seen better days since then, with much of its growth coming in the form of increasing online sales.

One reason for its success? 1-800-Flowers.com seems to be on a mission to offer the perfect gift to shoppers.

In the past few years, the company's product line has been extended by the merchandise sold through its many subsidiaries, including Plow & Hearth Inc. (plowandhearth.com), a direct marketer of home decor and garden merchandise; The Popcorn Factory Inc. (thepopcornfactory.com), a manufacturer and direct marketer of popcorn and specialty food gifts; Greatfood (greatfood.com), a direct marketer of gourmet foods; Ambrosia Wine (ambrosiawine.com), a direct marketer of California wines; Cheryl & Co. (cherylandco.com), a direct marketer of baked goods and cookies; Fannie May (fanniemay.com), an e-commerce site for chocolate lovers; Wind & Weather, a site for outdoor gifts; Problem Solvers (problemsolvers.com), a purveyor of organizational products; and The Children's Group Inc., a direct marketer of children's gifts, operating under the HearthSong (hearthsong.com) and Magic Cabin (magiccabin.com) brands.

Another advantage? It's a company that truly understands and embraces net-based selling. It was also a pioneer: Its first electronic storefront opened on CompuServ in 1992, followed by an AOL store in '94. Its website went live in 1995, which is early in internet time. 1-800-Flowers accomplished that by serving as a beta tester for what became Netscape's Commerce Server. While other leading businesses often stumbled when it came to jumping into the online world, 1-800-Flowers got it right from the start.

Does the site still work? Absolutely. And keep this in mind: Flowers are easier to sell on the visual web than they are by phone. Do you know what a "Memory Garden" bouquet looks like? Of course not. And even if you're told it has a half-dozen roses arranged along with floral favorites such as stock, alstroemeria and waxflower, you may be clueless about its looks. But on the website, you see the arrangement, which can usually be magnified.

A fast-loading site that includes text and plenty of imagery to capture the visuals of the floral business, 1-800-Flowers aims to make the shopping experience easy. Flowers appropriate for an upcoming holiday are noted. An "Occasions" section offers gift suggestions for common events—birthday, get well, love and romance—and if you still don't know what to buy, you can use an interactive "Gift Finder." The home page also offers weekly specials and product highlights. The most impressive thing about 1-800-Flowers is it offers up lots of information on a page that nonetheless doesn't seem cluttered or overwhelming. That is exceptional page design, and it is a goal every site designer ought to aspire to.

Another plus: If you are truly clueless about flowers or reach a roadblock in trying to make a purchase, it's easy to find a real person to talk to. Click on the "Customer Service" button at the bottom of the home page, and you'll be directed to a page with customer service FAQs, an e-mail link, a way to track your package and, of course, the 1-800 number.

PUSHING THE ENVELOPES
Staples Inc., Office Depot Inc., and OfficeMax Inc.
staples.com
officedepot.com
officemax.com

The three office supplies chains—Staples, Office Depot and OfficeMax—slug it out online every bit as vigorously as they do in the brick-and-mortar world. And think of the barriers to building a good office supplies site: The products are nonvisual (who wants to look at a ream of paper?) and inherently unexciting. Hardly anybody gets a tingle thinking about buying the month's toner, paper clips and envelopes. This is boring stuff, and, as consumers, we want to get in and out as quickly as possible.

That's good news for office supplies site designers. With some kinds of retail, shoppers actually enjoy the physical shops (fine jewelers, for instance), but with office supplies, if we never have to step into a brick-and-mortar store again, likely we'll all toast our good fortune. The trick for a site designer is making it all work on the web so that it's easy to make the purchases we need.

Unsurprisingly, all three of the office supplies giants take essentially the same route. In fact, Staples, Office Max and Office Depot have pages that are stunningly similar—heavily text-oriented, scant use of graphics, with an organization that revolves around imitating the aisles in a physical store.

Which site comes out on top? For my money, it's OfficeMax, but only by a nose. OfficeMax wins because it offers quick and simple product searches, helps save you money with "instant savings" buttons clearly positioned next to sale items, and, finally, it offers free shipping options. Staples is a close runner-up. By making it easy to replenish supplies with just a couple of mouse clicks, Staples takes some of the drudgery out of this chore.

IT'S IN THE MAIL
Stamps.com Inc.
stamps.com

The biggest challenge in selling is convincing people to do something new, something they have never done before. Witness escargots. You've seen them on menus. Have you ever eaten snails? If you have, you either like them or you don't, and you know without further ado if you'll order them again. But if you have never ordered them—never tasted a snail—it's difficult to be persuaded to order one at a restaurant. A freebie may help, but probably not. What would tempt you? Tough question, with no easy answer.

What do snails have to do with the web? Quite a lot, actually. Just look at Stamps.com, a site that has been around for several years but offers a service many people may have never used before. Of course you understand postage, but the way it has always worked is that you've gone to the post office with money and walked out either with a sheet of paper stamps or with credits entered into a postage meter. Stamps.com wants to change all that.

Its aim is to entice you to buy postage on the internet from a company you have never heard of and—somehow—to affix this postage to your outgoing mail in ways you do not yet understand. How could you ever be enticed into taking this deal? Simple: Sign up with Stamps.com, and your account automatically starts with $5 free postage and a free Stamps.com Supplies Kit (a $5 value). After your trial period, you will receive additional postage coupons ($20 value), plus a free Stamps.com digital scale ($50 value)—a total value of $80. Because it's free, you just might try it out.

Look closely at Stamps.com's front page. Its highest goal isn't to sell you; it's to tempt you to try out the service. For example, the first button on the page isn't "Sign Up Now"; it's "Learn More." Is that putting priorities in the wrong place? No, because you won't be sold into buying Stamps.com's service until you try it, and the smartest, fastest, best way to induce you to try it is to give it away.

Everything about this front page aims at achieving that goal, and that makes this a well-designed site. It's a lesson website designers should absorb. Sometimes the web merely offers new ways to do old things (as, for instance, Amazon adds a cybertwist

Smart Tip

Tip...

What can you give away? Stamps.com gives away free postage, among other things—which is something visitors know the value of and will use. But if you use this tactic, keep close tabs on both your visitor counts and the numbers that take advantage of any freebies you are offering. If the visitor count dramatically exceeds the number of folks who go for the freebie, maybe you are trying to give away escargots—meaning visitors don't know if they actually want what you are offering. The remedy? Think hard about finding a way to position what you are offering as both valuable and desirable, and keep tinkering with this value proposition until a healthy percentage of visitors are jumping on your freebie.

to book buying), but in other cases the web is about wholly new things to do, which is the case with Stamps.com. And the only way to get customers to plunge into uncharted waters is to tempt them with freebies.

The jury is out on the near-term viability of Stamps.com or any of its competitors, but for now the site wins applause for doing all the right things to persuade us to, at the very least, give this newfangled way of buying and affixing postage a whirl.

THE RIGHT DOSE
drugstore.com Inc.
drugstore.com

Who likes shopping for aspirin, soap, razor blades, prescription medicines and the rest of the stuff that

takes us to drugstores? Almost nobody, and that's why an early niche targeted by trailblazing e-tailers was the drugstore category. Imagine if you could save yourself a half-hour—maybe more—weekly by eliminating those shopping trips and instead clicking a mouse a few times.

That's the value proposition put forth by drugstore.com, a category leader that has won a variety of awards and accolades over the years. For example, it was ranked No. 35 in Internet Retailer magazine's Top 500 retail websites in 2007 (ranking based on internet retail sales volume each year). There is much to admire on the drugstore.com site: pages that load quickly; numerous tools for personalization ("Your List"); a well-organized store directory where you can shop by category,

Smart Tip

Tip...

How can you make your customers' shopping easier? Are there "ready-made lists" you can create? How about lists of the most ordered items? Can a customer save his or her own wish list and then forward it to a family member or friend? Face it: No matter what any tech headie says, web shopping lacks the buzz and fun of a mall (although it has other strong advantages). Build in tools that make shopping go fast, and your customers will thank you by spending more money in your store.

Smart Tip

Tip...

With whom can you forge alliances? Which companies will dress up your pages and build higher levels of visitor trust in your business? Make up a list, and start knocking on doors. For an online startup, these kinds of partnerships can spell the difference between a fast ramp-up into success or a swift plunge into failure. A few partnerships are plenty; put too many on your page, and you risk blurring your message and losing your identity.

such as "vitamins," "beauty" and "top sellers"; five-star reviews; and a search engine, which makes finding the necessities on your shopping list a snap. Plus, there are extensive customer reviews posted for products on the site, which help shoppers determine the best item for their needs. Special offers are also highlighted on the front page, which is always a favorite with consumers. The company also offers free shipping on orders of $25 or more for new customers.

Drugstore.com prides itself on transparent drug pricing, making it easy for consumers to comparison shop for their prescription medications.

The other distinguishing feature about drugstore.com is that it's leveraged upon joint marketing arrangements with well-known, brick-and-mortar businesses—notably Rite Aid and GNC. Its home page, for example, highlights the GNC brand in the "vitamins" category. Rite Aid, on the other hand, has an "online shopping" navigational tab at the top of its home page (riteaid.com) that leads to drugstore.com. Both of these companies have spent millions of dollars nurturing consumer awareness and comfort, and they rank high in their niches. In turn, drugstore.com gets to parlay its investments into a powerful play for consumers' trust and shopping dollars.

RIDING THE WAVE
Yahoo! Inc.
yahoo.com

No website comes close to Yahoo! in winning visitors. It was among the net's first websites but remained a powerhouse. In the April 2007 list of the top 50 internet properties by visitor count from comScore Media Metrix, Yahoo! was No. 1. That month, Yahoo's sites had more than 178 million visitors. White-hot eBay managed only 79.1 million visitors in the same period. Yahoo!'s performance is simply amazing, especially since this month-in, month-out leadership has lasted for years.

Surf into Yahoo, and what you find is a monument to an internet philosophy of less is more. Graphical elements are so few as to be almost not used at all, and the page is heavily text-based—but it somehow manages to remain both uncluttered and readable. This is as skilled as website programming gets: Yahoo! programmers manage to make an extremely sophisticated site design somehow look simple.

Now notice how many services and options Yahoo! offers, from personalized stock quotes to e-mail options, auctions—even a customized "My Yahoo" page where registered users can select exactly the information they want to see. It's a rich array of individualized information, and since it's free, smart users tap into it.

Especially when compared with some of its main competitors, Yahoo! has a better-looking site. For example, head over to the MSN site. You will see a very different look, consisting of more visuals and, strangely, both less information and more irrelevant stuff. On a recent site visit, I found an article titled "High-energy lifestyle tips" and an article called "Ultimate Holiday Entertaining Guide."

Tip...

Smart Tip

Surf around and visit all the portal or gateway sites that Yahoo has trounced in the past several years. Let's face it: Yahoo is clearly a winner when it comes to portal or gateway sites. This should lead you to ask, "What does Yahoo do better, and how can I adapt it to my site?" Odds are you can't duplicate the sophisticated programming or the high level of personalization offered by Yahoo. But keep surfing, and you'll soon be jotting down concrete ideas for your site.

While this information is interesting, Yahoo! manages to be sober and even more useful, compared with a kind of frivolity at MSN. Most users want to dispense with the frivolous and get down to business.

Learn from Yahoo! that less is definitely more, and information—useful, relevant information—is power. Give surfers facts, make the page load fast, and you are following in Yahoo!'s footsteps, which is an excellent path to take.

IT TAKES A VILLAGE
iVillage Inc.
ivillage.com

A site aimed at women, iVillage.com ranked 40th in comScore Media Metrix's tally of the top 50 internet properties in April 2007—pretty high for a special-interest site—and attracted nearly 17 million visitors that month. With the intense competition that's out there, what moved iVillage to the top of the heap?

Log on to iVillage and see for yourself. It's evident that the site strives to be a portal for women, the kind of page it hopes users will set up as their home page. That's because the site offers a full range of services, everything from horoscopes and quizzes to the latest gossip and iVillage widgets (content boxes) that you can add to your own site. There are recipes, beauty tips, pointers for parents and places to chat online.

The site is also well-designed and easy to read. For example, one of the first things a visitor sees is a list of categories—"Health," "Home & Garden," "Love" and "Pregnancy & Parenting"—that she can click on for more information. The most impressive thing about iVillage is it knows its target audience and gears everything to those viewers. Many sites are unfocused or try to be all things to all people, and that never works. What does work is knowing who your viewers are and gearing everything on the site to them. In this respect, iVillage excels. Looked at from a functional point of view, it is not fundamentally different from, say, the AOL home page, with the major exception that iVillage has defined its audience and pursues it.

KEEPING IT FRESH
FreshDirect Inc.
freshdirect.com

The odds are certainly against it, but FreshDirect Inc. (freshdirect.com), a New York–based online fresh-food retailer, is actually succeeding.

What is making this company succeed when other cybergrocers—such as Webvan and Kozmo.com—were among the most well-known dotcom flops? Well, for one thing, those companies were straightforward grocery distribution companies with hubs located all over the nation. Fresh Direct, on the other hand, is really a fresh food and meal solution company that just happens to deliver its products to New York customers.

The company, conceived in 1999 by Joe Fedele (a New Yorker who has started gourmet supermarkets), shortens the supply chain by purchasing fresh foods direct from the source and processing orders in a 300,000-square-foot manufacturing facility just outside New York City, using batch-manufacturing processes. Then it delivers its products to customers in parts of New York and New Jersey.

Its food-friendly facility lets the company do much of its own food preparation, like roasting its own green coffee beans, dry-aging its own prime beef, and baking its own breads and pastries. It also sells specialty foods and popular grocery brands. And because it doesn't have a retail location, it doesn't pay expensive rent for retail space. These factors help keep food fresh and costs low and allow the company to pass the savings on to its customers. As a result, FreshDirect says it can save customers up to 25 percent compared with local retail markets. The company is expanding rapidly and currently serves most of Manhattan and locations in Queens, Brooklyn, Staten Island and the Bronx, as well as parts of New Jersey, Westchester and Nassau County.

FreshDirect customers can shop anytime from work or home, and the company brings everything directly to you in a FreshDirect refrigerator/freezer truck so the food is protected all the way to your door. There is a $30 minimum total per order. Delivery costs $4.95—although that may vary in certain areas—and tipping is at the customer's discretion. Customers are advised to tell FreshDirect where and when they want their delivery by choosing a convenient two-hour delivery window on weekday evenings and all day on weekends.

Smart Tip *Tip...*

A key to FreshDirect's success is its graphics. It shows all its products in a clear and very appetizing way. Are you selling products that would benefit from appealing graphics? If so, spend the bucks, and make sure they look good. It really makes a difference to consumers. The better, more appealing something looks, the more likely people are to buy it.

The formula seems to be working: According to FreshDirect, the company has currently attracted more than 250,000 customers. There are numerous reasons for the company's success. One is the concept itself—fresh food sold at low cost and delivered to your door. Another is the company's focus on providing a robust shopping experience for incredibly fresh foods and meal solutions.

Another reason for its success is its easy-to-use website. FreshDirect's online store is a cinch to use and is loaded with great information. Learn about what you're buying. Compare products by price, nutrition and flavor. Get recommendations for foods to suit your taste. When you come back, the company remembers what you ordered last time so you can reorder in minutes.

Smart Tip *Tip...*

Navigation is key to a website—can users find what they're looking for on yours in a glance? Heavily monied corporations actually test and time users as they poke around rough-draft websites. You can do the same. Ask employees, friends or neighbors to navigate your site, and listen to their feedback. It does no good if you hide your gems—they need to be readily visible, even to casual lookers.

When you visit the home page, you'll see that it highlights its delivery information, which is important, especially since it must get many calls and questions from people about this important part of its business model. It also asks you to find out if the company is delivering in your neighborhood. All you have to do is enter your ZIP code.

Aren't located in an area where FreshDirect delivers? You can still browse the site and enter your e-mail address to receive a notice if FreshDirect will be coming to your area.

FreshDirect's home page is designed to make navigating its vast product offerings very simple. The home page is categorized by "Easy Meals Prepared By Expert Chefs," "Delicious Foods Treated With Love and Respect" and "Popular Brands and Everyday Pantry Needs." For the utmost convenience, customers can choose from a range of "Ready to Cook" meals, "Heat and Eat," or from the popular "4-Minute Meals," which employs special steam valve technology that cooks raw materials to perfection in under four minutes.

Departments such as "Fruit," Dairy" and "Meat" are clearly listed. Once you are in each department, you are treated to more graphics and details so you can easily click on the exact item you'd like. Prices are clearly listed here as well, which is a plus. As you go along, you are treated to even more details about each item. When I clicked on "Fruit," and then "Apples," and finally "Granny Smith," I was greeted with the following description: "The tartness of a Granny Smith piques your palate, but then its deep sweetness comes out to balance the flavor." I was also shown the price again. Also important: Checking out is easy as well—almost every page has an icon that lets you view your shopping cart or check out. All in all, it's a great experience.

TECH SAVVY
Dell Computer Corp.
dell.com

Michael S. Dell, chair and CEO of Dell Computer Corp., founded the company in 1984 with $1,000 and, back then, an unprecedented idea in the computer industry: Sell computer systems directly to customers. Michael, who is also the longest-tenured CEO in the computer industry, knew what he was doing.

Under Michael's direction, Dell has established itself as a premiere provider of products and services required for customers to build their information-technology and internet infrastructures.

Dell is also acknowledged as the largest online commercial seller of computer systems. The company is known for redefining the role of the web in delivering faster, better and more convenient service to customers.

To see how well it is serving customers, take a look at Dell's website. Navigation is very user-friendly. On the front page, online shoppers are also clearly presented with easy-to-read categories such as "Home & Home Office," "Small Business & Medium Business," "Large Business," and "Government, Education, Healthcare & Life Sciences."

Within each category, visitors can shop by type of product, and those products— servers, notebooks and desktops, or printers, for example—are clearly displayed by name and graphic image as well.

When clicking on the "Home & Home Office" button, shoppers are presented with a cleverly designed web page with options for product browsing, recommendations, checking out promotional specials—such as desktops from $299 after a $50 mail-in rebate and free shipping with the purchase of any Dell Home System—clearly displayed. They are also presented with a "Find It in Retail" section, where they can find information on Dell products sold at Wal-Mart, Sam's Club, Best Buy and Staples.

Unlike many e-tailers, Dell doesn't make it hard for shoppers to return their purchases. There is a clearly visible link to "Returns," which takes you to a page that spells out the return policy, and explains warranty coverage and what steps to take when returning a Dell product.

An important thing to remember: While Dell may have an elaborate back-end infrastructure, most of the elements on the site are pretty basic and could be done by a small e-tailer just starting out. In fact, the real beauty of the site is not anything flashy but how it's organized. It's user-friendly and shows that Dell really understands its customers. It gets, for example, that most of them probably want to know how much their tax and shipping are going to cost before they make their final purchase, so they give customers that information upfront, as soon as possible. This is a pretty basic—but important—concept that any e-tailer should think about before finalizing site design plans.

IF THE SHOE FITS
Shoebuy.com Inc.
shoebuy.com

Shoebuy.com is one of the largest retailers on the internet focused on all categories of footwear and related apparel. Shoebuy has partnerships with more than 400 manufacturers and offers more than 600,000 products from top brands including Dockers, Florsheim, Keds, New Balance, Reebok, Skechers, Tommy Hilfiger and many more.

Simplicity is the guiding principle of the Shoebuy.com website. There are several ways to find your shoes of choice quickly and easily, and they are clearly listed on the Shoebuy.com home page: You can browse departments for men, women, teens, children or sale shoes; browse by collection, such as "boots" or "bridal shoes"; or browse by brand. A search button at the top of the page also allows users to search by brand, size, wide shoes, narrow shoes or sale shoes. There is also an "Advanced Search" button.

Budget Watcher

How can you give away shipping and not go broke? While FedEx and its competitors negotiate highly favorable rates with big shippers, they won't necessarily do the same with small businesses. But that doesn't mean only big-bucks options are left. Use UPS standard delivery or the post office. Both are cheap. A 1-pound package can be shipped cross-country via the post office for around $4.60, and that buys two-to-three-day Priority Mail delivery. If that gets you a buyer who becomes a repeat customer, isn't it some of the smartest money you've ever spent? Don't be too quick to say you can't afford to offer free shipping for the right order amount.

▲

Shoebuy.com also offers a 110 percent price guarantee. If you find a product for a lower price on another website, it will refund you 110 percent of the difference between the lower price and Shoebuy's price. It will even refund the difference if it lowers the price at Shoebuy. Plus, the company has been offering free shipping on all its orders since January 2000, when its site was officially launched. This freebie is prominently displayed throughout the site.

The CEO and co-founder of the company, Scott Savitz, has said that he didn't want to enter into this business if he couldn't sell a product that offered free shipping because he believed it was part of the whole value proposition. He felt that just because Shoebuy.com was offering a product on the internet, that alone wasn't enough for somebody to make a purchase.

Shoebuy.com, Amazon.com, drugstore.com, Dell Computer Corp.—all of these companies and many more—are using free shipping promotions to encourage people to buy online. And why not? Experts have said that they lure more mainstream buyers to the internet—such as shoppers who are more price-sensitive, have lower incomes than frequent online shoppers and are more used to the brick-and-mortar world than surfing the internet. But there are some downsides to free shipping, and a major one would be cost. So before taking the free shipping plunge, run the numbers and make sure it won't have a devastating impact on your bottom line.

FILM AT ELEVEN
Netflix Inc.
netflix.com

Here's a novel idea: Launch a movie rental service with the goal of using the DVD format and the internet to make it easier for people to find and rent movies they will appreciate. This is what the founders of Netflix had in mind when they formed Netflix.com in 1997, and the site is now a success. Today, Netflix is the world's largest online DVD movie rental service, with 7.5 million members and 90,000 movie titles. Its appeal and success are built on providing an expansive selection of DVDs, an easy way to choose movies and fast, free delivery.

The concept is pretty simple. Members can rent DVDs and keep them as long as they want. Netflix also provides free, prepaid return envelopes so members can just drop their movies in the mailbox to return them to Netflix. And with 50 distribution centers across the United States, more than 90 percent of Netflix members receive their DVDs in one day.

Currently, Netflix has nine monthly plans, starting at $4.99 for a one-out-at-a-time plan with unlimited rentals. The most popular is three movies out at a time, with unlimited rentals, which is $16.99 per month.

The more you use Netflix, the more the site is tailored to your tastes. After you see a movie, for example, you can rate it by clicking on the stars that appear next to every movie's listing on the site, from one star if you hated it to up to five stars if you loved it. The more you rate, the more Netflix learns what you like, and it delivers personalized recommendations every time you log on. It also allows you to easily rent these DVDs by displaying a red "Add" icon beside each movie description.

Besides highlighting picks especially for each member, the Netflix home page also allows you to easily search by genre ("Action Adventure," "Comedy" or "Documentary," for example). You can also add other members as "friends" in your Community section to see what they are renting and read their reviews. The site clearly understands its audience— film lovers—and makes ordering DVDs a very pleasant experience.

Tip...

Smart Tip

A key to Netflix's success is that it truly understands its audience. It knows, for example, that its customers are films buffs, so it allows them to pick and choose films from genres that only true film buffs would understand and enjoy. What's more, it offers them fully personalized pages so they can rent DVDs that they would most likely pick. While Netflix's personalization capabilities are at a level that many e-tailers might not be able to achieve, they should still make an effort to get to know their customers in general and talk to them in their own language on their websites. It's not rocket science, just pure business sense.

The Future of
e-Commerce

Where is e-commerce heading? Tough topic, but to gain insight into the future, I asked Bruce Weinberg, chair of the marketing department at the McCallum Graduate School of Business of Bentley College and a visiting scholar at the McCombs School of Business of the University of Texas at Austin, for his thoughts.

A writer and thinker about the net, with particular expertise in online shopping and online consumer behavior, Weinberg is both a tough critic of present-day e-tailing and a bona fide optimist about the role of e-commerce in tomorrow's retailing mix. You may not always agree with the opinionated Weinberg, but his thoughts are well worth pondering.

Entrepreneur: What's the best e-tailing site on the web?

Bruce Weinberg: Amazon is still numero uno. eBay remains a great alternative for many buyers and sellers; although, the shine is off this rose a bit. In addition, I want to give a shout out to local merchants and wholesalers who have extended effectively to online retail (e.g., KidRobot at KidRobot.com, Outhouse Designs at OuthouseDesigns.com) and are providing value to customers by offering information online and/or items for sale.

Some key aspects of their approach to constructing and operating a business are:

- *Enabling customers to develop high degrees of trust in the exchange process, which, theoretically and practically, is critical for long-term success in any business.* As 1972 economics Nobel Laureate Ken Arrow said, trust reduces the friction in commerce.

- *They each offer great value by making it easier for customers to find a wide variety of items through a one-stop shopping experience.* The notion of value in a one-stop shopping process in an online environment may sound strange given the ease with which you can switch from one website to another. However, some factors at play that make this plausible are that time is relative and loyalty is an investment that keeps on giving.

- *Time is relative.* If I told you that you could be physically transported to the aisles of your favorite bookstore in five to 10 seconds, you would be elated. Normally this could take on the order of five to 30 minutes. However, waiting five to 10 seconds for a web page to download would drive you nuts (assuming the use of a high-speed internet connection). Normally, a web page loads in one to two seconds or less with a high-speed connection. In the physical world, one to two seconds is really fast; however, in the web world, one to two seconds is not so fast—it may even be annoyingly slow to some people. So time is relative. The few seconds it may take to type in another URL or search for another online store to visit may not be perceived as quick when operating in an online state of mind (with apologies to Billy Joel). One-stop shopping saves online consumers time.

- *Loyalty is an investment that keeps on giving.* On average, consumers continue to view shopping online as a very risky activity. This risk is reduced when consumers find a trustworthy and reliable merchant (or merchants, in the case of eBay). Consumers believe that the majority of online purveyors are untrustworthy, so when they find one they can trust, they are surprisingly likely to stick with it. One good experience after another increases customers' trust and loyalty. Consumers are investing their shopping hearts and minds into the online merchant. This results in a cycle that is difficult for a competitor to break. The loyal and invested customer is more likely to consider and value alternative offerings, such as those that could be offered in a one-stop shopping environment.

In general, a website—and the processes set in motion based on customer interaction with a website—should do the following six things:

1. Allow customers to perform some aspect of the buying process better than is possible through other means. If the purpose of the site is to provide information, then it should provide information either more effectively or more efficiently than was possible before the firm offered a website. If the site allows customers to order products, then it should enable a better experience in some meaningful way. For example, catalog retailers should make the online ordering process either faster or more convenient than ordering via telephone.

2. Clearly describe a product so that consumers know exactly what they are considering (check out a camera review at Dpreview.com, and you'll see an example of a site that leaves little to the imagination).

3. Put forth a sincere effort to truly understand a customer through communication and sincere interest, not exclusively based on clickstreams.

4. Provide full and accurate information upfront about what is being offered. For example, don't make customers go through the checkout process in order to find out whether an item is in stock or to find out the full cost of an order (which includes the costs of the product, sales tax and shipping).

5. Keep promises. Say what you mean and mean what you say. For example, deliver the next day when a customer pays for next-day service. And don't call something next-day service unless it means the product will be delivered to the customer on the next day.

6. Respect customers' privacy and security. Consumers have serious concerns about these issues. Once a person overcomes them to buy from you, do everything in your power to maintain the promised and expected levels of privacy and security.

Entrepreneur: Do you have a personal favorite website?

Weinberg: My favorite sites tend to be the ones that help me find effective solutions to my problems.

I'll mention two particular sites here, but I'll note a couple of experiences that speak to the general notion of a "favorite" website that helps me find effective solutions. For online shopping, my most preferred site is eBay, the online auction site. At eBay, I almost always find what I want, when I want it, at a price that I find reasonable (as I play a role in setting the price when bidding in an auction). In addition, I get a thrill from shopping at eBay; it is an affect-rich shopping and buying experience. First, there is the excitement associated with finding an item that I thought I would never find anywhere (e.g., a Rolls-Royce key case, a brand-new unit of an old version of a handheld solitaire game). Next, there is the delight associated with interacting with other bidders (though some would call this the rush of competition). Then, there is the agony of defeat or the thrill of victory (with apologies to the Wide World of Sports). Finally, I don't buy items on eBay; I win them. I love the feeling of getting a great deal when I win. But on eBay and other online auction sites, you should be careful of the winner's curse (in essence, paying too much for an item) and of the potential for addictively "chasing losses." Researchers at Harvard Medical School have observed some similarities between gambling and auction bidding with respect to human behaviors and emotions.

I also enjoy using Google. Two to four years ago, it probably would have sounded strange to have a search site as a favorite. Now, however, I suspect that Google is a favorite site for millions of people. In both my professional and personal life, I frequently find the need or desire to search for information online. Google typically leads me to information that will help me "find" what I am looking for or solve a problem, either now or down the road. For example, I easily reconnected with a long-lost friend from Sweden by "Googling" him. His name appeared in a few web pages, one of which included his e-mail address. We just got together in Boston for dinner at the end of February, and I'm now arranging for my family to visit his home in Sweden.

Google has also helped me find websites that addressed pressing problems for me. During the summer of 2005, my central air conditioning compressor unit stopped working. Most people would probably call an air conditioning repair company. Well, I was not sufficiently confident that I would easily find one that would act mostly in my best interest (and pocketbook). A new unit could cost thousands of dollars! So I hit the internet looking for, and finding, a place where I could learn how to diagnose and, as it turned out, repair my central air conditioning unit. I visited the "Cozy Community" of CozyParts.com, an independent Lennox dealer in Oklahoma.

Similarly, I recently had a problem getting my radio to work in my 1993 Lexus LS400 after I had disconnected and then reconnected a battery cable. I believe a Lexus dealer would have charged upward of hundreds of dollars to "help me out." In the end, I found a solution within a community of car owners at carKB.com, which cost me a few minutes of my time in the end. My approach to resolving a problem may not be effective for everyone, as I can be a bit of a do-it-yourselfer type.

Entrepreneur: What's wrong with all—or virtually all—e-commerce sites today?

Weinberg: Tough question. I'll stop short of saying that certain problems are associated with all e-commerce sites. But I will highlight some areas where firms should seriously reconsider the status quo.

First, I believe many sites could benefit from a greater appreciation of the consumer buying-decision process. The process has been the same for centuries, and it is unlikely to change in the foreseeable future. It details precisely what consumers do when engaged in the process of buying. They: 1) recognize a problem or need, 2) may search for information to reduce the risk associated with the buying decision to be made, 3) may evaluate alternatives and come to a decision about which one may be "best," 4) make the purchase, and 5) carry out a variety of post-purchase activities, such as consuming the product, spreading negative or positive word-of-mouth, returning the item and so forth.

Second, businesses should realize that humans engage in exchange and that the internet, the web, computers and other technologies are exchange tools for humans—not the other way around. Model your approach for exchange based on this simple and important principle. eBay brings together buyers and sellers. Match.com brings together people who want companionship. World of Warcraft, an online game with about 10 million subscribers, brings together people who like to interact through and explore fantasy worlds.

Third, scaling [growing your business] is a great way to garner more profits per dollar invested; however, scaling works only when a successful process remains a successful process in its scaled form. Don't assume that every business process that can be automated and scaled up in some way should be automated and scaled up. For example, using a Help/FAQ section as a means for scaling the availability of customer service may not be enough. Sometimes the customer or the situation requires more assistance than what is offered by a set of FAQs. Even mighty Amazon learned this lesson, as it now offers customer service over the phone.

All this being said, there are situations where scaling online may be extremely effective. For example, consider the case of viral marketing, or getting others to pass along your message or some message that will bring customers to your door. The internet can be extremely effective in this regard. In addition, the web is a great way to scale the number of interactions with a person and the number of people with which you have an interaction—for example, through an electronic newsletter. This can effectively support a permission marketing program.

Entrepreneur: What business principles hold in e-commerce?

Weinberg: Tried-and-true business principles hold in e-commerce. If your value proposition is weak, then your appeal to customers will likely be weak. In addition, to survive in e-commerce, it is critical to have a clear vision and reasonable plan for success, determination and discipline in execution, and the ability to understand and satisfy consumers. You must not only have a great idea, but also be able to "make it happen." There is a long history of entrepreneurs who developed "greater mouse-traps" that did not result in everyone beating a path to their door. In addition, understand that consumers, in both B2C and B2B, have more "power" and expectations.

Smart Tip

Where do eBay and Amazon excel? By enabling customers to develop high degrees of trust in the exchange process, offering great value by making it easier for customers to find a wide variety of items through a one-stop shopping process, keeping promises, and respecting their customers' privacy. Do you do these things? If so, you're on the right track to success.

Entrepreneur: What niches have yet to be fully attacked by e-tailers?

Weinberg: I have observed many small businesses filling niches. I still see a lot of opportunity in luxury goods. Some online luxury retailers are beginning to see significant growth. For example, Blue Nile, an online jeweler, has grown more than 50 percent since 2002 and is profitable. Many long-established and premier luxury purveyors, such as Gucci, Tiffany and Rolls-Royce Motor Cars, are online; however, their sites leave much to be desired. I see a great opportunity online for luxury providers.

A few years ago, I wrote that a great opportunity for online retailers was in the area of digital downloadable recorded music, that the record labels were scrambling to figure out a viable solution to this problem, and that I saw no reason why a new player could not devise a solution for this great opportunity. Well, Apple stepped up, and its iPod line and iTunes.com have been extremely successful; many experts have said that this revitalized Apple. There have been rumors that the Recording Industry Association of America [RIAA] is going to make some potentially crazy decisions that could end up derailing the success of iTunes. That would be a shame for relevant industry players and consumers. I'm not convinced that the RIAA has figured out how to operate effectively in a digital world.

I currently see a lot of opportunity in online (video) games. Some massive multiplayer games have been successful, such as World of Warcraft and Everquest, and many have failed, such as The Sims Online. However, I see the stars aligning in terms of consumers' experience with mobile devices and relevant technological advances in wireless devices and service delivery, and game development. The line between physical reality and virtual reality is going to increasingly blur. Consumers will be doing more, and spending more money, in virtual/digital contexts.

Entrepreneur: What will the next-generation sites offer that today's sites don't?

Weinberg: Sites in the future will offer increases in speed, fidelity (e.g., the ability to feel items and speech recognition), ease of use, and access for the physically or psychologically challenged. In addition, sites will facilitate or carry out decision making. The web has become a terrific place for acquiring information; it will evolve into a great place for not only this but also for using/processing that information, such as making decisions or evaluating/judging emotions for you.

Entrepreneur: What are two bad e-commerce sites? Why?

Weinberg: Pick any two that make your blood boil or bring out frustration. The most common causes are grounded in content (e.g., limited product information, limited product availability), functionality (e.g., navigation, checkout, customer service), and privacy or security. A site that bothers me is that of Hermès, one of the world's leading luxury good brands. The site provides an irritating shopping experience. Navigation is neither intuitive nor pleasant, and information is minimal.

Entrepreneur: What has fundamentally ailed the prevailing B2C website business models?

Weinberg: I see many problems. Here are a few:

- Systems should be structured [according to how] consumers think and behave.

- Great ideas are wonderful things. They stimulate other great ideas. A great idea, however, is not enough to build a sustainable enterprise.

- Many firms got hung up on giving product to consumers. Some initial promotions effectively generated awareness and trial. At some point, however, these promotions should have stopped. Aside from credit card fraud, shipping charges are one of the most-mentioned [negatives] for those who have not shopped online (and even for some who have shopped online). If organizations were to provide free or flat-rate shipping and drop the ridiculous promotions, I bet sales would do just fine and profits would be improved. As I understand it, Amazon Prime—an "all you can eat" shipping service for $79 per year—has been successful.

- Websites lack personality; they can be sterile. Let's see some faces or caricatures on these sites. Provide cues that bring out human affect—we humans like emotion.

- Word-of-mouth is the most powerful and persuasive form of communication. Organizations should more actively look for ways to integrate this into their websites. Allow customers to share their opinions/ratings and reviews, to read those of others, and to interact with one another. Sure, it means giving up some control, which can be frightening. But it can also be liberating and improve the customer experience and the bottom line.

Entrepreneur: Is Jeff Bezos still the smartest e-tailer around? Why or why not?

Weinberg: Two years ago, I wrote that, in my opinion, he and Meg Whitman [eBay] were the smartest online retailers and marketers who were leading internet companies. Jeff Bezos has primarily earned his reputation through Amazon. He was an e-commerce groundbreaker and has inspired and taught millions of people to engage the internet as buyers, sellers, surfers, etc. I see great nerve and genius in what he has done. Jeff cleverly helped Amazon evolve into more of an e-tailing platform provider where, like eBay, it leveraged its technology and understanding of the marketplace to bring buyers and sellers together while outsourcing much of the physical (and harder to scale) aspects of the buying/selling process.

Entrepreneur: Are any small e-tailers safe from Amazon now that Bezos has extended his retailing empire into more new categories?

Weinberg: Amazon can flow on and on. I love its model of involving everyone and helping him or her get a piece of the online pie (e.g., individuals, small companies, affiliates, other leading retailers). The internet is partly about creating connections, sharing information, helping people identify their passions and realize their dreams, getting people involved to use their brainpower and voice, and providing access.

Tip...

Smart Tip

Remember: Amazon offers many ways for you to succeed by helping it get more successful. There are auctions, the low-cost Shops—instant storefronts with fixed pricing—and, of course, the slick Amazon affiliates program. By all means, Jeff Bezos wants to be the top dog on the net, but he is shrewd enough to see that your success can forward his goals. So do as Bruce Weinberg suggests and find ways to help yourself while helping Amazon.

I believe that Amazon does most of this reasonably well. Increasingly, however, Amazon customers will be asking what Amazon can do for them. A few years ago, I wrote that Amazon would need to evolve well beyond its retailing roots and offer its very loyal customer base a set of solutions to the variety of everyday-life problems that they have and that were not being addressed by Amazon [see next question and answer for more elaboration]. Indeed, Amazon has evolved through such offerings as Amazon Connect and photo, financial and web services.

Entrepreneur: If e-commerce is different in the near future, how will it be? How will it be the same?

Weinberg: I mentioned multichannel marketing before. Many aspects of e-commerce will be integrated into the ways business gets done and customers are served. It will no longer be perceived as a process that dominates the entire way a firm does business; rather, it will be considered an element in an overall business process. The government will play a greater role in regulating e-commerce and will more effectively enforce laws that are violated in an e-commerce context. Issues of privacy and security, particularly identity theft, will remain important. I expect to see a huge increase in the number of "digital" security companies. In the physical world, American life transitioned from a time where people left the front door open to one where you'd be crazy to leave your house or car without setting the alarm. I expect the same to hold in the virtual world. Digital security will become increasingly complex and lucrative as more aspects of our lives become connected online/electronically, such as the home, cars and—yes—people. A variety of devices will begin to get connected via the internet. Think back to the 1967 movie

Wireless Wonders

In the movie *The Graduate*, the future revolved around plastics, or so the young grad was told. Today, the future definitely revolves around wireless technologies. Find your niche in wireless, and you are on a very fast track to success. "The opportunities today in wireless are much, much bigger than what I saw in the computer business back in 1983," says Phillipe Kahn, a leader in the imaging and wireless arena and the former CEO of LightSurf, a global leader in multimedia messaging and interoperability solutions for the wireless market. (LightSurf was acquired by VeriSign, a Mountain View, California-based provider of infrastructure services for the internet and telecommunications networks, in 2005.)

When Kahn says this, it's a meaningful mouthful. Back in '83, Kahn was a pioneering software developer who created a couple hits—SideKick and Turbo Pascal—for a company he founded called Borland. In 1994, he founded a company called Starfish Software, where he developed a technology called TrueSynch for synching data between devices such as a cell phone and a computer. The possibilities in front of the rugged pioneers who are today defining the wireless information landscape are vastly richer than what he saw in 1983, for one very simple reason: "The numbers were so much smaller back then," says Kahn, who in 1998 sold his TrueSynch technology to cell phone giant Motorola for an undisclosed amount. In the early '80s, PC users were sparse, and that meant the market upside was tiny. But nowadays, explains Kahn, the potential audience for wireless web products and services is already in the tens of millions of users. "Today's landscape is explosive," he says.

Again, the numbers have it: The wireless web soon will be in more hands than the conventional web is. Seem incredible? Well, it's not. In-stat, a company that tracks the communications industry, found through its Consumer Mobility Survey that 61 percent of the 131 million wireless subscribers in the United States are also wireless data users. And internet-ready phones have become so commonplace that the company no longer tracks them. You can tap into this. Don't stop thinking until you've found six ways to exploit this technology—then get busy implementing the best. Wireless is a wave that hasn't crested yet, but when it does, in just a few years, it will be a monster.

The Graduate and say the word "wireless" instead of "plastic" (see "Wireless Wonders" in this chapter).

One big change I see is the powerful force of large players dominating various aspects of e-commerce and internet media. For example, just as ABC, NBC and

▲

CBS were dominant when television broadcasting was emerging and maturing, I expect to see Google, Yahoo!, Microsoft, AOL and, perhaps, in some shape or form, eBay, dominating internet information/functionality delivery. These sites, in many respects, have become one-stop gateways for consumers' internet needs (e-mail and other forms of communication such as VoIP, search, geography mapping, shopping, etc.). Many consumers will become accustomed to the signature look and feel of the various tools offered by a specific portal and will likely return most often to that portal for various internet needs, which, increasingly, is becoming most everything.

Glossary

Advertising network: a company that connects advertisers with publishers that want to display ads

Affiliate programs: a program that allows companies to earn revenue by advertising and selling the products of another company

Angel investor: a private individual who invests his or her own money into an entrepreneurial company; angels can be affiliated (meaning they are familiar with you or your business beforehand) or nonaffiliated

Banner: a graphic image used on a website as an advertisement; the information superhighway's version of billboards

Beta site: a test site, usually erected in the authoring phase of a website

Blog: a website that publishes a running archive of dated entries

Bot: a robot, or program, that automatically does specified tasks

Brick-and-mortar (B&M): a term describing traditional businesses with a physical storefront rather than a cyberbusiness

▲

Business to business (B2B): companies that seek businesses, not consumers, as customers

Business to consumer (B2C): companies that market to consumers

Clip art: off-the-shelf images anyone can use; website authoring programs usually include lots of clip art

Common gateway interface (CGI) script: a simple program that runs on the net; guest books, for instance, often are CGI scripts

Cookie: data created by a web server that's stored on a user's computer to identify that user on return visits to the website

CPC (cost-per-click): a method of advertising that pays money to website publishers only when an online ad is clicked on by a site visitor

CPM (cost-per-thousand): a method of advertising in which advertisers pay website publishers a certain amount of money for every 1,000 ads displayed on their website(s)

CSS (Cascading Style Sheets): a language that's used to style web pages; it takes the information in the markup language used to build the website (such as HTML or XML) and presents it to the user

CRM: stands for "customer relationship management"

Domain name: the name that a company or individual registers to use as a location on the internet; it's what comes before the ".com," ".net" or ".edu," all of which are known as top-level domains

File transfer protocol (FTP): the system used to transfer files over the net; you FTP files to your web host

First-mover advantage: the built-in advantage of being the first business in a particular category

Flash: multimedia technology that allows you to add interactive and animated components to a website

Host: a company that provides space for storing (hosting) a website

Hyperlink: a connection between one object and another; also known as a link

HTML (hypertext markup language): the code that creates web pages

Internet service provider (ISP): the company that provides the connection that lets a user connect to the net; typical connection methods include DSL, wireless broadband, dial-up, Ethernet and cable modem

Keywords: terms that advertisers bid on through PPC (pay-per-click) ad programs like Google AdWords; meta keywords also are terms used on a web page that factor into its search engine ranking (see also Metadata)

Log: a record of all visits to a website; a log usually gives a click-by-click report on a visitor

Look-to-buy ratio: a common measurement used in analyzing the effectiveness of an e-tailer; ideally a 1 to 1 ratio—one looker produces one buyer; look-to-buy ratios of less than 10 to 1 are desirable

Metadata: different HTML or XHTML meta elements (or meta tags) are used to specify data about a web page, including title, description and keywords; this information is used by search engines to display a website's information when displayed in search results

Mind share: consumer awareness and loyalty

Newsgroup: an internet message board or bulletin board

Ping (Packet Internet Groper): a net utility that tests websites

Podcasting: to record audio or video files and make them available online so they can be downloaded and listened to rather like an "on-demand" radio show

Portal: a web "supersite" that offers links to substantial amounts of information and often to other sites; Yahoo! is a premier portal

Pure play: a company that does business exclusively on the web (it has no brick-and-mortar stores)

ROI: an acronym for return on investment

RSS feed: RSS is a family of web feed formats, specified in XML and used for web syndication

Search engine: a website that exists to help users find other websites; Google (google.com) is the most popular search engine

SEM (search engine marketing): the process of increasing traffic to a website through paid methods, such as pay-per-click ad programs AdWords and adCenter

SEO (search engine optimization): the process of optimizing the content of a website, including its use of keywords, in order to improve its listing in search engine results organically

SMB: an acronym for "small to midsize business"

Social bookmarking: sites that allow users to store, organize, share and comment on bookmarks of webpages; for example: Digg.com

Social networking: community-oriented websites that allow users to create their own home pages, "friend" other users to create social networks, interact with one another, and join communities of interest; for example: MySpace.com, LinkedIn.com, Facebook.com

Spam: unwanted, unsolicited commercial e-mail

Spider: spiders (also known as crawlers) search the web for information; search engines use spiders to find web pages

Template: a pre-designed document; a web page template, for instance, requires the user to simply fill in some blanks to produce a publishable document

▲

Term sheet commitment: a written offer from a venture capitalist that sets out how much money the firm will invest in a startup in return for a percentage of ownership

URL: an acronym for universal resource locator or, more simply, a web page's address

Venture capitalist (VC): a professional money lender who seeks out high-potential startups to fund and usually receives an ROI via the startup's IPO or acquisition

Web 2.0: refers to the ongoing transition of the World Wide Web from a collection of websites to a medium for self-publishing, creativity and collaboration among web users

Web designer: someone who creates the graphics and the content that contributes to the look and feel of a website

Web developer: someone who builds a website using programming languages; he or she is responsible for the framework behind the content you see on a web page

Widget: miniature web applications that allow users to view information such as news headlines or weather forecasts, view photos and play music and video

Wiki: a collaborative website that allows readers to add content on a subject, which can also be edited by others; for example: Wikipedia (http://en.wikipedia.org)

Wireless application protocol (WAP): the standard underlying programs that run on cell phones

Wireless markup language (WML): the underlying computer code that produces pages that display on the wireless web

Wizard: a help tool (usually in step-by-step format) that steers the user through to completion of a task

WYSIWYG (what you see is what you get): when the computer screen reflects exactly what the final output will be for a printed page or a web page

XML (Extensible Markup Language): a markup language that was designed to transport data, as opposed to displaying it, as HTML does

Appendix
Online Business Resources

ere's the blunt truth about e-commerce: Most of what you need to know will not be printed in books or even in magazines and newspapers. One medium that is successfully tracking the rapid developments online is the web itself. When you want to know more or need answers to questions, log on to the web and go searching. The information you crave is rarely more than a few mouse clicks away. Here you will find dozens of the sites that deserve tracking.

Competitive Intelligence

Fuld & Co.'s Internet Intelligence Index

Fuld & Co., a research and consulting firm in the field of business and competitive intelligence, has compiled this free index of information from a wide variety of public services. It contains links to more than 600 intelligence-related internet sites, covering everything from macroeconomic data to individual patent and stock quote information.

fuld.com/Tindex/I3.html

Hoover's

The best content is available for a fee, but there is ample free content for anyone who surfs in. Research competitors, track stock market performance and keep tabs on IPOs.

hoovers.com/free

KnowX

The savvy engine ferrets through public records and reports on bankruptcies, liens, judgments and such against individuals and businesses. Reports range from free to $24.95.

knowx.com

Thomas Register

This is the sourcebook on U.S. and Canadian companies; the book in print or on CD or DVD is free to companies in the United States and Canada, not including shipping and handling charges, and the content on the web is free as well.

thomasnet.com

Yahoo! Finance

This all-inclusive website has everything from up-to-the minute market summaries to stock research to financial news—and much of it is free.

finance.yahoo.com

Consumer Websites

BBBOnLine

The Better Business Bureau's e-tailer monitoring site

bbbonline.org

E-Commerce & the Internet

Interactive advice from the FTC that provides advice on avoiding common online frauds and security risks

onguardonline.gov

How to Protect Yourself: Shopping on the Internet

Counsel from Florida's attorney general; click on "Protecting Yourself From Consumer Fraud," and then "Internet Shopping"

myfloridalegal.com/consumer

Internet ScamBusters
This is a website and a free electronic newsletter designed to help people protect themselves from internet scams, misinformation and hype; much of the information focuses on internet merchants and consumers.
scambusters.org

SafeShopping
Created by the American Bar Association, this site bills it as "the place to stop before you shop."
safeshopping.org

WebAssured
An e-tailer evaluator
webassured.com

Direct Marketing and Mail Order

The Direct Marketing Association
This association's website offers lots of great information for companies starting out online or in mail order.
the-dma.org

Lists for Marketing
From the National Mail Order Association, this website includes basic information, tips and suggestions about how to best use mailing lists.
listsformarketing.com

National Mail Order Association
This association also has a great website, and it is targeted to smaller online/mail order companies.
nmoa.org

Domain Name Sellers

All Domains
alldomains.com

The Domain Name Aftermarket
tdnam.com

Go Daddy
Godaddy.com

Network Solutions
networksolutions.com

▲

e-Commerce Solutions

Amazon's WebStore
Create your own store and use Amazon's payments system.
amazonservices.com/webstore

eBay
Offers successful auctioneers a storefront within eBay
stores.ebay.com

osCommerce
Free open-source online e-commerce solution
oscommerce.com

ProStores
e-commerce solution owned by eBay; users can run their stores independently or list their inventory on eBay as well
prostores.com

Web.com
A full suite of tools for building and hosting a complete e-commerce storefront
web.com

Yahoo! Merchant Solutions
A simple and fast way to get an e-commerce store up and running
smallbusiness.yahoo.com/ecommerce

Global Commerce

GlobalEDGE
Michigan State University's International Business Center's vast library of world trade resources that includes an outline of the business climate, political structure, history and statistical data for more than 190 countries; a directory of international business resources categorized by specific orientation and content; and much more globaledge.msu.edu/resourceDesk

Going Shopping? Go Global! A Guide for E-Consumers
A report from the FTC on online shopping overseas
ftc.gov/bcp/conline/pubs/alerts/glblalrt.shtm

Planet Business
Business resources, arranged by country; a good place to look for foreign contacts, partners and information
planetbiz.com

Miscellaneous e-Commerce Information

ClicksLink

For exploring offbeat affiliate programs—astrology, watch stores and more
clickslink.com

Constant Contact

A leading e-mail marketing service provider targeting small businesses; the company helps set up and run an e-mail list
constantcontact.com

Keynote NetMechanic

For checking your site for bad code and broken links, free of charge
netmechanic.com

LinkShare

For signing up for affiliate status with name-brand e-tailers
linkshare.com

Microsoft Small Business Center

A great resource for anyone starting a new business, with lots of information about Microsoft's products and services
microsoft.com/smallbusiness/hub.mspx

ReveNews.com

A leading blog that covers topics such as affiliate marketing, online marketing, contextual advertising, search marketing, online publishing and spyware; the blog has very knowledgeable writers that offer fresh commentary on current events
revenews.com

Online and Offline Publications

Business 2.0
money.cnn.com/magazines/business2

E-Commerce Times
ecommercetimes.com

Entrepreneur magazine
entrepreneur.com

Internet Retailer
internetretailer.com

MIT Technology Review
techreview.com

Wired
wired.com

Search Engines

Ask
ask.com

Dogpile
dogpile.com

Google
google.com

Google Adwords
adwords.google.com/select

MSN
msn.com

SearchEngineWatch.com
searchenginewatch.com

Yahoo!
search.yahoo.com

Yahoo! Search Marketing
searchmarketing.yahoo.com

Shopping Bots

BidFind
bidfind.com

BizRate
bizrate.com

BottomDollar.com
bottomdollar.com

eSmarts
esmarts.com

Google Product Search
google.com/products

mySimon
mysimon.com

Social Networking

Bebo
Most popular social networking site in the United Kingdom; was recently purchased by AOL
bebo.com

Facebook
Originally for college students, this juggernaut is now open to everyone.
facebook.com

LinkedIn
The social network for businesspeople
linkedin.com

Mashable
Leading social networking news blog
mashable.com

MySpace
The granddaddy of social networking sites
myspace.com

Ning
Online service that allows you to create, customize and share your own social network
ning.com

Orkut
Social networking site owned by Google
orkut.com

Twitter
Hyper-caffeinated social networking where users post 140-character-or-less messages from their phones or computers
twitter.com

Software

Dreamweaver CS3
The new version of the popular, higher-end web design software
macromedia.com/software/dreamweaver

CoffeeCup
The easy-to-use web design software
coffeecup.com

Download.com
Allows users to download trial and full versions of software
download.com

Photoshop Elements
Consumer-friendly "light" version of Photoshop
adobe.com/products/photoshopelwin

WebExpress
Robust, powerful software with a free trial available
mvd.com/webexpress

ZyWeb
Web-based tools for creating your own site; results can be first-rate
zy.com

Statistics and More

ClickZ
Net-related stats in a readable format
clickz.com/stats

eMarketer
A great news source with an e-commerce focus; lots of stats
emarketer.com

Traffic Reports and Ratings

Alexa
Measures the most popular sites on the web
alexa.com

comScore Media Metrix
ComScore Media Metrix, the audience measurement division of comScore
Networks, offers an internet audience measurement service that reports on website
usage
comscore.com

Internet Traffic Report
Measures router volume at various points around the world
internettrafficreport.com

Nielsen NetRatings
A leader in internet media and market research
nielsen-netratings.com

Venture Capital Information

The Center for Venture Research at Whittemore School of Business and Economics at the University of New Hampshire
The center has created a nationwide list of venture capital resources to help entre-
preneurs find early-stage capital. You can order the list online for $40.
wsbe.unh.edu/Centers_CVR/about_us.cfm

Kauffman eVenturing
A website from the well-known Ewing Marion Kauffman Foundation that can be
tapped for timely, practical information on how to start, manage and expand your
business
eventuring.kauffman.org

MoneyHunt
The home page for the TV show that helps entrepreneurs link with VCs and angels
moneyhunt.com

National Venture Capital Association
This association's website contains industry statistics and lists of venture capital organizations and preferred industry service providers.
nvca.org

VFinance.com
A directory of venture capital resources and related services; a good site for getting info on who's who in the VC world and how deals get cut
vfinance.com

Web Art

About.com: Web Clip Art
webclipart.about.com

Clip-art.com
clip-art.com

Clip Art Searcher
webplaces.com/search

Free Graphics
freegraphics.com

iStockPhoto
istockphoto.com

New Visions Technology
nvtech.com

Web Hosts

1&1 Internet
1and1.com

Blue Genesis
bluegenesis.com

Compare Web Hosts
Web host comparison site
comparewebhosts.com

Dreamhost
dreamhost.com

Go Daddy
godaddy.com

▲

Hostway
hostway.com

Interland
interland.com

IPOWER
ipower.com

TopHosts
Another web host comparison site
tophosts.com

Web.com
web.com

Website Building Tools and Help

123 Webmaster
More than 4,500 free resources for web development
123webmaster.com

Builder.com
A source for web developers by web developers
builderau.com.au

How to Build Lame Web Sites
An insightful—and sometimes funny—look at bad site design
webdevelopersjournal.com/columns/perpend1.html

Jakob Nielsen
The guru of web usability, Nielsen particularly revels in pinpointing the "must nots" of website architecture. If Nielsen says don't do it, don't do it.
useit.com

W3Schools
Free source for web-building tutorials
w3schools.com

Web Development Journal
Another useful site full of web design and development tips
webdevelopersjournal.com

Web Site Resource
Links to web design tutorials, affiliate program guides and webmaster resources
wsresource.com

WebDeveloper.com
One-stop shopping for advice and tools for building better websites
webdeveloper.com

Webmaster Tools Inc.
Directory of webmaster resources
webmastertools.com

Wireless Web

Open Mobile Alliance
This organization is designed to be the center of mobile service standardization work, helping the creation of inter-operable services across countries, operators and mobile terminals that will meet the needs of users.
openmobilealliance.org

TagTag
A free tool that will help you make your site wireless and web-ready.
tagtag.com

Wap Catalog
A directory of wireless websites
wapcatalog.com

The Wireless FAQ
A site where programmers for wireless devices share information
thewirelessfaq.com

Index